OUTSOURCING IN THE UK

Policies, Practices and Outcomes

Janice Morphet

BRISTOL
UNIVERSITY
PRESS

First published in Great Britain in 2021 by

Bristol University Press
University of Bristol
1-9 Old Park Hill
Bristol
BS2 8BB
UK
t: +44 (0)117 954 5940
e: bup-info@bristol.ac.uk

Details of international sales and distribution partners are available at bristoluniversitypress.co.uk

© Bristol University Press 2021

British Library Cataloguing in Publication Data
A catalogue record for this book is available from the British Library

ISBN 978-1-5292-0960-0 hardcover
ISBN 978-1-5292-0961-7 ePub
ISBN 978-1-5292-0962-4 ePdf

The right of Janice Morphet to be identified as author of this work has been asserted by her
in accordance with the Copyright, Designs and Patents Act 1988.

All rights reserved: no part of this publication may be reproduced, stored in a retrieval system,
or transmitted in any form or by any means, electronic, mechanical, photocopying, recording,
or otherwise without the prior permission of Bristol University Press.

Every reasonable effort has been made to obtain permission to reproduce copyrighted
material. If, however, anyone knows of an oversight, please contact the publisher.

The statements and opinions contained within this publication are solely those of the author
and not of the University of Bristol or Bristol University Press. The University of Bristol and
Bristol University Press disclaim responsibility for any injury to persons or property resulting
from any material published in this publication.

Bristol University Press works to counter discrimination on grounds of
gender, race, disability, age and sexuality.

Cover design: blu inc
Front cover image: iStock/Achisatha Khamsuwan

Bristol University Press uses environmentally responsible print partners.

Printed in Great Britain by CPI Group (UK) Ltd, Croydon, CR0 4YY

Contents

List of Abbreviations   v

Preface   vii

1	Introduction	1
2	The Legal Basis for Competition in Public Services	15
3	Competition in Utilities	35
4	Preparing to Outsource Government Services	51
5	Local Government: Compulsory Competition and Best Value	69
6	Creating the Public Services Market	85
7	Outsourcing Central Government Services	103
8	Liberalising Health Services and Functions	119
9	Outsourcing in Education	133
10	The Third Sector and Social Value	149
11	Taking Back Service Delivery	163
12	Conclusions	179

References   195

Index   243

List of Abbreviations

BT	British Telecom
C and W	Cable and Wireless
CCT	Compulsory Competitive Tendering
CRC	Community Rehabilitation Companies
CSR	Comprehensive Spending Review
DfE	Department for Education
DHSS	Department of Health and Social Security
DLO	Direct Labour Organisation
DSO	Direct Service Organisation
EA	Environment Agency
EC	European Commission
EEC	European Economic Community
ePIMS	e-Property Information System
ERDF	European Regional Development Fund
EU	European Union
FMI	Financial Management Initiative
GATS	General Agreement on Trade in Services
GATT	General Agreement on Tariffs and Trade
GDPR	General Data Protection Regulation
GIS	Geographical Information System
GP	General Practitioner
GPA	Government Procurement Agreement
GPC	Government Procurement Code
HMT	Her Majesty's Treasury
IRC	Immigration Removal Centre
IMF	International Monetary Fund
LEA	Local Education Authority
LGA	Local Government Association
LGR	Local Government Review
MoJ	Ministry of Justice
NAFTA	North American Free Trade Association
NAO	National Audit Office
NHBC	National Housing and Building Council

NHS	National Health Service
NLGN	New Local Government Network
NOMS	National Offender Management System
NPM	New Public Management
NSA	Next Steps Agencies
OECD	Organisation for Economic Co-operation and Development
Ofcom	Office of Communications Regulator
Oftel	Office of the Regulator of telephony
Ofwat	Office of the Water Regulator
OGC	Office of Government Commerce
PFI	Private Finance Initiative
PHE	Public Health England
PPP	public–private partnership
RIEP	Regional Improvement and Efficiency Partnerships
RWA	regional water authority
SEA	Single European Act
SEM	Single European Market
SGEI	services of general economic interest
SGI	services of general interest
SNA	Single National Accounts
SoS	Secretary of State
SSP	Shared Strategic Partnerships
TfEU	Treaty on the Functioning of the European Union
TUPE	Transfer of Undertakings (Public Employment)
UKBA	United Kingdom Border Agency
UN	United Nations
VFM	value for money
WTO	World Trade Organization

Preface

This has been an interesting book to write and it has once again reminded me of how little we have engaged with the international agreements that have been used to shape the UK state since the 1970s. We have attributed outsourcing to the domestic ideology of the Thatcher years and membership of the European Union (EU). We have lived within the mantras of efficiency and effectiveness, performance management and austerity without looking behind them at the continuing application of international agreements made by our government with the World Trade Organization. While there has been vilification of EU for procurement practices and state aid rules, we have failed to understand how these have been applied because the UK has agreed to them as part of its wider international commitments, beyond the EU. They will not be removed by Brexit. Our failure to engage in these agreements and practices has meant that the reforms of the state that have been delivered as part of their implementation, reinforced by the inevitability of these international agreements providing protection for their delivery, have not been challenged – but there were choices. As demonstrated here, central state administrations seek out international agreements to provide camouflage for the changes they wish to make to retain control. We need to question, investigate and understand more of what is being undertaken so that it can be challenged and called out when necessary. We do not have to accept that the narratives of the state are always as they seem, and we can do better.

This book came about through a coffee break conversation with Stephen Wenham at a Political Studies Association annual conference. I would very much like to thank Stephen for all our rare similar exchanges and for his challenge to me to write this book. My first book for Policy Press came about in a similar way after sitting next to Alison Shaw at a conference and subsequent books with Emily Watt have been hatched over coffees and dinners. What a great team to work with, and Caroline, Susannah, Jessica and Laura have all been there to provide support and encouragement to relate these issues to a wider world. Thank you.

1

Introduction

The introduction of competition and outsourcing in the UK since the early 1970s has had a profound effect on the role, delivery and content of public services. It represented a major policy punctuation that shifted public services from direct to indirect delivery for the user (Gyford, 1991; Walsh, 1995). This has created a sense of detachment between organisations that remain responsible for the service and recipients (Kelly, 2007). Public organisations have mediated their understanding of service requirements with the quality of delivery and performance. However, public organisations never lose their responsibility for services purchased from third parties. Their accountabilities remain the same.

These changes in public sector delivery are frequently termed as privatisation although nothing in the international agreements and their associated legal frameworks for public sector liberalisation have required specific service transfer from public to other sectors. Rather there has been an agreement that they should be open to competition (Jackson et al, 1982). While the introduction of outsourcing is strongly associated with Margaret Thatcher's ideology in favour of the market over the state (Gamble, 1989; Marsh, 1991), the agreement to liberalise the public sector, exposing public services to competition, was made by the Labour government in 1976 (Morphet, 2013). This decision came after the government had been forced to seek financial assistance from the International Monetary Fund (IMF) in 1976 (Burk and Cairncross, 1992; Parker, 2009; Lowe, 2011). However, the international framework for liberalising the public sector had already been discussed and set as part of a longer term process of international trade discussions within the World Trade Organization's predecessor, the General Agreement on Tariffs and Trades (GATT). These discussions were part of the Tokyo Round of trade negotiations that lasted between 1973 and 1980 (Hoekman, 1995).

While the Conservative Party had always been in favour of reducing the welfare state and replacing it with the private sector (Lee, 2015; Mount, 2020a), Thatcher was more cautious about this before she became Prime Minister. Her 1979 manifesto included a commitment for local authority tenants to have the right to buy their council homes, but there was no commitment to privatisation (Seldon and Collings, 2014). Thatcher's election could also be seen as a temporal convenience (Goetz and Meyer-Sahling, 2009) that allowed the civil service to use a change in Prime Minister to implement the liberalising elements of the GATT agreement, developing and harnessing Thatcher's ideology. This would have been much more difficult policy turn under a Labour government. This GATT agreement also provided an opportunity for public sector changes in the way the state operated (Parker, 2009; Lowe, 2011). It introduced disruption into the post-war consensus for the welfare state (Timmins, 2001) and provided policy and career openings for those in Whitehall trying to find ways of adjusting the UK economy. The UK's membership of the EU from 1972 also left civil servants seeking a new domestic policy role (Buller, 1995; Wilks, 1996; Morphet, 2013).

This book discusses the ways in which outsourcing became a dominant mode for the provision of public services for the period 1980–2010, just as the welfare state had been the consensual model for the preceding period 1945–1980. It examines how the approaches to outsourcing changed as it was introduced into different sectors by successive governments. When these outsourcing initiatives were introduced, they were frequently presented as a way of solving sectoral problems – within local government (Boyne, 1998; Wilson, 1999), health (Broadbent et al, 2003; Confue, 2019), probation (Kirton and Guillaume, 2019) and immigration (Bacon, 2005) – rather than as part of an overarching programme that introduced parts of the public sector to outsourcing in successive and planned waves. Sectoral policy narratives were important to support the introduction of change, particularly when services were cast as 'failing' or 'inefficient' (Lynk, 1993; Mennicken, 2013). These tropes used by successive UK governments became the narratives of outsourcing. The banners of efficiency, effectiveness, citizen and customer focus, and austerity (Cunningham and James, 2014; Gamble, 2015) have been associated with each wave of outsourcing, and in most cases, these overarching narratives have been found to be overoptimistic (NAO, 2012, 2015a, 2015b, 2015c, 2019a, 2020a, 2020b).

At the same time, outsourcing has become a convenient way of disrupting and loosening regulatory practices for the private sector (Beesley, 1983). Liberalisation has also been used to change service provision by reducing funding and eligibility (Lethbridge, 2017). Outsourcing has become a method for reforming failing services although, again, this has been less effective in practice (Kirton and Guillaume, 2019). Privatisation has been regarded as a means of dealing with poor public management (Boyne et al, 2010). Contracted staff are considered easier to manage than direct employees and can be instructed to observe decision rules that directly employed staff, including professionals, might wish to determine case by case (Robinson and Burnett, 2007). However, the quality of service delivery still depends on the client organisation's management of the contract (Grimshaw et al, 2002). If there are weaknesses in the organisation that have led to outsourcing a service, these are likely to continue in the management and delivery of the subsequent contracts (Hood, 2011).

In this book, the role of neoliberalism in the development of public sector outsourcing is considered. Through the UK's involvement in international agreements with the GATT and its successor the WTO, the introduction and development of outsourcing is considered through a lens of statecraft and policy narrative. The implementation of international agreements has maintained and increased the strength of Whitehall through redefining some of its responsibilities as peripheral to save core government functions from competition or outsourcing (Haddon, 2012; Talbot and Talbot, 2019). The UK central state has never considered that its own role in outsourcing has included any requirements to give up power (Rhodes, 2001). Central government departments have maintained power relationships with their peripheralised institutions, apportioning blame when these agencies fail (Hood, 2011) while continuing to argue that departmental accountability to Parliament overrides any contractual considerations. This has meant that little attention is paid to managing contracts as there is an assumption that they can always be changed by using central government power and paying off contractors, even when contracts have gone badly wrong (NAO, 2020b).

Nevertheless, some parts of public sector service delivery are changing. Public service and social value are emerging as greater influences in outsourcing, particularly in local government (LGA, 2019). Meanwhile, central government's response to COVID-19 in England has demonstrated the weaknesses of reliance on an outsourced state that has excluded public sector partners (Monbiot, 2020). Allegations of 'crony' contracts, let without competition for respirators, vaccines, personal protective equipment (PPE), food parcels, tracing apps and track and trace systems that have failed from the outset, have left England with the highest death toll in Europe (King's Fund, 2020). This outsourced approach has been used despite WHO advice and experience of countries successful in dealing with the virus working through local government and health organisations (WHO, 2020). Will the increasingly centralised state learn from this or will ideology prevail?

Government Procurement Agreement, General Agreement in Trade in Services and neoliberalism

Neoliberalism is used to describe the shift away from a Keynesian public provision model of the operation of the state and the economy to one where the private sector is favoured for the provision of public services (Marsh, 1991). It was introduced into public discourse in the late 1970s, at the same time as the GATT Tokyo Round was agreed for implementation (Harvey, 2007; Palley, 2005). The trends to open the public sector to the markets started earlier in the late 1960s, when the Tokyo Round terms of reference were negotiated. As Harvey (2007) demonstrates, neoliberalism had its origins in the 1930s and could have gained an earlier foothold in the operation of markets if the 1939–1945 war had not taken place. However, the physical, social and economic damage of this period, accompanied by the military covenant made to the returning soldiers, meant that direct public expenditure was a mechanism of state rebuilding by providing employment and social infrastructure (Kynaston, 2008). The UK Conservative Party never expected this to be the permanent state (Parker, 2009). The cross-party post-war agreement to the welfare state in the UK was more fragile than it was perceived to be (Timmins, 2001).

The Tokyo Round was preceded by the Kennedy Round, which concluded in 1967 and had focused on non-tariff barriers to trade (Jackson et al, 1982). It had been important in recognising the EU as a trading entity although powers to negotiate on behalf of its members were not granted by the GATT (Meunier, 2005). By the 1970s, Milton Friedman was a major proponent of market liberalisation (Shleifer, 2009). Harvey (2005) argues that his approach was part of the wider anti-communist narrative in the US in the 1950s that extended into US international influence over the UK in the 1970s. Neoliberalism remained at the margin until the early 1970s when Friedrich Hayek, in 1974, and Friedman, in 1976, won Nobel prizes in economics for their work on monetarism and deregulation. Hayek's work stretched back to the 1930s and related to the information communicated through price (Hayek, 1944; Hayek and Hanson, 1984). Friedman's work was also on the theory of money and was regarded as a major disruptive turn away from the widely accepted post-war Keynesianism (Shearmur, 1997). Friedman described the Keynesian model of the welfare state as 'embedded liberalism' (1962).

These Nobel prizes give some indication of the change in economic orthodoxy and provided the underpinning approach of the Tokyo Round (Winham, 2014). This was also influenced by the concerted effort of the US Chamber of Commerce to change the public's views on the role of the corporation and business in society in 1971 (Harvey, 2007, p 43). It did this by expanding its membership and lobbying capacity, buttressed by the creation of new think tanks including the Heritage Foundation and the Hoover Institute (Ashford, 1990; Stone, 2000). At the same time, the opening of UK think tanks in favour of neoliberal policies began, through the creation of the Institute of Economic Affairs (1955), the Centre for Policy Studies (CPS) and the Adam Smith Institute that all started to influence Conservative Party policy (Heffernan, 1996). Sir Keith Joseph, who later became one of Thatcher's ministers and who supported her into power, was a co-founder of CPS, writing its first pamphlet on 'Why Britain needs a social market economy' (1974). This change in direction was not taken into the political mainstream and the opening of the public services to competition was not anticipated (Pliatzky, 1988). Despite her views, Thatcher remained initially unconvinced that such an approach would be appropriate for all public services (Holmes, 2019).

The post-war reconstruction phase in the UK was being undermined by an economic recession by the mid-1970s (Morgan, 1997). The Labour government could no longer fund capital investment such as housing and social infrastructure (Timmins, 2001). The introduction of private sector funding to support public services, including construction, was regarded as a measure that could provide public investment (Crosland, 1956; Meredith, 2005). This approach assumed that costs to public bodies commissioning services would be less. However, while there were pull factors from the public sector for the injection of private sector funding, there were also push factors from the private sector to expand their domestic and international markets (Parker, 2009). In the 1960s, there were private sector concerns that market saturation was being reached and, without an expansion into new markets that were closed, companies could no longer grow (Tiefer, 1996). The Tokyo Round was initially focused on non-tariff barriers to trade (Jackson et al, 1982), but in the longer term, access to public sector markets and eventually to public services as well as goods created a major new sector.

Did public sector liberalisation stimulate economies and provide public funding in the shorter term? Has the dominant narrative of the market changed the public sector? Harvey (2007) discusses the development of the neoliberal state where government is turned into governance, assets are the subject of enclosure (Christophers, 2019) and elites and private interests are included within formal decisions with democratically elected politicians (David-Barrett, 2011; Dávid-Barrett and Fazekas, 2019). The liberalisation of the public sector in a succession of services has extended the role of private interests in developed and developing markets (Kochanek, 1996). While liberalisation and outsourcing were promoted as tools of efficiency and effectiveness that would be achieved through market competition, there has been a reduction in competitors, through mergers and acquisitions that were not anticipated. This has been through a coalescence between modes and types of provision, for example in energy and transport (Cowie, 2002; Price, 2005).

Statecraft's role in implementing competition in UK public services

The implementation of public sector liberalisation in the UK has a continuing relationship to the practices of statecraft. Statecraft is the way in which governments and their officials seek to implement their policies as set out in their election manifestos (Stivers, 2008). However, this diminishes and neglects other international sources of policy that are also on any government's delivery agenda and form part of a continuous policy framework that stretches over government and Parliamentary terms (Kingdon, 1993).

The presence of a continuing set of policy commitments is a particular issue in the UK, where the constitution requires that each Parliament is sovereign and cannot be bound by commitments made by preceding Parliaments (Bercow, 2019). While this is the case within domestic policy, the UK also has a continuing set of international agreements and commitments that stretch over the bridge of Parliamentary change. These include those with the GATT, WTO, EU and UN together with a wide range of specific agreements that accumulate over time (Aust, 2013). Treaties may include commitments for taking domestic action in the future such as the UN Paris Climate Accord (2015) and are not removed at each general election when a new Parliament is formed. While these international agreements are in the public domain and transparent when concluded, their associated implications are incorporated into domestic policy (Jackson, 1992; Kadelbach, 1999; Wilkins, 2017). The ways in which these longstanding agreements are translated into government delivery can be identified as statecraft. How are the actions that arise as a consequence of these agreements made palatable to governments and the public?

Bulpitt (1986) introduced the role of statecraft into an examination of how governments and officials manage political agendas into delivery.

While Bulpitt (1982, 1986) examined statecraft in relation to a range of issues including territorial politics and finance, here, these discussions on the application of the theories of statecraft have extended to the implementation of outsourcing policy in the UK. Bulpitt (1986) identified the ways in which political elites and their advisors seek to retain power through successive electoral cycles; they pursue policies that will make this more likely to occur. For civil servants, aware of international commitments, such as public sector liberalisation, the use of statecraft is central to their success. When overcoming the potential political unacceptability of the application of these external commitments, there is a need to tailor their delivery in ways that are more politically acceptable. This also requires policies that fit within a contemporaneous and overriding ideological narratives. Bulpitt's work has been criticised for a range of reasons but Buller (1995) reassessed and recalibrated statecraft within 'realistic' frameworks. This critical realism (James, 2016) accounts for the statecraft actions that are also integral to the implementation of long-term delivery but are not explained directly in the public domain. Another dimension of statecraft is to use constructed narratives that align party political ideology with these commitments (Buller, 1999). These ideologies can be recalibrated when the party in government changes while the underlying policy remains the same (James, 2010; Diamond et al, 2016). The requirements of international agreements can be drivers to shape domestic policies to support their implementation but may also be carriers of other institutional objectives. Policy design, including the selection of specific solutions above others, have wider significance than achieving treaty compliance (Lodge and Wegrich, 2012). These international agreements provide power to the central state to underwrite and guarantee reforms by providing requirements for action that cannot be undermined by the short termism of immediate political considerations.

Given the usefulness of these international agreements as carriers of wider public reform, which are more impervious to immediate political agendas, central government managers have often been the 'midwives' of internationalisation to help them implement domestic change (Weiss, 1999; Hirst and Thompson, 1999). This has allowed the centre of government to manage issues in its own interests (Convery, 2014) while providing ways that the civil service can use to progress change when it has not been in tune with any government's specific political agenda.

The use of statecraft to manage the delivery of public sector liberalisation has been through a significant range of narratives to buttress institutional reform over 40 years. Through the use of statecraft, the programmatic approach to implement liberalisation in different parts of the public sector has been a key determinant of institutional change. Yet, these reforms have been attributed to other narratives, associated with different governments with attempts to analyse the provenance of public policy without understanding its underlying momentum. New Public Management (NPM) (Common, 1998) and performance management (OECD, 1994) were used as tools to support the reshaping of public services to meet the requirements of the Tokyo Round's resulting Government Procurement Agreement (GPA) and later the General Agreement in Trade in Services (GATS). However, without this understanding of the overriding policy and the role of statecraft in its implementation, the purpose of these reforms was projected on to political ideology. This meant that the policy design of the implementation of the GPA and GATS went unchallenged in the UK. There were other ways to implement this market liberalisation, which have been demonstrated, including the use of concessions in France (Bel and Foote, 2009) and social value models in Sweden, Germany and the Netherlands (Nicholls, 2007; Bovis, 2015; Halloran, 2017), but through the use of statecraft, academic and policy debates were diverted to metanarratives such as efficiency and effectiveness as policy drivers (Cowie, 2002; Micheli et al, 2005). The UK's membership of the EU was made to carry a public policy burden of public sector liberalisation (Torres and Pina, 2002) that was derived primarily from the UK's membership of the GATT and WTO. These investigations into policy change focused on *how* rather than *why* they were being implemented and diverted attention away from the more fundamental policy options being purposefully ignored by the central state. The extent of this diversion can be exemplified through the initial denial by the UK government of the application of the Transfer of Undertakings (Protection of Employment) (TUPE) Regulations (Kerr and Radford, 1994).

As this book demonstrates, statecraft has used a succession of metanarratives to drive institutional reform in government based on the agreement to implement public sector liberalisation. These have included the need to save money, as a political ideology during Thatcher's first government 1979–1983 (Bulpitt, 1986), as efficiency (the Rayner scrutinies 1983–1990) (Warner, 1984), as effectiveness (major market testing and agencification 1990–1997) (Rittenberg and Covaleski, 1999), as performance management (NPM/Labour government 1997–2010) (Demirkaya, 2006) and as austerity (successive Cameron governments 2010–2016) (Fairclough, 2016). The role and use of policy narratives as mechanisms and carriers in the implementation of statecraft objectives are also important. While statecraft can be a process of misdirection and obfuscation of public understanding of the underlying and on-going political dimensions of public policy, it is frequently the policy narratives that are carrying the weight of this.

Public policy narratives blend the underlying agenda setting issues (Kingdon, 1993); this is why the policy is of high priority for implementation, with the optimal dimensions for communicating the justifications for these policies within their ideological framing. These policy narratives carry a major load in political justification within the frame of government political ideologies (Shanahan et al, 2011). They are also associated with civil service expectations for opportunities to revise policy at the time of changes in political leadership or the party in power. General elections are less disruptive and easier to use than sharp shifts in direction in the middle of a government's term in office (Franklin, 2003; White and Dunleavy, 2010). Such changes can be engineered by using shocks such as economic or health crises but these can be unpredictable and less easy to control in practice. However, for implementation of policy change to meet external agreements, including the implementation of the GPA and GATS, civil servants prefer electoral cycles to political disruption. As the practical effects on public sector liberalisation in these international agreements on the GPA and the GATS have not been in the public domain, they have remained hidden in plain sight. The regulations for compliance are laid in Parliament and monitoring returns are made to the WTO and the Organisation for Economic Co-operation and Development but are not introduced into public discourse.

All public policy is socially constructed but is generally examined within specific policy contexts (Jones and McBeth, 2010; Shanahan et al, 2011). The alliance between changes in policy to meet external commitments and political parties in power can be understood as being an outcome of a specific political event − that is an election. If there is a change in the party in power then the electorate expects a change in expressed ideology accompanied by a narrative of why change is needed. These changes can appear abrupt (Baumgartner and Jones, 1993) but, where governments have continuing international commitments, it the role of statecraft to create new narratives to deliver existing policies where this is required. Here policy narratives have a performative and presentational role that distracts people from the lack of change between two governments of different parties, in a form of 'old wine in new bottles'. Where international agreements need more fundamental change to achieve compliant implementation, general elections also have a pivotal role.

This underlying policy continuity for public sector liberalisation has been a design feature of governments from 1976 onwards. The challenge for the civil service has been to find metanarratives that can provide ideological alignments with the party in power but also deliver the underlying commitments. One of the interesting features of this approach in the UK has been the way in which agreements with the WTO and EU have been separated through political communication and the media despite the core agreement being the same (Abbott, 1990; Meunier, 2005). Much of the EU's policy for the Single European Market and procurement has been for the application of international agreements made by member states with the WTO and its predecessor, GATT. One of the key benefits that was expected after Brexit was an end to the EU public procurement regime, including adverts in *OJEU*, procurement thresholds and packaging regulations (Morris and Kibasi, 2019). However, the UK has made these legal agreements with the WTO and they will continue after Brexit (Morphet, 2017).

The specific actions by government departments to deliver these international agreements might be described as being at the meso or micro levels (Shanahan et al, 2011) and have been used to convey how the metanarrative is translated into specific policy delivery (Morphet, 2013). While efficiency and effectiveness are metanarratives that have been used by successive governments, the mesonarratives might be denationalisation, right to buy, citizen's charter, best value or social value. These convey the overriding principles into programmes of action before being translated at the micro level into specific policies.

While metanarratives convey belief or ethical ideologies, these are incorporated within the policy design of delivery. This has been particularly important within public sector liberalisation because the overriding ideologies of parties in government and the civil service have chosen to exclude some legal options within the framing narrative in order to make it conform to overriding political expectations. This has had a considerable effect on the way in which outsourcing has been implemented in the UK. This is particularly apparent since devolution in 1999, where all four nations are operating within the same liberalisation regime. Scotland, Wales and Northern Ireland have strengthened the welfare state using the wider opportunities contained in GPA and GATS procurement regulations (Mooney and Wright, 2009). In England, these lessons have been learned by local authorities, pressured into innovation and policy divergence, from each other and the government, to survive austerity (Morphet and Clifford, 2020). UK central government's response to the COVID-19 pandemic has been entirely focused on outsourced delivery through over £1bn expenditure on contracts awarded without competition (Monbiot, 2020). This has been despite civil service objections, where 11 ministerial directions have been given (NAO, 2020d). It is also an approach that has not embraced the experience of countries more successful in managing the death rate and moving from lockdown (OECD, 2020). The comparative death rate demonstrates the significant differences in the UK, particularly England, where outsourcing has been the primary mode and death rates have been much higher (King's Fund, 2020). Local authorities and their directors of public health in England have increasingly taken over from these centrally failing approaches whether for testing, provision of PPE and test, or track and trace while the funding for these activities has remained with the private contractors (NAO, 2020d).

Policy failure

The development of the neoliberal state has been changed by private sector delivery – through financial failures such as Carillion (NAO, 2020b) or in the ways service design, specification and performance management regimes have run counter to service objectives (Whitfield, 2012). These failures have occurred in railways (NAO, 2015b), back office services (NAO, 2015c), probation (NAO, 2019a), migration services (NAO, 2014a) and deportation centres (NAO, 2012).

The failures of the market and service companies have demonstrated that while public sector organisations can contract their service to other providers, sharing some of the risks, they are not able to pass these responsibilities to contractors (Harvey, 2007, p 79; NAO, 2020b). This continuing responsibility has been demonstrated following the Grenfell Tower fire (Gorse and Sturges, 2017) and in railway disasters (Tyrrall, 2004). While private health care can deliver routine procedures, any difficult, non-routine cases are transferred to the National Health Service (Williams et al, 2001). Where there are contract failures or costs rise, public bodies terminate contracts at a loss to the taxpayer (NAO, 2020b). When service contracts end, services can be taken back into direct delivery rather than recontracted. When the public sector in the UK had to demonstrate opening their services to competition, these choices were less available (Walsh, 1995a). Now that these have been achieved, they have not resulted in a greater use of the private sector to deliver public services but rather there is a return to more direct provision and a mixed economy (LGA, 2019).

Outsourcing, liberalisation, offshoring, externalisation or privatisation?

One consideration for this book is what is meant by outsourcing and how this term works with more popularly used terms of liberalisation, privatisation and externalisation. In much of the public sector literature, these terms are used interchangeably. What is common is that they indicate a degree of policy or political will on the part of the public sector organisation that is implementing them. These terms also imply that there is an expected outcome – that is that the services cannot be operated directly by the public sector, despite their role in funding and ultimate accountability (NAO, 2019a; NAO, 2020a). These terms incorporate the view that the status quo cannot continue and, in the future, services will be delivered in a delegated or arm's length way on a contractual basis. All approaches are associated with neoliberal ideologies that favour market methods above direct delivery, which has traditionally been used in the public sector (Stewart and Walsh, 1992). It is useful to unpack what is meant by each term.

Liberalisation

The term 'liberalisation' refers to the removal of restrictions, generally but not exclusively in trade. Market liberalisation in the public sector occurs when the services that are funded by public institutions are opened to being provided by third parties – from the public, private and third sectors (Ascher, 1987; Parker, 2009). The process of liberalisation is generally through competition and different bodies make a tender to undertake the service or provide goods within the specification provided by the organisation purchasing the service.

Privatisation

Since the adoption of the GATT Tokyo Round GPA, the use of the private sector to deliver public services has increased across the world and has been accompanied by the trope of poor performance of public bodies (Boycko et al, 1996). There have also been assumptions that, at times of economic decline, publicly owned bodies were more interested in their role as employers rather than as efficient providers. In the UK, the term 'privatisation' has been regarded as a metaphor for tactical political strategy to change the nature of the state by a section of the Conservative Party that favoured the market (Graham, 1995). Privatisation was a preferred political strategy to implement the GPA and GATS (Pliatzky, 1988; Ridley, 1992) although not an approach that was required in the agreements (Bovis, 2019). The word 'privatisation' is used as an expected outcome of competition rather than as a verb describing a process that has followed open market competitive tendering as it is pejorative.

Externalisation

Externalisation is the process of providing organisational services by contracted third parties (Goe, 1991; Torres and Pina, 2002).

Outsourcing

The term 'outsourcing' is used when an organisation hires another to perform functions on a contractual basis that were previously undertaken 'in-house', that is inside the organisation. The contracting organisation may be from the public, private or third sectors. The object of outsourcing is primarily expected to be a cost reduction to the client organisation based on reducing labour costs by using the outsourcing process to reduce service specifications or changing the nature of the service more fundamentally (Bovaird, 2016). Outsourcing began to be used as a term in the late 1980s but this was not when the provision of services within organisations by third parties began (Parker, 2009). In the private sector, outsourcing has been associated with a globalised approach to providing delivery suppliers – sometimes called offshoring (Oshri et al, 2015). This has generated an international supply market that has been a central element of globalisation (Aron and Singh, 2005).

Outsourcing can also be focussed on reducing direct costs such as accommodation and employee costs including national insurance and indemnity insurance (Schulten et al, 2008). The contractor may be able to use cheaper accommodation and employ people on zero-hours contracts or through service companies (Brinkley, 2013). These reduce direct employment costs for the contractor by transferring risks to the labour force who are no longer legally defined as employees. Organisations started to consider the separation of activities by moving back office functions such as accounts, customer management systems, production and servicing to less expensive locations in the 1960s (Stringfellow et al, 2008). This started in the UK with financial services such as insurance and mortgage finance, which were moved out of the city into back office locations such as those in Basildon and Witham in Essex and extended to other central functions in organisations including central government (Marshall et al, 1991; Rydin, 1998). In some cases, services such as procurement and payroll have been outsourced to other similar public organisations (LGA, 2016c).

One major driver for outsourcing, in addition to cost cutting, was stated as improving performance or achieving guaranteed delivery times (Ruddock, 1994). Some organisations have chosen to outsource their services to contractors where they are required to deliver a response within a fixed period of time and have used this to transfer risk of non-performance to a third party (Bing et al, 2005). This transfer of risk has costs associated with it that are included in the supplier's contract valuation (Hellowell and Vecchi, 2012). Organisations argue that outsourcing is a strategic choice and can help them focus on their business rather than the processing and delivery functions (Quinn and Hilmer, 1994). However, detachment from the organisational responsibilities can lead to distancing and loss of understanding of the business (Rhodes, 2001). There can also be a breakdown of communication between the organisation and the contracting party (NAO, 2020b). In manufacturing and other consumer businesses, there can also be concerns that the distance between the contractor and the responsible organisation has an influence on the ethics of the supplier. Where there has been an outsourcing of call centres to other parts of the world, there have been concerns about cultural misunderstandings (Grossman and Helpman, 2005).

In government, the processes of relocating back office services outside central London started in the 1950s and then accelerated in the 1960s as part of regional policy (Glasson and Marshall, 2007). The distribution of central functions to areas needing economic support and new towns was accompanied by a ban on the development of office accommodation in London that was reinforced through the 1972 Industry Act (Marshall et al, 1991). Her Majesty's Revenue and Customs moved its operations to Cumbernauld in Scotland, and other regional centres, and later was further decentralised (Carter et al, 2012). The Rural Payments Agency was moved to Newcastle and the Driver and Vehicle Licensing Agency to Swansea, and other tax centres were established. These were approaches to regional economic policy but they had already identified back office work as non-essential and suitable to be transferred to a peripheral location. This meant that the later practices of identifying less important activities for potential agencification or outsourcing was already established within the civil service.

2

The Legal Basis for Competition in Public Services

Introduction

The legal agreements and constructs that provide the operating framework for outsourcing in the UK are seldom discussed and more frequently regarded as the result of neoliberal ideology being applied by successive governments (Harvey, 2007). The opening of public sector procurement for goods and services from 1980 gradually replaced a direct delivery model, which had prevailed as the norm in the UK since the 1880s. The liberalisation of the public sector has had a long and international tail (Jackson et al, 1982). In any international policy, agreed within a treaty, each signatory state is bound to apply what has been included within it, which may stretch into the future (Aust, 2013). In this case, the Labour government in 1976 agreed that the UK would adopt the Government Procurement Agreement (GPA), which was then in negotiation as part of the Tokyo Round (1973–1980) of the General Agreement on Tariffs and Trade (GATT) (Jackson et al, 1982; Winham, 2014). Through this decision, the government entered into obligations to liberalise public sector procurement, of goods and then services, opening it to competition from domestic and international organisations (De Graaf and King, 1995).

As with all international agreements, each signatory state starts from a different point and has to determine its own domestic policy agenda to achieve the delivery of terms of the international agreement (Jackson et al, 1982; Bown, 2004). The discussions on how to implement such agreements can be in the public domain, but for those that will operate over decades, different cultural and institutional frameworks and policy redesign from those prevailing at the time of the agreement may be required (De Graaf and King, 1995). Governments, supported by civil servants, will apply the tools of statecraft to embed these changes using all available means (Smith and Jones, 2015). They will attempt to implement the easiest options first, often described by management consultants as 'low hanging fruit' (Thorburn, 2020), both to make some early progress and to show the holders of these international obligations that a start has been made to comply with agreed commitments. This was the case for the GPA in the UK. The progress towards opening public services to competition and outsourcing was undertaken in a programmed way, leaving the most politically contentious services to later – education and health. Those activities that were within the government's control, such as transport and the nationalised industries, were the first to be tackled in the 1980s (Parker, 2009). The pressure on local authorities to open their services to outsourcing came in the second wave in the late 1980s as the GPA was extended to include their activities and construction while services were added at the adoption of the General Agreement on Trade in Services (GATS) in 1994 (Kuijper, 1995).

In the UK, before 1980, competition in the market and its regulation was primarily confined to the private sector. The public sector, including the industries nationalised after 1945, local government, the National Health Service (NHS) and other services held in the public interest like the Crown Agents were all delivered by directly employed staff with some supplementary contracting for construction growing in the 1960s (Ball, 1983). The UK was regarded as having a strong legacy in the management of monopolies and restrictive practices (OECD, 2002), through the establishment of an investigative commission in 1948 (Utton, 2000). This commission undertook a range of reviews of the private sector, focussing on restrictive practices and fair trading. However, government departments were defensive about enquiries into sectors that were within their remit. These approaches to reviewing competition were not considered to be wholly effective and annual studies on monopolies and on restrictive practices, published in 1978 and 1979 and based on the collected commission evidence, found the UK economy to be dominated by large firms. These were operating in oligopolistic markets, to a greater extent than any other major industrial power, and were identified as having 'characteristic monopolising practices' (OECD, 2002, p 9).

These issues were addressed in the Competition Act 1980 that was also used to consider the operation of the nationalised industries and utilities. In retrospect, this can be viewed as preparation for their privatisation. There were 35 reports under the Competition Act from 1980 to 1993, including postal services, rail, electric power, water, steel and coal (Parker, 2000,

2009). The privatisation of these state monopolies became the focus of the government rather than maintaining watch on the practices of the wider private sector (Ridley, 1992). There was a long delay between announcing the intention to reform the private sector competition assessment in 1988 and the reform in 1998. The Organisation for Economic Co-operation and Development (OECD) (2002) suggests that this was because the UK was awaiting the development of the EU approach. After the 1998 Competition Act, the UK approach was consistent with that set out by the EU (McCarthy, 1999) and was adopted with very little public comment or discussion in the UK. The timing of both Competition Acts in 1980 and 1998 coincided with the coming into force of the GPA and GATS agreements in 1980 and 1995 and changes in governments.

GATT GPA 1980

The development of the Government Procurement Code (GPC) that was put into the GPA was part of world trading agreements established in 1947 as the GATT. This has continued, becoming the World Trade Organization in 1995 (Preeg, 2012). Initially GATT was focused on trading agreements between states. It was extended to include plurilateral agreements between groups of states that had the objective of establishing customs unions – that is trading areas without tariffs for trade between them. Some sectors such as agriculture operate within the wider agreements while keeping their distinctive character (Anderson, 2005). For EU member states, both the GPA and the GATS are set into the EU's Customs Union and Single European Market (SEM) (Abbott, 1990). The EU has acted as a facilitator and enforcer of the implementation of these international agreements within member states although the agreements made within the GATT (and later the WTO) are made on an individual state basis (Meunier, 2005).

The Tokyo Round of the GATT (1973–1980) introduced the liberalisation of the public sector market to the private sector (Jackson et al, 1982). It did this by extending fundamental trade obligations of non-discrimination in national treatment and most favoured nation status to include government procurement (Winham, 2014). This GPA was accompanied by requirements for transparency and dispute resolution procedures through the use of international courts. Until the GPA, governments had virtually no restraints on their procurement policies and practices (Audet, 2002). The work to develop the GPA was supported by the OECD, which circulated a Draft Instrument on Government Purchasing Policies, Procedures and Practices in November 1976.

The GPA is a plurilateral agreement applying to signatory states, rather than all members of the GATT. Initially it was limited to the purchase of goods above a specified value threshold of $195,000. The GPA was later renegotiated and extended to construction, services, local authorities and public undertakings during the Uruguay Round (1986–1994) (De Graaf and King, 1995). From the outset, the GPA included a range of options for selecting a contractor's bid against specific evaluation criteria set in any procurement process either based on lowest price or quality. While it was recognised that a quality-based approach to evaluation of contracts could still lead to domestic preferences, it was regarded as doubtful that a quality approach could be removed from international agreements (Mattoo, 1996).

The extension of the GATT to include public procurement was based on several issues (Jackson et al, 1982). Firstly, there was concern that the private sector had reached its full market potential. While new products might be developed, it was assumed that there would be market saturation. The public sector offered a potential opportunity to expand private markets. Public sector expenditure had not been considered as a market in the post-1945 consensus but was rather viewed as state expenditure to provide public goods and services (Timmins, 2001). In some parts of the public sector, such as local government, there were joint organisations for the management of services and facilities including cemeteries and parks and the provision of computer services and public health laboratories. However, this provision of services was not considered in the same way as the market for goods, services and assets in the private sector (Gingrich, 2011). Local government had also been subject to reorganisation in the early 1970s that created more self-sufficient, larger local authorities suitable for direct service provision (Greenwood et al, 1975). The UK government anticipated that local authorities would take on much of the implementation of any EU agreements, when the UK joined in 1972, leaving central government activity largely untouched (Rippon, 1973; Haigh, 1996). However, it had not considered the implications of this scaling up of local authority size for subsequent competition thresholds within the GPA, although this was also emerging through negotiation at the same time.

Secondly, there was a push towards globalisation (Woolcock and Hodges, 1996) where companies wanted to supply their products and services across a range of countries without the additional costs of specific regulatory regimes that could act as non-tariff barriers to trade. While many companies operate as multi-nationals across different countries, globalisation offered the opportunity for greater efficiencies in production through the use of common standards and labour regulation. This was particularly the case within the SEM (Wallace and Young, 1996) and had considerable effects on domestic markets, production and user expectations that were socially and economically disruptive (Cavusgil, 1993). As globalisation has developed, companies have also become more adept in their use of different locations for transfer pricing, taxation and reporting of profit as companies (OECD, 2017b).

Thirdly, the scale of public sector procurement has been estimated to form between 10 per cent and 20 per cent of the world's trade (Audet, 2002). The internal direct delivery of services by public sector organisations meant that they were not exposed to any process of competition and the form of this type of service delivery was regarded as a non-tariff barrier to trade for domestic preferences that excluded both domestic and third country organisations (McAfee and McMillan, 1989).

In the 1960s, both the private sector and right of centre governments started to push for change. The argument for liberalisation was also emerging on the left, with a consideration of the practical limits on state ownership (Bockman, 2011). In the UK, there were emerging discussions about whether the economy could continue to grow without some major changes in industrial practices, focussed initially on the utilities and transport sectors (Shanks, 1961). These changes may have been easier to envisage in the sectors that had been taken into state ownership in the immediate post-war period (Parker, 2009). Crosland (1956) suggested ways that a mixed market could be developed where private and public sectors could co-exist in the support of the economy and efficient running of industry. However, Crosland did not envisage liberalisation of state expenditure on public services, even as the country was having a financial crisis in 1976 (Burk and Cairncross, 1992; Wass, 2008). The same was true of Margaret Thatcher before her first term of office as Prime Minister in 1979 (Seldon and Collings, 2014).

For governments, if public services were to be delivered at increasing levels as expected by the electorate, the associated growing costs implied increases in taxation. The introduction of the GPA, including the injection of private sector knowledge, experience and funding, might help governments maintain service delivery levels and standards without the accompanying levels of cost to the public purse. When the GPA came into effect in 1980, after a long period of development and negotiation, it included defence and central government but not sub-national governments (Graham, 1995). The GATT policies also tackled the preferences for domestic suppliers and the protection that they were afforded against external competition from the market and abroad (Foy, 1992). Before the GPA, Australia had a 20 per cent preference for domestic suppliers and New Zealand 10 per cent (McAfee and McMillan,

1989). Some countries, such as Sweden, initially resisted the GPA, but the Scandinavian model adopted different approaches to competition in public services (Larsson et al, 2012) and by the 1990s had developed a range of privatised services (Blomqvist, 2004). There were also critics of the 'McDonaldization' of public services (Ritzer, 1983; Caputo et al, 1998; Gingrich, 2011).

The GPA public sector liberalisation negotiations did not enter UK public discourse in parallel with their progress. Between 1970 and 1974, during the Edward Heath government, pressures to liberalise the public sector were already emerging (Taylor, 1996). In the US, Milton Friedman had won the Nobel prize for economics in 1976 for his work on monetary policy arguing against Keynesianism, indicating that the economic orthodoxy that framed the discussions of international economic and trade policy were changing. There was also a movement towards increasing liberalisation and deregulation of competition (Harvey, 2007) including the changes implemented by Clinton such as the removal of the Glass–Steagall Act 1993 that deregulated the banking sector (Hendrickson, 2001). This was characterised by the US state as 'steering' rather than 'rowing' (Osborne and Gaebler, 1993) – directing rather than delivering – in a powerful internationally adopted management metaphor that captured the change introduced by the GPA but without associating it with opening services to competition (Morphet, 2008).

While there may not have been an expectation of the private sector running public services, there was an increasing rhetoric about the need for efficiency and the embedding neoliberalism in government (Taylor, 1996). This was also a mantra of 'less government', which was another mechanism for reducing public expenditure. As former Thatcher minister Nicholas Ridley later recalled, this started to usher in the era of privatisation (Ridley, 1992; Mount, 2020a). Ridley was the president of the Selsdon Group, a think tank in favour of promoting privatisation founded in 1973 (Selsdon Group, 1973). It took up Friedman's approach and started to lobby for its application in the UK (Charmley, 1998).

Before the 1979 election, Ridley's confidential report on the privatisation of the public utilities was leaked through *The Economist* (27 May 1978, pp 21–2). Although there was some immediate public rowing back on its ideas by the leaders of the Conservative Party (Seldon and Collings, 2014), this did not represent a movement away from the ideas but more 'soft testing' to gauge public opinion and prepare for change. While Ridley's report promoted liberalising the public sector, it also set an important political agenda by characterising the public sector as the enemy of the Conservatives in power (Dobek, 1993), which has since been a persistent mantra of Party ideology.

In 1976, the UK suffered a major financial crisis when the Chancellor of the Exchequer had to go to the International Monetary Fund (IMF) for financial support (Harmon, 1997; Wass, 2008). The IMF brought funding to the UK together with a review and overhaul of the internal operation of its public sector expenditure (Parker, 2009). In the post-war period, the UK continued paying down war debts that were not repaid until 2004. It was using these funds to fulfil the military covenant to provide its returning soldiers with public housing, the NHS and new schools (Addison, 2011). The economy also needed to be supported by investment in transport infrastructure, where roads were favoured over rail or other public transport projects (Parker, 2009). However, by the mid-1970s, the funds had started to run out, and while there had been significant public investment, run down older industries and the closure of the docks in East London meant that by 1976 some places in the UK had male unemployment rates of over 25 per cent. The UK was in recession and entered a period of stagflation where prices increased as the economy stagnated (Harvey, 2007). For the public sector, this meant the end of public capital investment and post-1945 rises in standards of public services.

The potential for private investment in public services through their partial privatisation, as offered through this new GPA approach, seemed to be the only option available where there were no public funds. No political party in the UK wanted to take the same approach as 'Red' Bologna, which took more assets and services into public control as an alternative economic strategy (Jäggi et al, 1977; Green, 1978). However, despite the pressure on budgets, private investment in public services was not a pathway that the Prime Minister, James Callaghan (1976–1979), seemed disposed to implement with any enthusiasm (Morgan, 1997). The 1979 general election saved Callaghan from making these choices. While Thatcher was the harbinger of liberalisation, the general election in 1979 allowed a political change to deliver GPA commitments. There was a coalescence between the UK's implementation of the GPA and the Prime Minister's burgeoning ideology that could be harnessed to achieve these changes.

The UK implementation of the GPA needed a major change in the previous public service approaches that were set in direct provision. Public servants were expected to use fair decision making in their selection of contractors for works or in the allocation of council housing. When Thatcher came to power, her ideology represented a major opportunity for public policy to change: the government implemented the GPA without having to publicly admit that this was an undertaking that had been entered into by the previous Labour government (Morphet, 2013).

The Thatcher programme included two major sets of actions (Gamble, 1989; Burton, 1987). The first was to start a process of privatising public utilities including gas, electricity, the post office, the British rail, coal and the provision of water (Parker, 2009, 2012). These were nationally owned and controlled activities and could be progressed with a strong Parliamentary majority.

The second set of actions was more preparatory, in the expectation that there would be an extension of the GPA into internal services within public sector bodies (De Graaf and King, 1995) through the development of the GATT Uruguay Round, which officially started in 1986. There were issues to confront here. Firstly, there had never been any consideration of public services as a market and how they might be specified before they could be open to competition. Secondly, there was no understanding of their operational costs and the sunk cost in their assets (Hoekman, 1995). Thirdly, there was no private sector set of companies ready to compete for public services (Croome, 1996). While functions and staff could be switched into new organisations, this could be commercially risky. Potential contractors would not have the appropriate experience on which to base a tender for services. There would be sensitivity in transferring government services to start-up companies. One approach was adopted in the BBC where transitional 'sweetheart deals' were arranged, with proportions of programming being switched over a five-year period (Born, 2011).

Implementing the GPA in the UK

When considering the ways in which the UK responded to the implementation of the GATT Tokyo Round, there is very little to indicate that it was being delivered. These decisions and any subsequent action taken to implement these GPA commitments are not addressed in the *Official History of Privatisation* (Parker, 2009, 2012). This may have been because the UK had joined the European Economic Community (EEC) as the Tokyo Round had started in 1973 and there was intentional conflation of issues in the negotiations (Winham, 2014). There are issues for governments and their civil services to consider when adopting international agreements and their application within domestic policy. In the UK, a choice was made to submerge both EU and GATT negotiations within Whitehall while developing domestic policy to match the political ideology of any government in power or likely to win the next general election (Wallace, 1973; Morphet, 2013). The UK's approach differed from other countries, such as the US, where there were public discussions about whether the GPA would lead to changes in the Machinery of Government (Jackson et al, 1982).

Rather than have any public discourse on the liberalisation effects of EEC and GATT memberships, the UK central government chose to internalise negotiations and preparations, using them as an ideological tool to change domestic policy. The preparation to introduce government competition and privatisation offered opportunities to change the state. The civil service, which has a focus on continuity while governments change, may have considered that any acknowledgement of influence on policy that was directed by international agreements, including GATT or the new relationship with the EEC, may have made them and the UK appear weak (Bulmer and Burch, 2005). There were also power struggles between the European Commission (EC) and the member state governments on trade (Meunier and Nicolaïdis, 2005). The GATT negotiations were pivotal in this, particularly in the roles played by France and the UK (Hanley, 1996). Ownership of the application of these agreements by Whitehall rather than Westminster allowed the civil service to offer specific policy tools to incoming governments that matched their political priorities. By 1974, public discussion of all EEC matters had been submerged (Morphet, 2013). As there was a clear relationship between the EEC and the GATT Tokyo Round negotiations, this might be regarded as a continuation of the same approach. Further, civil servants considered that, as a new member state of the EU with existing international standing, the UK could bring both expertise and influence (Wall, 2008). It was also an opportunity for the UK to take a distanced and quasi-colonial stance on the implementation and application of these agreements (Haigh, 1996). There was an early assumption in the civil service that these EU agreements would apply to delivery by local government rather than central government policy making (Rippon, 1973).

For the civil service, there had been reviews of their fitness for purpose by the Fulton Committee, 1966–1968, which it had managed to thwart (Fry, 1990). With the introduction of the potential opening of government procurement to competition, the civil service did not want any further undermining of its position through airing these changes in public (Theakston, 1995). As the Tokyo Round negotiations continued through the 1970s, there were also opportunities for the civil service to 'change the weather' on the policy debate on the extent to which governments should remain owners of nationalised industries (Pendleton, 1997). Through a range of think tanks created in the 1950s, supportive of liberalisation and increasingly funded by like-minded bodies in the US, including the Institute of Economic affairs and the Adam Smith Institute, there was an opportunity to introduce these ideas. The response to the

IMF financial crisis of 1976 included conditions for assistance placed on the UK that the government should spend less (Wass, 2008). Civil servants were casting around for the means to introduce change, and these interventions in the national debate on public ownership created the opportunity for action (Harmon, 1997).

While international agreements have most public focus at the point when agreed, governments have a fuller understanding of the predicted outcomes during the negotiations and use this period to prepare for eventual implementation (Wallace, 1973). Even before the start of the Uruguay Round of negotiations in 1986, the Thatcher government adopted three different models to prepare for the implementation of the GATS. The Rayner scrutinies by the Efficiency Unit (1979–1983) advised on ways that the central government could be made more efficient through scrutinies focused on recommended action rather than reviews and reports (Haddon, 2012). This was supported by the Financial Management Initiative in 1982 (Gray and Jenkins, 1986; Fry, 1988). Permanent Secretaries, who were heads of the government departments, found ways of using scrutinies that served their own ends or diverted scrutiny attention to minor issues such as the office canteen (Rhodes, 2001). Structural reform was introduced through the creation of the Next Steps Agencies following the Next Steps report in 1987 (Kemp, 1990; Gains, 1999). By this time, more clarity was emerging on the content and approach of the Uruguay Round. An internal review of the Efficiency Unit (Kemp, 1990; Haddon, 2012) provided an opportunity to change direction to prepare for the GATS, which was going to have a more direct influence on the liberalisation of central and local governments. This would require a more fundamental reform of government institutions.

Implementing the GATS

The pressure to open the trade in services to competition had been growing following the conclusion of the Tokyo Round in 1980 and was regarded an 'unfinished business' (Croome, 1996). Initially, the GATS did not include government procurement of services but it was agreed that negotiation would be commenced within two years by the WTO when it took over at the end of the Uruguay Round in 1994. This commitment was included within an extended version of the GPA in 1987, although there was an agreement that there could be no prescription in the mode of supply in the public sector (Preeg, 2012). The role of governments, in determining which services should be identified for priority exposure in relation to the potential benefits to their economies, was central to this process of introduction of the GATS (Hoekman, 2000). For services in the private sector, governments would expect to be influenced and lobbied by interest groups on the operation of the GATS (Kochanek, 1996). For public services, there was an expectation of reverse lobbying in favour of opening up the public sector to providers of services and to exclude bids for work by public employees.

For governments, one of the benefits of the GATS approach was that in setting programmes and schedules for the implementation, it could be associated with a domestic reform agenda (Hoekman, 2000). This reflected the approach taken by the UK, as a form of statecraft. The implementation of the GATS agreement in 1996 coincided with the closing of the Conservative period of government (Audet, 2002). This presented an interesting challenge for the civil service to consider how the GATS could be implemented in ways that would sit within the ideology of the incoming Labour government in 1997.

EU, competition and the WTO

The experience of the EEC in the GATT Tokyo Round 1973–1979, with a lack of clarity of the power of its negotiating position on behalf of all member states, had a significant influence on the conduct of the Uruguay Round for services when it started in 1986 (Kuijper, 1995). In the application of the agreements in the Tokyo Round, some were put into effect by the EEC through Regulations, others by Directives and some remained for member states to implement individually (Woolcock and Hodges, 1996). This reflected the extent to which the Treaty of Rome (1957) could be interpreted as passing powers to the EC (Jackson et al, 1982). As a response, some reform of the EEC legal basis was expected that would clarify the extent of its negotiation powers for the Uruguay Round (Meunier, 2005). Within the context of the GPA, the EEC had developed an approach to the procurement of goods and services within the SEM implemented in 1992 (Audet, 2002). The same approach had been adopted through the creation of the North American Free Trade Association (NAFTA) in 1994.

One of the stated reasons for the UK joining the EEC in the 1960s was economic (Wall, 2008). The UK wanted access to markets to trade goods. The market for services was not developed then although the ways in which Harold Macmillan, when Prime Minister, opened up household financing through the extension of credit and the mortgage markets in 1962 enabled the UK to become a leader in financial services (Aveyard et al, 2018). As Woolcock and Hodges (1996) point out there has always been a tension in the development of EU policy through potential conflict between national and community interests. This is particularly the case of trade where different member states have longstanding strengths and investment in specific markets (Meunier and Nicolaïdis, 2005; Moravcsik, 1994). While these differences can offer the benefit of trade-offs within internal negotiation, the role of the EC in negotiating on behalf of all members in external trade agreements can be more difficult (Meunier, 2005).

Initially, the main focus of the EEC was to create a market within its own members so that the economic and trading benefits could be retained internally. The internal approach to competition had been first established through the Treaty of Rome (1957), and as integration studies in the 1970s demonstrate, there had always been an intention to create a full economic union that was beyond a customs union (Baldwin, 1994). There was also an expectation that creating a larger market for the purchase of goods and services would establish a more influential bargaining position when dealing with third countries in an international market (Meunier and Nicolaïdis, 2005).

The development of the SEM 1985–1992 was a mechanism to achieve international influence and increase the benefits of internal trading (Wallace and Young, 1996). In the adoption of the GPA and GATS, there was an opportunity for the EC to shape policy and delivery compliance across the member states (Allen, 1996). Before 1985 there had been attempts to harmonise legislation in member states but this was a slow process and eventually the economic crises at the beginning of the 1980s put pressure on the EEC to deal with these issues in a more fundamental way. It was agreed through the Single European Act (SEA) 1985 that there would be a more embracing and formal process to create the single market (Schildhaus, 1989). This process was led by Lord Cockfield, the UK's EU Commissioner (Cockfield, 1994). The SEA 1985 created a programme to achieve a SEM in 1992, in the year that the UK would hold the rotating presidency of the EU.

The SEM also provided an opportunity to adopt a unified approach to a single welfare state across all member states (Morphet and Clifford, 2020). This encompassed workers' rights, health care, transferability of these rights across member state borders and unifying standards for EU citizens that extended beyond their life at work (Wallace and Young, 1996). The SEM was based on the four freedoms of good, services, capital and people. The SEM also included EC powers to regulate market functioning, market access, competitive conditions and sectoral policy (Moravcsik, 1994). The competition aspects of the SEM are upheld by the European Court of Justice, which has contributed to competition policy through its judgements (Allen, 1996). The SEM has developed incrementally and has been able to adapt and extend to new markets as they emerge such as social media and IT platforms including a standard for data protection and privacy as set out in the EU Regulation CEC 2016/679.

The SEM was also associated with increasing efficiency in the provision of goods and services within the member states (Moravcsik, 1994). This was implemented through a single regulatory framework that would reduce costs on business. This allows cross-border movements and increasing 'just in time' manufacturing processes without delays at internal member state borders for companies, manufacture and assembly (Cockfield, 1994). The regulatory framework also extended to increasing mutual recognition of professional qualifications (Blitz, 1999). In the development and implementation of the SEM, Prime Minister John Major considered that there was a strong case for European Enlargement related to the GPA (Higashino, 2004). The increase in the number of member states would enhance the market's size, and for a period of time, the high-skilled, low-wage economies of Eastern Europe would give the new EU SEM a significant international competitive edge (Pellegrin, 2016).

The role of the OECD in applying the GPA and GATS

The OECD is a membership organisation that uses soft power rather than legal agreements to influence the actions of governments and other undertakings. It was set up in 1947 as part of the post-war settlement and establishment of other international institutions including the GATT. It has a concern for the interaction between social, environmental and economic policies. While it undertakes work on trade, it is also concerned with the impacts of poverty, environment, living standards and the effects on economic policies on the lives of the citizens of its members (Porter and Webb, 2008). Its membership stretches across the US, the EU, Australia and Canada as well some South American and South East Asian states. However, some countries such as Singapore have not been allowed to join because their political and governance regimes have not been judged as meeting the democratic standards of other member countries (Armingeon, 2004).

The OECD develops its own policies in conjunction with its members but also works with the major international economic institutions such as the IMF and WTO and with trade groupings such as the EU and NAFTA. The WTO maintains close links with the OECD, attending

Council meetings, and there is regular interaction between staff of the institutions. The OECD can provide a mechanism for sounding out members, who are all members of the WTO, about their priorities and objectives for change (OECD/WTO, 2019). The WTO can also use work undertaken by the OECD to inform their own policies and programmes (Lyal, 2015; OECD, 2017b). The WTO and OECD have worked together on specific programmes such as transfer pricing and aid for trade. In 2019 both organisations launched a joint study into the WTO's role in supporting international regulatory cooperation (OECD/WTO, 2019), in recognition of the globalisation of the economy and international business organisations.

The relationship between the OECD and WTO, in the operation of public procurement of goods and services and the liberalisation of the market, is one where the OECD is an adviser both to the WTO and to its own members (OECD, 2018). In 2015, the OECD adopted a policy on public procurement (OECD, 2017a). In the study undertaken to provide guidance on implementing these changes, the OECD found that considerable action was required to improve the role of procurement in public services (OECD, 2019). The key criticisms related to the objectives set for the procurement process and whether these are met in practice and delivered through a contract, if a service is outsourced. The study found that civil servants were not adequately trained and skilled in procurement and questioned whether they had the appropriate capacity. Only ten members of the OECD undertake capacity assessments of their procurement staff and this does not include the UK. The OECD has also provided advice on procurement to include SMEs to ensure these are part of the process (OECD, 2018) and how to procure innovation (OECD, 2017a).

The OECD undertakes comparative studies of member states to support their agreed programmes. Through case studies, there can be an exchange of good practice, policy transfer and benchmarking between states to support improvement and to provide an underlying climate and culture of compliance (OECD, 2019). In 2019, the OECD estimated that 12 per cent of member states' GDP was spent by public bodies in procurement (OECD, 2018, 2019). To support their activities, the OECD has agreed on principles and provided a toolbox for members. It relates public procurement to the principles of good public governance and applies it as a barometer of efficient and effective operation within the state. This does not mean that the OECD is in favour of privatisation but does support the application of fair competition as a mechanism for the improvement of public services (OECD, 2017a). In undertaking its case studies, the OECD considers different types of public procurement including goods and services and individual projects as well as multiple purchase. The OECD recognises that the procurement environment can be complex and has undertaken specific projects on major events, major infrastructure (OECD, 2015a, 2015b), health and energy (OECD, 2011).

Services of general public interest

Services of general economic interest (SGEI) are those the EU classify as having a wide general interest to society and are regulated in order to support their role in operating in the public interest. These services can be supplied by the public or private sectors. These SGEI are also subject to state aid rules, which were updated in 2011 by the EU. In addition to SGEI there are services of general interest (SGI) such as the police, justice and social security that are not subject to single market and competition rules within the EU. Finally, there are social services of general interest such as social housing. In 2011 the EU agreed on quality frameworks for SGEI and SGI.

State aid

The role and regulation of state aid has been a core feature of the GPA and GATS since their agreement (Smith, 1998). It is a requirement that all states should notify the WTO of any proposed direct or indirect state aid that has the effect of supporting prices and reducing imports into their territories. It also includes subsidies to exports (CEC, 2015a). These agreements are included in the Subsidies and Countervailing Measures agreement of both the Tokyo and Uruguay rounds. As all EU states are members of the WTO, they are subject to the state aid rules.

Although state aid was included within the Treaty of Rome (1957) its importance increased with the introduction of the GPA. It is now regarded as the backbone of the EU's competition policy (Cini, 2001) and has been developed further since the agreement of the GATS. The EU state aid rules exceed those in the GPA and GATS. This was initially because the EU was receiving external challenges on trade liberalisation (Cini, 2001). State aid rules also impose a wider level of discipline on states. While cases of state aid infringement are passed to the WTO after they have occurred, the EU requires that state aid be considered prior to any award of public funding (Ehlermann and Goyette, 2006). The role of state aid in the EU has developed further since the beginning of the SEM and has been regarded as a hard rather than soft law approach (Cini, 2001). Like other EC approaches to regulation and legislation it is rule-based (Van Middelaar, 2013), and one of the issues that emerge in the application of the GPA and GATS is the understanding of state aid rules and how they operate in practice as demonstrated in the EU–UK post-Brexit trade negotiations (Morris and Kibasi, 2019).

Within the UK, state aid is generally understood to be a tool of EU policy that restricts the government from providing support to localities and businesses, while the provenance of that policy within the wider international agreements that the UK has signed is often misunderstood (Morphet, 2017). The UK government states, in guidance, that the UK and EU strongly support state aid (DBIS, 2015a, 2015b). This was an issue of contention during the Brexit referendum campaign and was seen to be part of 'taking back control'. This issue re-emerged when the COVID-19 business support packages were announced, with some journalists alleging that these packages would not meet the EU's state aid regime, although they had already been agreed by the EU (Stojanovic, 2020). Nevertheless, the government had to obtain formal approval for its measures as part of the Brexit transition arrangements for 2020. Despite claims that the EU state aid rules prevented the UK from having any kind of industrial strategy, Morris and Kibasi found that the UK chose not to use state aid interventions to the same degree as other member states: 'in 2016 state aid expenditure in the UK was €8.6 billion, compared with €14.5 billion in France and €41.1 billion in Germany' (2019, p 5).

State aid is a mechanism of financial and other support provided by governments to any undertaking that, when paid, has the potential to distort the market. These funds or support can be in the form of tax incentives or preferential borrowing rates and extend beyond subsidy into a wide range of aid (Davies, 2013). As in the COVID-19 pandemic, there are rules that permit the use of state aid in specific circumstances that are prescribed by the WTO and operated through the EU. These include providing funding and assistance to economically lagging regions that receive EU structural funds, where there is market failure or where the amount involved provided to a wide range of sectors of less than £200,000 over three years (CEC, 2015a). This is defined as *de minimis*, although this does not exempt those who are in this position from retaining appropriate records of the purpose and destination of funding. The EU has also provided class exemptions through the 2014 General Block Exemption Regulation for certain kinds of activity such as natural and environmental disasters, broadband infrastructure and transport for remote regions (DBIS, 2015a). This can be interpreted as areas where non-market values are upheld (Davies, 2013).

There has also been discussion about state aid for natural monopolies, which include water supply and other environmental infrastructure where competition cannot be easily applied. Although there were doubts about this initially in the UK (Parker, 2009, 2012), competition has been extended to these natural monopolies although there have been concerns about monopolistic conditions for the providers and the profits they have been able to return to shareholders (Harvey, 2007; Haughton, 2002). The class exemptions also include investment in local infrastructure, culture, heritage sport and recreational facilities. State aid can also be applied in the business sector for research and development or venture capital, support for public services and SMEs, although all uses of these exemptions have to be notified to the EC (DBIS, 2015a). The provisions of the state aid rules and exemptions are set out in the EU's state aid handbook (CEC, 2015a) and the UK produced its own version of this manual (DBIS, 2015b).

There has also been some discussion about the role of the EU in developing state aid rules and its attitude to market making in the implementation of the GPA and the GATS (Blauberger, 2009). Different member states have contrasting cultures on opening up their public expenditure to international organisations and the private sector, while others have been more liberal in tone but more conservative in their practice such as Sweden (Siverbo, 2004). There are also issues about the ways in which markets for goods and services are perceived to be constructed, which can have some influence on the application of state aid rules that might also reflect a wider view of external competition for public services (Davies, 2013).

While the provision of state aid was included in the Treaty of Rome (1957), it is also included in article 104 in the Treaty on the Functioning of the European Union (1992) as part of the implementation of the SEM and is reviewed on a regular basis. The last review was in 2013 and the EU has extended the operation of state aid rules beyond those within the WTO agreements including providing powers to the EC to report on member states and investigation of any infringement (Smith, 1998). These powers were taken in 1992 at the start of EU Enlargement processes and there may have been fears that the administrative and political practices of new member states may have continued. While there were considerable differences in pre- and post-accessions state policies for state aid, all new member states complied with the EU's rules (Blauberger, 2009). This was a particular issue, not least as the EU anticipated the investment of considerable amounts of aid in the enlargement states. While lagging regions would be exempt from many of the state aid rules, this was not expected to be in perpetuity and there might also be exceptions that international undertakings could locate within these member states to obtain favourable terms for taxation regimes and premises (OECD, 2017a).

The EC has pursued some cases on this basis, including the issues of tax provisions for international companies in countries such as Ireland, the Netherlands and Luxembourg, which have been sites of transfer pricing by international companies such as Amazon, Apple and Starbucks (Lyal, 2015). The OECD has a set of agreed rules on transfer pricing that are not mandatory in their application but the way in which they have been developed across countries has led to them being used as a basis of the EU's approach. In some applications, transfer pricing has been determined to be a form of state aid (Lyal, 2015). However, it is unclear whether the domestic practices to provide taxation holidays or reduced rates for these companies break state aid rules, as some forms of taxation lie outside EU treaties. The EC's approach has been to start to regulate the finances of companies within the EU that operate their finances in tax-friendly states. This has had a particular impact on Switzerland that is regarded as a secure location for financial privacy but is also the largest non-member state recipient of EU funding for projects such as transport (Banister et al, 2000). This also has led to some of the Swiss banking sector to be opened up (Linder, 2011, 2013). The approach to offshore locations for taxation is being gradually brought within EU regulations although a number of member states are moving slowly. This is a particular issue for public service companies bidding for public contracts but then not paying tax within the state where the contract is awarded including, for example, Virgin Care in the UK (Boffey, 2015). As part of the COVID-19 response several EU member states including Denmark have decided not to offer bailout packages to companies that do not pay tax in their jurisdictions.

Following the EU review of state aid (CEC, 2015a) the UK government issued new guidance, which extended state aid investigations for the EC into sectors and across countries as well as specific cases and projects (DBIS, 2015a, 2015b). The EC has powers to investigate any case of state aid and complaints can be made directly by those who consider that state aid might have been provided. The UK government advice on state aid (DBIS, 2015a) is not to attempt to redesign a project so that it does not comprise of any state aid but where it cannot be avoided to take a 'well-trodden path' (p 7). In the UK, there have been cases when the government has sought EC agreement for state aid rules to be set aside. These include the purchase of Lloyds Bank during the 2008 financial crisis although the government was required to sell off part of this, HBOS, as part of the grant of its state aid request (Lyons and Zhu, 2013). There are some grey areas where state aid cases have focused. These include sales of school land for development with the income supporting the school and the support for regional airports as part of the economic development strategy (Wishlade and Michie, 2009).

Outside the EU, any member of the WTO plurilateral GPA and GATS agreements will need to comply with the procedures included within them. This is contained in the WTO's Subsidies and Countervailing Measures agreement that was reached as part of the Tokyo Round and has subsequently been amended (Coppens, 2014). This is based on a country-to-country procedure without the same resort to EU remedies. The country-to-country procedure will use the WTO dispute settlement procedure although in 2020 this is in abeyance due to the failure of the US to agree to changes. There have been international moves to change this position but state aid disputes have to await the resolution of the US approach to the WTO before these can be invoked. Outside these, the WTO agreements allow for individual countries to undertake their own investigations and if they find that there is an infringement of the state aid rules then they can apply tariffs to the sectors and companies that have been implicated. It is also the case that in any trade deals between the EU and the UK state aid rules would be part of the EU's negotiation position and will be applied in the future (Morris and Kibasi, 2019). The membership of the WTO by the UK and member states suggest that this is expected and would retain some dispute resolution process in the future. This approach was agreed in the EU/UK (Irish) Protocol in 2019.

3

Competition in Utilities

Introduction

At the start of the 1970s, the UK state owned or had controlling shares in a large range of companies and activities (Parker, 2009). Many of these had been taken into public ownership after 1945. As both concerns for the UK economy and international discussions about the role of the private sector in running of public business started to mount in the early 1970s, there was a change in attitude towards their retention (Parker, 2009). The links between monetary theorists and the newly established think tanks in the UK such as the Institute of Economic Affairs and the Adam Smith Institute meant that these ideas were starting to cross the Atlantic (Ridley, 1992; Shleifer, 2009). They found a political home that could have some influence on Conservative Party thought about future economic policy for the time that they would next be in government (Selsdon Group, 1973).

While these influences were developing as a prelude to the General Agreement on Tariffs and Trade (GATT) Tokyo Round that started in 1973, they did not resonate with Edward Heath, Prime Minister between 1970 and 1974, who primarily focused on the UK's entry to the EU and the consequent institutional reforms associated with this, such as the reorganisation of local government (Campbell, 1994). This focus allowed those in the Conservative Party, who were against EU membership and more Atlanticist in their orientation, to consider how these monetarist approaches could be harnessed and developed in the future in the UK (Overbeek, 1993).

The first moves to implementing the Government Procurement Agreement

The Conservative Party entered a period in Opposition in 1974 and established a review of the future role of the nationalised industries led by Nicholas Ridley, who was expected to take on the job of a junior trade minister in the forthcoming government when elected (Ridley, 1992; Taylor, 1996). Its terms of reference were 'to consider future policy regarding the existing nationalised industries, the scope of denationalisation and conditions required for the proper management of the industries remaining in a competitive economy' (1968, quoted in Taylor, 1996, p 143). This report did not recommend that there could be a complete rolling back of the state in the operation of the nationalised industries but concluded that they could be run more effectively if privatised. The study identified that, as services of general public interest, there would always need to be a back stop of a government guarantee. Ridley and his group proposed that there should be a greater separation of responsibility between the nationalised industries and the state with guidelines that would indicate what the government wanted them to deliver and also be clear about defence and political requirements. Ridley suggested that there should be holding companies between the state and the nationalised industries and that there should be five-year rolling plans for their operation.

While the Ridley report was prepared, the underlying context of the GATT Tokyo Round discussions were progressing. Sir Keith Joseph favoured other methods of opening up these nationalised industries to competition such as fiscal incentives to business through tax cuts (Denham and Garnett, 2014), while Heath supported an efficiency approach to public sector cost saving through the reduction in red tape (Campbell, 1994). When it came to power in 1974 the Labour government was immediately concerned with the state of the economy and established the National Enterprise Board in 1975 to take into ownership or support companies (Hindley and Richardson, 1983; Kramer, 2019). In 1976 the Labour government agreed to the approaches within the GATT Tokyo Round including for a Government Procurement Code (GPC), which eventually became the Government Procurement Agreement (GPA). Neither the Conservative Party nor the Labour government discussed the role of the GATT agreement in relation to implications for the liberalisation of the public procurement market. Rather, politicians were focussed on some of the more traditional sectoral approaches related to the trade discussions as part of the agreement including textiles and the exclusion of agriculture (Hansard, 1979, vol 969, col 832).

For parts of the Conservative Party, these international discussions provided momentum for their approaches for denationalisation. Ridley's report was considered as preparatory work for what might follow. At the same time, there was less interest on the part of the Labour Party that had been focussing on dealing with the financial crisis in 1976, the party split in 1978 and the public sector worker strikes in 1978–1979 (Morgan, 1997). The International Monetary Fund settlement in 1976 also focused on the reform and reduction of state-owned enterprises in the UK and it would be implemented through public policy (Burk and Cairncross, 1992). If the Labour Party had been returned as the party of government in the 1979 general election, the change of political direction required to liberalise public services would have been a considerable ideological challenge for the civil service.

On the creation of the Selsdon Group in 1973, Ridley proposed selling off some nationalised industries to the private sector with a particular focus on steel, British European Airways and the Upper Clyde shipbuilders while the Labour Party's proposals to nationalise the docks were put on hold (Wilson, 1983). The Ridley report also recommended that nationalised industries should be prevented from diversifying and so the National Coal Board should end North Sea gas exploration and British Rail should withdraw from its interests in shipping and hovercraft (Parker, 2009). It also recommended that postal and telecommunications services should be separated. The Ridley group was less certain about gas and electricity but thought that BP could be subject to a public–private partnership approach (Parker, 2009).

Another report, *Conservative Opportunity* (1976), prepared for the party by John Redwood, later a major proponent of privatisation, concluded that denationalisation would be too disruptive and instead the nationalised industries could manage whatever responsibilities they had been given. The key industries identified for privatisation by the Ridley group's updated report in 1979 were coal, buses, British Rail, electricity, gas, telephone service and Cable and Wireless (Parker, 2009). Ridley's was a far more reformist approach, although the Shadow Cabinet's support for this was rapidly distanced when it was leaked in the *Economist* in May 1978 (Ridley, 1992; Parker, 2009). The Conservative Party chose a more pragmatic approach to the policy. However, much of the Ridley report's approach was included in the Conservative Manifesto for the 1979 general election, although buried within wider policy statements.

When Margaret Thatcher came to power in 1979, the government was committed to a programme of economic reform and removing the more centralised approach to the economy as characterised by the National Enterprise Board (Parker, 2009). However, there was no unanimity within the Conservative Party about how Thatcher's economic reform would be accomplished (Holmes, 2019). The commitments to denationalisation and moving these industries into the private sector were 'particularly limited' (Parker, 2009, p 49). While lacking any specific commitment to privatisation, the 1979 Manifesto did offer some commitments to selling back recently nationalised aerospace and shipbuilding companies. Other existing nationalised industries were expected to raise their levels of productivity. The Conservative Party was uncertain about whether there would be any support among the electorate for the privatisation of public services and focussed rather on getting elected before they determined their detailed priorities.

On 29 June 1979, not long after taking office, the new Conservative government reported to Parliament that the GATT had concluded the Tokyo Round, recognising the start of these discussions in 1973 had been led by a Conservative government. Cecil Parkinson, the minister who made this statement, also informed Parliament that the negotiations for the UK has been undertaken by the European Economic Community (EEC), although UK was an individual signatory of the GATT treaty. However, the focus of the Parliamentary statement (Hansard, vol 969, col 832) was on the effects of the agreement for less developed countries and the UK textile industry rather than on the other liberalising provisions that were included in the GPA. The statement took place in the House of Commons on a Friday afternoon with few MPs present, and the paper, which the minister promised as a background to the agreement, had not been made available at the time of the statement and debate. In respect of the GPA, the minister stated:

> The Government Procurement Code brings in a limited measure of liberalisation for Government purchasing. It thus creates new opportunities for exporters, but it will make some formerly "safe" markets for manufacturers more open to competition, although much of the purchasing concerned has already been liberalised within the EEC. There are important exclusions such as local authorities, most nationalised industries and what are described as warlike stores. The important element is again transparency—more open procedures to prevent "fixing" or covert discrimination. (col 839)

> I hope that the Government will pay close attention to monitoring the Government procurement code to see that it is carried out in practice as well as merely by adherence to the principles involved in the negotiations. (col 851)

While the final text of the Tokyo Round on the GPA was agreed just after the general election in June 1979, there is no evidence that this was part of any consideration of future policy in the general election, as there was in the US (Jackson et al, 1982). However, it must have been a serious consideration for the civil servants who participated in these negotiations and were required to prepare for its implementation within the UK.

For Thatcher's government, the first consideration for the introduction of liberalisation was the sale of the government's land and property assets to generate income and meet the deficits that the incoming government inherited (Burton, 1987). This issue gradually increased in importance. If the government could find resources through the sale of the nationalised industries and other government commercial holdings, it could retain current levels of taxation rather than implement increases. From the outset, government departments were put under pressure by the Treasury to dispose of assets to find income although this was not defined as a privatisation process but more of a 'sell-off' (Burton, 1987; Parker, 2009). However, as there were also concerns about whether the government had the authority to pursue the disposal of assets without specific legislative powers, each disposal was taken as a separate programme, led by different departments supported by specific legislation (Marsh, 1991). The government was also concerned about the power and influence of the trade unions to undermine their policies and proposals, as they had done with Heath's government in 1974 (Marsh, 1992).

In the search for assets to put up for sale, the first identified were those related to energy, the government's BP shares, the assets of New Towns Corporations and the British Sugar Company (Parker, 2009). There were also assets held by the National Enterprise Board together with land and buildings. Health assets, like other land sales, offered some quick wins although the funds derived from the sales did not go to the health trusts that controlled them. By 1981 Thatcher was regarded as a very unpopular Prime Minister (King, 1985). While these sales could provide some easy wins, the progress in privatising government assets was not going well and the economy had still not improved (Seldon and Collings, 2014).

In 1981, Thatcher reshuffled her Cabinet to assemble a group of ministers more aligned with her thinking (Holmes, 2019), generating a new focus for the privatisation agenda, particularly on the removal of the monopoly of nationalised utilities. This coincided with the conclusion of the GATT Tokyo Round and the agreed implementation of the GPA. The period between 1979 and 1981 could be regarded as a preparation for this larger agenda. The economic framework that was established by the Treasury and the preliminary work had demonstrated that a more radical approach to liberalisation would be needed if the financial shortfall and requirements of the GPA were to be met. The parallel processes were significant. The narrative driver for progressing the privatisation of nationalised utilities was said to be their inability to manage their finances since 1979 (Parker, 2009, p 78), but there appears to be no mention of the GPA in underpinning this move.

The pressure to achieve clearer accounting and financial processes has been at the heart of all successive waves of outsourcing that have been progressed by governments (Pliatzky, 1988). There was a requirement to identify their worth to provide potential purchasers with an indication of their running costs, assets and income prior to sale when new markets were being created (Gains, 1999). There were also emerging limits on external financing as the potential precursor to state aid rules and practices emerged. The government was aware that some utilities such as water had already benefitted from state aid but any change in their status might have some significant implications for their financing (Parker, 2009).

In the sale of nationalised industries, there were issues to consider. Firstly, they had been nationalised after 1945 because they were all essential to the nation's economic, social and environmental wellbeing and had public support for this reason (Parker, 2009). Secondly, nationalised industries depended on major capital investment in fixed infrastructure that is repaid over a long period, if at all, and this might be a barrier in attracting the market for their purchase. Thirdly, outsourcing nationalised industries that were important for national security was a concern (Cabinet Office, 2017). These are also services of general economic interest and cannot rely on monopolies to create scarcity for price manipulation as in other markets (Sauter, 2008). The costs of the infrastructure meant that it was difficult for new entrants to the market to provide services and there was considered to be no economic case for providing parallel networks for rail, water or energy to provide alternative services to the same locations (Parker, 2009). However, how can two competing providers use the same networks, particularly if the network is owned by one of them? Also, how can investment in maintaining and improving supply networks be incentivised if the provision of service had been privatised? How can states maintain their competitiveness with others if they are reliant on private sector investment when they have no control over it?

Maintaining control? The role of the regulators

As part of the institutional architecture of outsourcing publicly owned utilities, regulators were appointed for each sector. Each has an associated office and their role has evolved (Booker, 1999). The regulator acts as an independent authority whose responsibility is to protect the interests of the consumer and customer through regulation of price, investment and competition. These regulatory roles also reflect the definition of utilities as services of public interest within EU law and the requirement that the public interest is protected while allowing competition in delivery (Sauter, 2008). This provides specific powers for intervention in markets, which is not permitted otherwise. Nevertheless, the energy and water companies, which have been able to generate significant profits for their shareholders, complain about required investment and some have paid fines after investigations by the regulator Ofwat. Regulators take different factors into account within individual services although there are some common features. As well as safeguarding the interests of consumers and competition, they are also important in regulating delivery standards.

A key issue for all regulators is how independent they will be from the state. As Booker (1999) reflects, all government departments are expected to retain a policy interest in the sectors for which they are responsible (NAO, 2020b). The regulators are also responsible for ensuring compliance with international and domestic standards. In the UK, regulators are held to account by the Parliament through Select Committees and questions to responsible ministers. Regulators can be challenged in their decision making through judicial review. However, the relationships with their sponsoring government departments are informal and not open to scrutiny. Booker (1999) has suggested that the departments and the regulators require some form of consensual agreement in order to function. While the regulators remain notionally independent, this working relationship with their sponsoring department remains a challenge across all government services that have wholly or partially been separated into arms' length organisations – private or public. The role of the customer and consumer is contained within the regulators' remit but is detached from ministers and civil servants in practice. The regulators are also members of the senior civil service and do not have independence of employment.

Since the regulatory framework for utilities within a privatised market was established, much of the operation and institutional structure of providers has changed (Parker, 2012). At the time that competition was launched for each of these nationalised utilities, there was an expectation of the maintenance of a diversified market, comprising a range of providers and owners, including many individuals who bought public shares as in gas (Kemp, 2013). However, over the period since privatisation, there has been reduction in providers so that some markets have become duopolies for consumers (Graham, 1997). In some areas such as consumer banking, the government has supported challenger banks to extend the competitive market (Lu, 2017). In utilities, the government policy was to privatise rather than to outsource from the outset and there has been a cross-sectoral shift in ownership so that some companies own more than one means of energy or transport supply (Cowie, 2002). In some markets, such as telecommunications, BT has been allowed to operate in a monopolistic way in comparison with other providers and be both a core network and a commercial provider and other companies have no choice other than to use their networks (Parker, 2009).

There are a number of weaknesses in the system of regulators. Firstly, regulators treat the variety of providers within their responsibilities as silos. In energy, the regulatory process does not allow for a comparison between types of energy use within a climate emergency framework (Helm, 2020). Secondly, there are no methods of examining the differences between modes in sectors where there are different methods of provision and regulation like transport. Thirdly, there are concerns that the regulators are considered to be too weak in the face of business and finance interests and have been 'captured' (Stern and Cubbin, 2005; Helm, 2006). Fourthly, there are concerns about the ability of regulators to control the rates of reinvestment and profit margins and these are particularly an issue in the water industry (OECD, 2002).

There are also issues for new types of activities in sectors that are primarily regulated but, for specific technical or delivery responses, fall outside regulatory frameworks for a period of time before they are reregulated. These include the activities of Uber and Airbnb, which operate in a mostly deregulated way within a regulated sector such as for taxi licensing and licensing of homes used for tourists and short let accommodation (Edelman and Geradin, 2015). There are also concerns where the government provides subsidies through its agencies such as to housebuilders through the Help to Buy scheme that the regulatory framework is too weak and allows the funding to pass into the hands of shareholders and employees, as profit and bonus, rather than to increase access to homes for those on middle and lower incomes (Carozzi et al, 2019).

Water

The development of the transfer of the water supply provision from the primary provision by the public sector to the private sector in the UK was undertaken as one of the first within the GPA and as part of the EU single market (Dore et al, 2004). The movement of water provision outside the public sector also happened alongside wider environmental reforms that the government made in order to meet environmental agreements made within the EU (Haigh, 1996). When the UK joined the EU, there was an assumption that most of the relationship would be conducted through environmental issues (Haigh, 1996). This may have been an unintended consequence of the focus of the negotiations that were taking place with the Scandinavian countries for membership at the same time (Morphet, 2013). The reorganisation of local authorities into larger units was managed by Heath's supra ministry, the Department of Environment expected to deal with the implementation of agreements made within the EU without having much effect on the practices of central government (Rippon, 1973; Morphet, 2013).

As part of local government reorganisation in 1972, the government moved responsibilities for water away from local authorities into nine regional water authorities (RWA) in the 1973 Water Act. This retained strong local government involvement, and the RWA operated within a National Water Council in England and a single authority for Wales that was regarded as a tenth RWA in practice by Whitehall (Parker, 2012). These RWA provided water and sewerage for their areas by absorbing the services that local authorities owned. Where these services were provided by private companies, these continued to operate independent of the RWAs, as the Conservative government did want to take them into public ownership (Parker, 2012). The provision of water services remains in public ownership in Scotland, albeit through a publicly owned company since 2002, and in Northern Ireland. As these RWAs developed, there was an increasing focus on relating water charges to the costs of provision without any subsidy from the government and also an equalisation of charges within each of the RWA areas. Private water companies provided 25 per cent of water services although there were regional variations and in some this provision was much higher (Lynk, 1993).

However, as the civil service started to recognise its commitments both within the EU to regulate environmental services and to meet the agreements made within the GPA, this initial approach was changed to remove local authorities entirely from the provision of water services (Parker, 2012). The Water Act 1983 also abolished the National Water Council that had been established in 1973. There were increased pressures from the EU to manage the control of pollution, and the role of RWAs, as both operators and regulators, was unsustainable. The RWAs also had a number of public duties for the management and access to their land that extended beyond those required of the private sector. It was these public good functions that initially kept water services outside the privatisation programme adopted by the Thatcher government 1979–1983. It was also said that there was no evidence that private sector water companies were more efficient than the public ones even though an injection of private funds for investment might be welcomed (Lynk, 1993).

After the 1983 general election, a further review of public services that could be privatised was conducted by the Treasury (Pliatzky, 1988). This review concluded that water remained a natural monopoly and transferring its assets to the private sector would not result in more competition – a finding that would also be made after 30 years of operation of a privatised water market in 2020 (NAO, 2020c). The issue of market making for a natural monopoly varied in comparison with other public sector privatisation and was a specific challenge that delayed competition. However, the approach to market making had been supported by international financial institutions such as the World Bank (Haughton, 2002).

As the UK's membership of the EU started to develop further, through the creation of the Single European Market (SEM) between 1985 and 1992, it was becoming clear that more fundamental changes would be needed in the organisation of environmental services (Haigh, 1996). There were also further sectors that would require some exposure to competition as a consequence of the GPA. In the UK, this was regarded as an opportunity to link the management of waste and water within these changes (Parker, 2012). There was a use of statecraft (Bulpitt, 1986) to bundle together these necessary reforms through the agencification of the government's environmental responsibilities that could all be grouped together and the 1990 Environmental Protection Act created the Environment Agency (EA) (Helm, 1992).

The privatisation of water has been particularly shaped by both WTO and EU forces (Gilardi, 2001). One of the major concerns for the government in the privatisation of water supply was the extent to which the industry had been a beneficiary of the European Regional Development Fund and the required matched funding that the government had to supply in order to access the funds (Parker, 2000). Water was privatised in 1989 in England and Wales through the sale of the ten RWAs, which was planned immediately after the 1987 general election (Parker, 2012). Water continued in public ownership in Scotland and Northern Ireland. The water and sewerage companies are now primarily owned by private equity companies that pay some of their taxes outside the UK (Helm, 2020). The role of the new water companies was set within a regulatory framework determined by the government, in this case through the Department of Food and Rural Affairs (DEFRA), focused on meeting consumer needs, compliance with EU legislation and capital investment in new and existing systems. It is regulated by the office of the Water Regulator – Ofwat.

As in other privatised services, there was an expectation from the outset that investment in extending and repairing water infrastructure should be funded by the service users rather than through government investment (Parker, 2012). This also meant that when there are problems of drought the companies ration supplies (Haughton, 1998) but the state, through the EA, has to manage flooding. When considering the role of pricing and the consumer, Ofwat has undertaken five yearly reviews and the NAO (2015a) examined the approaches that water service providers have adopted and the effects on consumer value. The NAO found that water services had improved since privatisation and in the 2014 pricing review there had been more incentives for the water companies to focus on consumer benefits including efficiencies in service (NAO, 2015a). However, when considering the pricing of water, the NAO found that there had been an increase of 40 per cent since privatisation and that the approach of Ofwat still needed to be tightened to ensure that pricing levels are appropriate. The NAO concluded that the water industry is not achieving value for money.

Water continues to be a natural monopoly that gives advantages to the companies in their areas and there appears to be little pressure or sanction on these companies to repair leaks and manage their supplies and services more in the public interest. Swyngedouw (2005) argues that since privatisation, water had been commodified and that these policies for water provision remain disconnected from land management and urban policy. At the same time, the EA, set up to regulate and provide flood management, have had their actions framed by successive governments reluctant to act to enforce management and reflect planning challenges (NAO, 2001, 2011a, 2014b). Flooding is occurring with increasing frequency and the EA has been tasked with building physical barriers that are barely complete before they are broken again. Ofwat and the EA are sponsored by DEFRA while policy for land use remains in a different government department.

As with other privatised government services, the contemporaneous ideology of efficiency and effectiveness as a narrative driver for privatisation has been espoused without any wider discussion of other EU, GPA or GATS agreements (Ogden, 1995; Dore et al, 2004). The civil service exercised a successful statecraft approach to the privatisation process. While the level of compliance with EU water standards improved to 92 per cent from 78 per cent following privatisation, this investment was reflected in the bills paid by consumers. However, it is also the case that the profits made by water companies privatised in the UK increased by 142 per cent and were much larger than those in any other country (Dore et al, 2004). Meanwhile, have water services become independent of the state in the UK? Haughton (2002) found that the level of engagement by the government in innovation in the water industry has remained at a high level.

Other countries did not expose their water services to competition (Lobina and Hall, 2008; Helm, 2020). In France, for example, the water supply remains in public ownership and there is competition between private companies in its management (Dore et al, 2004). There were multiple contracts at the local level with no overall organisation to ensure that they operated and were regulated. Helm (2020) finds that there is little evidence that privatisation has made the provision of water services more efficient. He argues that it is not the ownership of water services that matter, either public or private, but that it is the regulatory framework and its mechanism for ensuring compliance that are fundamental to the effective and efficient delivery of water services. Helm argues that Ofwat's role, as other regulators, is to maintain the public interest and it therefore cannot reinforce a fully privatised model. However, Helm does not address the role of regulators in upholding services of public interest and the specific issues that are accompanied with the privatisation of monopoly services.

Has water privatisation been successful and how can this be examined? There are various ways this can be undertaken including considering original claims for efficiency and investment but the main drivers were agreements within the GPA. As Helm (2020) demonstrates, evaluations of success of privatisation are undermined by a failure to understand both the international agreements and the role of statecraft in their implementation. He acknowledges the role of EU water directives in driving up the requirements for investment in water services and the government's objective to transfer this investment away from government to the citizen/consumer.

Government's role in water security has also increased since the initial processes of privatisation (OECD, 2013b; Morris and McGuinness, 2019). The privatised service contracts ended in 2014, which gave an opportunity to reconsider the configuration of the industry started by reviews in 2008, when both Ofwat and an independent review by Cave (2011) asserted that regulation would also be second best to competition in the market (Lobina and Hall, 2008). The Water Act 2014 separated the consumer provision of water services from the infrastructure and its maintenance to bring this into tighter control. The Cabinet Office (2017) has included drought on the national risk register. While protecting the interests of citizens at a national level this may not be so supportive of citizens as consumers.

Overall Ofwat, as the regulator, has been regarded as being weak when dealing with the water companies since privatisation, particularly over issues such as profits, charges, reinvestment and managing water leakages (Haughton, 1998; Morris and McGuinness, 2019). The consumer focus and pricing has been a driving consideration in privatisation and its subsequent operation; however, it remains the case in the water industry that the main consideration for the consumer is in the investment of infrastructure and supply (Lobina and Hall, 2008) while for the water companies it remains focused on financial returns.

Telecommunications

The discussions on the privatisation of telecommunications were initially framed by the same considerations as water. Telephony was initially considered to be a natural monopoly and it was not possible to offer alternative service providers (Parker, 2009). Although this assumption proved to be unfounded, the way in which BT was privatised and the government's subsequent approach to it as a provider of telephony has retained BT's underlying monopolistic position. This has enabled the maintenance of some Whitehall control over telecommunications in addition to that provided through its regulator, Ofcom, which has recently been led by former senior civil servants. This maintenance of government control of telecommunications was also in response to the concerns of the Home Office and Security Services (Parker, 2009, pp 244, 268) who continued to require that BT, whatever its status, public or private, should be led by civil servants. Regulators at Ofcom are employed as civil servants and the regulator's post has been occupied by politicians and more recently by career civil servants who have spent time in the Treasury. When privatised, BT was held in a public corporation established in 1979 but when it was clear that increased investment would be required to provide for demand in services and innovation, this would be challenging for the financial limits set on the corporation (Parker, 1991). At the same time, there were increasing strikes and customer resistance to higher charging for a monopolistic service. BT management was antagonistic to any competition in telecommunications despite the government's attempts to introduce a rival provider, Cable and Wireless (C and W) (Moon et al, 1986). C and W was reliant on the use of BT's infrastructure but the resulting agreement in 1984 left both BT and C and W unhappy with the outcome, with considerable uncertainty left for C and W about its ability to operate as an alternative service (Parker, 2009).

As a strong monopoly, BT had a government dependent on it both for delivery of service and for meeting the future needs of business. It was in a strong position to bargain on the methods and means of privatisation and the framework within which it would operate. This was different from water, another monopoly supplier, where the provision was linked to natural water catchment areas. BT appeared to withstand all the pressures placed on it by the Treasury and the Business Department (Parker, 2009). It made the government's initial approach to change its monopoly, through the introduction of C and W services using Mercury, ultimately difficult (Moon et al, 1986). When establishing the regulator Oftel, later to become Ofcom, it was recognised that the existing approaches to monopolies and competition would not be adequate to cope with the powers that would be vested in BT through privatisation (Stern, 2004; NAO, 2010). Up to the point of privatisation, BT had been a regulator and a provider that also included the power to license its competitors but the main change in privatisation was to prevent it making monopolistic profits (Parker, 2009). Yet, the whole process of privatisation was dominated by haggling between the government and BT rather than the government setting the terms of outsourcing, as in other sectors. This has remained as a continuing tone in the relationship between BT and the government. After the Office of the Regulator was established, BT sought to undermine its role by appealing to the Secretary of State (SoS) to ask the regulator to back off; the SoS refused but this was a continuing relationship of attrition.

Despite this early and complex privatisation and the resulting asymmetrical duopoly between BT and Mercury, it became clear that by 1991 the operation of BT had remained stable in terms of productivity, outputs, profits and revenues (Florio, 2003). This consistency would not satisfy wider competition requirements that would be introduced through both the SEM in 1992 and the GATS in 1994. While BT was protected by a universal service obligation, it could use government support to withstand competition from TV cable companies that offered telephony using their cable connections by making a requirement that calls had to be connected through BT exchanges. BT consistently resisted the laying of fibre connections into homes so that an alternative system that challenged their broadband network could not be provided. It has subsequently been required to change its policy by the government and introduce fibre across its network by 2027. The introduction of mobile telephony and broadband services has largely continued using the same network principles. While mobile phone companies have constructed their own mast systems, which are increasingly shared on a cooperative basis, they are still dependent on the BT network.

BT has also started to diversify its range of services to include 'pay for view' services for sport including football to the point where the company is significantly dependent on this income (Whalley and Curwen, 2017). This is an interesting return to the type of diversification and cross-subsidy used by nationalised industries including energy and transport providers that Ridley sought to end in the 1970s. Ridley (1992) was concerned then about the benefits accorded to companies through cross-marketing and subsides that reduced competition based on real costs of operation. It is interesting to note the same strategy has emerged in a privatised company, BT, that has remained largely unchanged despite privatisation.

Reinforcing competition compliance

While compliance with the GPA/GATS is concerned with the volume of government work exposed to competition, it is also important how this is put into practice and monitored. The Organisation for Economic Co-operation and Development (OECD) (2002), in examining performance, considered that the UK's practice of monitoring compliance was weak. The Labour government's Competition Act 1998 was the first measure to put this on a legal footing by establishing the Competition Commission to study and address issues of market dominance, monopolies and enforcement. The OECD also commented that the structure of UK compliance to the GPA/GATS had been through institutional and incremental reform rather than an overall design and that this has also generated some issues particularly when considering sectoral mergers. The OECD comments that although the 1998 reforms were not put into effect until 2000, they were immediately followed by further reforms to strengthen the system. Commenting on this, the report suggests that this approach 'just displays the characteristic pragmatic search for incremental perfections' (OECD, 2002, p 6).

In the utilities, the OECD (2002) view is that the approach taken in the UK has had unexpected consequences. In bus deregulation, they argue that the approach has followed a pre-1988 monopolistic position that has not been able to be addressed within the legislation. There is also an issue that the sectoral approach in the UK, which reflects the relationships between activities and their sponsoring departments, has not led to an overall approach to competition compliance and regulation (NAO, 2019b). There are concerns about capture and incorporation through the informal relationships that have been established between the private sector and the government, both politicians and officials, that are reinforced through social events, secondments and an objective to ensure that government policy is successfully implemented. There has also been continued political interference in decision making in regulation, which has allowed the process to be seen to be not independent but one of clashing personalities (OECD, 2002, p 54).

Windfall taxes

While successive governments may not be willing to reopen contracts that have been agreed, there are actions that they may take if they consider that the contracts have been too generous to the contractor. In some cases, such as the franchised railway service and probation service, the government has taken back the contracts because the performance was poor or the contracts could not be delivered within the policies agreed. In other cases, there may be a view that the surplus accumulated in the contract should be adjusted through some kind of claw–back (NAO, 2015b). It is difficult for government to use this provision if is not contained in the original contract and private sector bodies would be less willing to include this as part of the tender process (NAO, 2015a). In this case, the government has used another mechanism – that of the windfall tax (Waelde and Kolo, 1998). This recognises that the market conditions at the time of contract offer may have been depressed and the final price paid was less than might otherwise have been achieved. The incoming Labour government in 1997 decided to apply a windfall tax (Waelde and Kolo, 1998).

However, are privatised and regulated businesses, which have been opened to competition under international agreements, including the GPA and GATS, able to dispute this as unfair treatment and interference with the market? The EC's view was that the operation of the windfall tax did not create a market distortion or state aid. Another consideration is whether actions like this, by a government, will lead to reduction in prices offered at point of sale or whether this windfall tax is then collected through price rises to consumers. If so, what action could a regulator take to prevent this from occurring? Waelde and Kolo (1998) argue that this is a risk that needs to be factored into any future acquisition of a service of public interest by a purchaser of the assets or rights to operate services.

4

Preparing to Outsource Government Services

Introduction

While the first stages of the implementation of the Government Procurement Agreement (GPA) focused on those government-owned activities that required capital investment in infrastructure, the second wave of government preparation was in anticipation of the application of the General Agreement on Trade in Services (GATS) that came into effect in 1994. The Uruguay Round 1986–1994 was concerned with the extension of procurement into the liberalisation of public services and to other parts of government, including local government (Walsh, 1989). There was also some preparation to open these markets through the parallel development of the Single European Market (SEM) from 1985 that came into effect in 1992 (Cockfield, 1994). In the EU, the negotiation of the GATS was undertaken by the European Commission (EC) for member states, although each was an individual signatory of the agreement (Meunier, 2005). While these General Agreement on Tariffs and Trade (GATT) negotiations had an external, international focus for world trade, they also informed the development of the SEM (Abbott, 1990).

The UK government prepared for the implementation of the GATS and the SEM by restructuring its institutional governance arrangements. It did this by separating policy making and ministerial responsibilities from services with a direct public interface, businesses or service providers (Haddon, 2012). This separation between policy and delivery led to distancing and deskilling within the civil service (Theakston, 1995; Rhodes, 2001). Preparations for liberalisation took both practical and cultural approaches. The practical steps included a gradual approach to preparing government delivery services for potential exposure to competition (Pliatzky, 1992). This was accompanied by a change in the cultural narrative of the public sector's role and abilities to undertake its work by moving away from the assumption that public services can only be delivered by public service providers. This was a major challenge, as Margaret Thatcher found (Marsh, 1991). By her second term in office, 1983–1987, the costs of government had increased rather than reduced and it was proving very difficult to wean the public away from expectations of public services and the ways in which they were to be delivered (Fry, 1988).

The Thatcher period 1979–1990 introduced and then intensified the narratives of financial efficiency – she argued that there was a need to reform public service delivery to save the public purse (Gamble, 1989). When John Major became Prime Minister in 1990, the change in leadership offered the opportunity to use a different narrative to implement liberalisation. This promoted private or third-party provision of services through a more citizen-centred approach (Gyford, 1991). This shifted the focus from efficiency to effectiveness in public service management and delivery (Pollitt, 1994). The approach paralleled that of the Clinton administration in the US, where citizen leadership was promoted and government's role was said to be 'steering' and not 'rowing' (Osborne and Gaebler, 1993; Morphet, 2008).

Stewart and Walsh (1992) argue that this change in emphasis in the narrative, from efficiency to effectiveness, was symptomatic of a government wanting to introduce an ideological shift in the way in which public services were delivered, rather than any specific need to do so. However, this view fails to recognise two major changes in public service procurement and delivery – the implementation of the EU Single Market in 1992, which already incorporated the GPA, and the GATS from 1994. The switch in narrative was a mechanism to make the outsourcing of public services more palatable to the electorate. While popular public share ownership for energy had been regarded as a success in changing public opinion about the operation of utilities (Chapman, 2011), the opening of public services to competition, such as those provided by local authorities, health services and in education, on the grounds of price reduction, was much more likely to face widespread opposition. The change in Prime Minister, from Thatcher to Major in 1990, was a useful opportunity to reset the narrative to one that was expected to be more acceptable to the public. This new narrative was not focused on cutting costs but getting more for the funding provided through gains in effectiveness (Haddon, 2012). This reflects a statecraft approach to implementing these agreements (Bulpitt, 1986), where private sector management methods were promoted as being better for public service delivery than traditional models (Gyford, 1991).

The potential for market making to create a plethora of new providers of public services meant that there could be change (Gingrich, 2011). In service delivery, this would allow separation between politicians, who were ultimately responsible for public services, and delivery organisations (Kemp, 1990). This distancing was argued to be another means of improving the quality of service, so that there was no political interference and an increase in managerialism (Walsh, 1995). It was also argued that it would be a fairer system as services delivered on a contractual basis might reduce the need for decisions about who should benefit from them (Pollitt, 1994). There was no evidence that the private sector would be more efficient, not least as some services had never been operated by organisations other than public bodies. On the other hand, after a decade of Thatcherism, confidence in public sector organisations to deliver efficiently with reduced budgets had already been undermined. After 11 years of Thatcher, the public had been readied for this narrative and willing to believe its promises.

The preparation for outsourcing of some public bodies was undertaken through institutional separation including between purchasers and providers (Bailey and Davidson, 1999), an approach that was also used in other countries such as Sweden (Siverbo, 2004) and New Zealand (Ashton and Press, 1997). The approach to agencification in the civil service was initially considered by the Fulton Commission (1968) impressed by a visit to Sweden, which already had this division between policy and delivery. There was also a suggestion that this division was introduced into the civil service structures in Hong Kong in 1971, as a potential experiment (Talbot and Talbot, 2019). Agencification provided a detached means of public accountability for delivery. Creating agencies and identifying the services to be provided and the ways in which they were to be delivered anticipated a period when there would be a need for service specifications within a contracting environment (Talbot and Talbot, 2019).

The agencification narrative was also promoted as a mechanism to improve delivery for citizens. This was supported by the introduction of the Citizen's Charter initiative in 1991 (Stewart and Walsh, 1992) where specific service standards were to be displayed to the public at the point of delivery. This also allowed the introduction of specifications that could later be used for competitive tendering. The wider performance culture for local authority public services was included within a White Paper (Cm 1599, 1991) followed by the 1992 Local Government Act and overseen by the Audit Commission. The White Paper focused on setting standards, the provision of information, the right to choose, privatisation and competition, redress, and inspection and regulation. The means to achieve 'The Principles of Public Services' were:

1. Standards
2. Openness
3. Information
4. Choice
5. Non-discrimination
6. Accessibility
7. Redress

(Cm 1599, 1991, p 5)

In this approach, the public was regarded as having acquired rights to services through the payment of taxes rather than citizenship. The model of the state's relationship with the population became one of contract rather than embodying any idea of commitment and responsibility as in the welfare state (Timmins, 2001). The state's role was being redefined to guarantee specific rights rather than provide services. The justifying basis was one of liberal individualism rather than civic republicanism (Oldfield, 1990) and accountability was now regarded as market-based (Stewart and Walsh, 1992) rather than being held by politicians.

Framing outsourcing

The preparation for the introduction of the GPA and GATS occurred over a period of time and through a range of initiatives after 1980. These included the Rayner scrutinies (Beesley, 1983; Warner, 1984) and the Financial Management Initiative (Gray and Jenkins, 1986) followed by the establishment of Next Steps Agencies (NSA) after 1986 (Ascher, 1987; Haddon, 2012). However, as Theakston (1995) stated, the potential to introduce privatisation into new arrangements for running the civil service through NSA was there from the outset. The Next Steps approach was seen as a mechanism to prepare government services for privatisation and outsourcing so that there would be the opportunity for some soft market testing once agencies had accounting systems based on commercial models. Major supported this preparation for outsourcing by allowing the private sector to participate in the agency reviews in 1993 (Theakston, 1995). This gave them access to accounts, operational models and softer information that would be useful when given any opportunity to tender.

Policy narratives

The application of statecraft in the implementation of the GPA and GATS that had started under Thatcher continued into the 1990s, although the policy narratives were changed. While Thatcher was concerned with saving money, the Major narrative focussed on making services work better for citizens. In a continuation of the Next Steps managerialism, the process of taking forward privatisation, or at least preparation for the market, was taken outside Parliament. This would not have been the practice in other European countries (Theakston, 1995, p 141). However, this change in the public narrative was accompanied by continuity of purpose by central government departments, particularly the Cabinet Office, which was increasingly important in translating EU and international policy into domestic delivery (Morphet, 2013), and the Treasury.

The preparation for the implementation of the GATS after Thatcher continued on the same path of agencification for those parts of the civil service that were outward facing and were responsible for public service delivery (Talbot and Talbot, 2019). The Thatcher government started this process in 1980 by commissioning the Pliatzky Report (1980) from the Treasury. Pliatzky identified four key reasons for introducing agencification into government departments. He argued that government agencies were needed:

> Because the work is of an executive character which does not require ministers to take responsibility for its day to day management; because the work is more effectively carried out by a single purpose organisation rather than a government department with a wide range of functions; in order to involve people from outside government in the direction of the organization; in order to place the performance of a function outside the party political arena. (Quoted in Flinders, 1999b, p 29)

While there has been discussion about the growth of agencies and quangos in the UK state, there is little in this commentary on the role of agreements made within the GATS and GPA. Flinders (1999b), for example, argues that an underlying reason for creating agencies and quangos was the extent to which the state had grown between 1945 and 1979. This account argues that the state was involved in matters that it was not good at delivering or should not be in the public domain. This fails to recognise the statecraft narrative that accompanied the external impetus that was underlying reform of the state and its institutions. Pliatzky later associated his approach to the establishment of agencies to the need to prepare for public service change. While Pliatzky considered the sale of council housing had been a success, he was less certain that health and education could be subjected to the market (Baldwin, 1999), not least as there needed to be a market made for competitors to exist before this could occur.

The argument in favour of agencification was based on value for money and efficiency through the introduction of private sector management methods (Radnor and Johnston, 2013). Loosening the organisational and management ties between operational government functions and the civil service could introduce expectations of change (Rhodes, 2001). A major factor in the selection of services for agencification was the identification of those that were operational activities. Policy-orientated civil servants did not consider these to be of high status (Landers, 1999) and, with their greater staffing levels, required more 'hands-on' management. By moving large groups of staff into agencies, it was possible to reduce departmental staff headcounts while retaining control (Flinders, 1999b). Distancing a service through the creation of an agency could offload management responsibilities, particularly as direct services generated more complaints to MPs when things went wrong. An agency could be held to account and provide distance between the service failures and ministerial accountability (Hood, 2011; King and Crewe, 2014). However, because the civil service had low regard for these services, there was an assumption that despite this agency distancing they could continue to dictate policy, appointments and projects in a continuation of current practices.

Institutional strategies

In the centre of government, the civil service advises ministers on their commitments and obligations through international and EU agreements and then on how these policies should be delivered in practice through legislation, funding and institutional restructuring (Morphet, 2013). However, these policy targets were frequently to be implemented by others such as local authorities. When the implications of the GPA extension and GATS started to emerge in both the initial and expected extended forms, anticipatory planning was undertaken to identify those parts of government that were more likely to be subject to these new rules. The civil service also identified intermediate functions that were delivered through other bodies or required a regulatory role to ensure compliance, particularly to EU commitments in the environment. Once semi-detached, these functions could be available for outsourcing, if there was pressure to do so, without compromising the policy heart of Whitehall (Theakston, 1995).

The preparation for agencies started during Thatcher's first weekend in office (Talbot and Talbot, 2019) through the Rayner Efficiency Unit. This undertook its work through short three-month scrutinies of parts of the civil service, identifying potential areas for efficiencies but also providing some indication of which parts of government might be suitable for outsourcing through the GPA. The Efficiency Unit had completed over 300 of these scrutinies by 1987. The Rayner approach was not a 'grand scheme' approach to service redesign (Thompson, 2000, p 199) but rather an internal incremental approach. In this way, Rayner believed that change would be acceptable and more likely to be successful. The purpose of the scrutinies was to promote value for money, remove obstacles to good management and encourage quick and effective changes (Gray and Jenkins, 1984). The underlying narrative of the programme was that services could be improved by defining their purposes with greater clarity, understanding how they were delivered and beginning to understand the costs of delivery. While the Rayner scrutineers identified potential savings and efficiencies, they also encountered strong internal opposition within the civil service. Beesley (1983) states that while a range of inefficiencies were identified these did not include any understanding of the relationships between cost and effort in delivery and there were no proposals to streamline processes, including the use of technology.

The scrutinies were focused on the processes that were concerned with direct public delivery such as employment benefits, where the Department of Health and Social Security (DHSS) already had an agency arrangement with the Post Office for payments (Warner, 1984). In this case the scrutiny team drew on evidence from the US and the EU on benefits payment methods and frequency. They recommended that the weekly Post Office order method should be replaced by a longer time period that would cut operational costs to the government. However, the achievement of scrutiny savings was frequently determined by a narrow approach that did not consider the wider implications of their effects if implemented. The DHSS budget recommendations did not fully consider the financial dependency on cash of those receiving benefits nor the role of the benefits system in maintaining the post office and sub-post office networks throughout the country.

The civil service used a range of institutional strategies to prepare their services for liberalisation including quangos and agencies. A quango can be defined as 'any body that spends public money to fulfil a public task but with some degree of independence from elected representatives' (Flinders,

1999a, p 4). This type of financing would now be considered to be a tool of depoliticisation where both the use of time (Goetz and Meyer-Sahling, 2009) and restructuring have the effect of removing scrutiny of central government activities from democratic accountability and the public gaze. As with other strategies of the civil service to prepare for the application of the GPA and GATS, an outward distancing of control made them less visible and decisions could be made under the guise of management and operation. By 1997, a number of quangos that had been created since 1979 were criticised as being undemocratic and a danger to the state (Marquand, 1999). While the government stated that the number of quangos had fallen during the 1979–1996 period, in practice there was a reduction of 45 per cent of Non-Departmental Public Bodies, as they were officially designated, but an increase by 300 per cent in the expenditure of those left (Flinders, 1999a, p 5). In practice this type of criticism also created the opportunity for further change, particularly in those service areas in government where there were perceived to be challenges. These were either because there had been an inadequate amount of opening of the service to the market or because the structures created meant that there was a loss of civil service control.

While much of the focus of the Rayner scrutinies was on their potential usefulness and whether or not they were difficult to implement both politically and practically, Warner (1984) reflects that there were considerable benefits in having the administrative arm of the civil service, usually focussed on policy advice, spend their time being focused on the delivery of the services that followed these policy decisions, albeit short lived. Most administrative civil servants, once legislation, finance and institutional arrangements for new policies have been completed, move on to develop other policies and have little or no further relationship with the delivery of their policies. This means that the policy learning though developed was not absorbed and used next time (Dunlop and Radaelli, 2013).

Financial Management Initiative

The role of the Rayner scrutinies in identifying shortcomings in the management of costs and the use of financial systems in running the government together with a low organisational status ascribed to this kind of activity led to the implementation of the Financial Management Initiative (FMI) (Fry, 1988). There were also other tensions in the civil service that had arisen from the conduct of the Rayner scrutinies but also from Thatcher's impatience about a lack of progress (Gamble, 1989).

These resulted in civil service strikes, the closure of the Civil Service Department and an increase in early retirements from the home civil service (Theakston, 1995). The scrutinies were interpreted as a mechanism to undermine the morale and strength of these officials and to improve, what was regarded as, the climate for change (Fry, 1988). The FMI was seen as a further opportunity to restrict the freedoms of civil servants in running their departments, reduce resistance to pay cuts and offer pay increases for those recruited from the private sector.

When the FMI was launched in 1982, it was focused on associating government delivery policy with finance and particularly cost management. At the time, Rayner stated that no one in government knew in detail what it cost to deliver services (Fry, 1988). The FMI already had some antecedents in the management information system set up by Michael Heseltine when he was Secretary of State for the Department of Environment. Heseltine later wanted to see this management information system for ministers (MINIS) extended across Whitehall (Likierman, 1982). However, the head of the home civil service considered that it would be up to individual ministers to determine whether or not they wished to apply it (Fry, 1988). While MINIS was not adopted, the FMI was one of its outcomes and this was applied across the whole of Whitehall. The head of the home civil service was retired early to be replaced by someone who was more in favour of centrally led approaches.

The FMI provided a mechanism to disaggregate costs in anticipation of the application of the liberalisation of public services. This was a government-wide approach in stark contrast with the Rayner model, which was intended to devolve financial decision making to operational level (Pliatzky, 1988). Here the opportunity to identify specific service budgets and give local managers the experience of their operation was a potentially significant contribution to the preparation for the introduction of competition. However, this approach was undermined by a strong civil service culture that did not favour these changes either at the strategic level of the Treasury or within departments (Zifcak, 1994). Further the pro-policy and anti-management culture of the civil service, where civil servants seeking to reach the highest levels avoided those roles that were directly related to responsibilities for delivering services, had a significant effect (Thompson, 2000).

The FMI required each department to draw up a priority plan for its activities to define the costs associated with them and then to allocate budgets to manage their delivery. The work of the FMI was led by the Treasury that established a Financial Management Unit to specifically manage these tasks (Gray and Jenkins, 1984). While this was expected to be a long-lasting initiative, implemented through stages that started with each department, it was clear from the outset that it was regarded by the civil service as an exercise to be undermined (Theakston, 2000). Government departments made statements about their objectives in very general terms and continued to describe their responsibilities and functions rather than describe how their organisations worked to meet their objectives. While the Treasury provided leadership through the FMI, it also regarded the FMI as a mechanism for seizing more control over departmental expenditure (Fry, 1988). In particular, this process removed the ability of departments to move funding without recourse to Treasury agreement.

Next Steps Agencies

The National Audit Office (NAO) found the outcomes of both the Efficiency Unit scrutinies and the FMI were only partially successful. They did not deliver results in their first years, and the NAO found that of £215m scrutiny 'savings' that had been identified less than a quarter had been delivered (Talbot and Talbot, 2019). The general election in 1987 was a major opportunity to reset these approaches particularly now that the GATS approaches were emerging (Wallace, 1988).

The NSA were first established in 1988 and represented a major change (Haddon, 2012; Talbot and Talbot, 2019) that included an acceptance that the liberalisation of the public sector would be applied in central government. When the report of the failures of the Efficiency Unit and FMI was ready in 1987, Thatcher delayed its publication until 1988, not least because she did not want to show that her efficiency policies had been less successful than anticipated (Theakston, 1995). The programme to establish the NSA was set out in *Improving Management in Government – the Next Steps* (HMG, 1988) and represented a separation of responsibilities in a principal–agent model (Gilardi, 2001). The distinction could have been for a number of purposes, including the separation of operational departments from their regulatory quasi-judicial roles. After preliminary work examining the civil service and how it could be classified into policy and delivery functions, the Next Steps approaches advocated that this separation should be operationalised through the establishment of agencies (Kemp, 1990) that were to remain within the policy and budgetary control of their sponsoring departments that would act as their client (Audet, 2003). The executive or delivery elements would be established as agencies at arm's length. There was some indication that NSA should then be responsible for determining how best their functions could be delivered, but the expectation was that they remained within departmental control, not least as Permanent Secretaries were responsible to Parliament for their expenditure (Black, 1993; Lewis, 1997).

The NSA started to mirror the potential structures that might be adopted if these functions were undertaken by third-party external bodies (Gains, 1999), in an unacknowledged preparation for potential competition. In order to develop new markets, the purchaser–provider split was identified as a key requirement of these new working relationships within all types and tiers of government (Stewart and Walsh, 1992). Even within organisations outside the NSA programme, such as health, this split established internal trading relationships, separating policy making from delivery (Calovski, 2018). The implementation of the NSA also allowed the introduction of different accounting practices. The government used cash rather than accrual accounting systems as in the private sector and was considered rudimentary in comparison. This was particularly in the case of identifying and allocating costs and assessing performance that could not easily be verified (Hyndman and Anderson, 1995). It also did not include capital accounting where infrastructure investment could be funded over longer time periods secured against the asset. If these agency services were to be eventually subject to competition, a financial accounting system was required that the market could assess before making bids to run any service (Seal, 1999).

The implementation of the NSA continued for a decade. Initially, 12 candidate services were identified but by 1998 there were 140 said to be operating on these lines and by 1997 3 out of 4 civil servants were employed in an agency (Talbot and Talbot, 2019). However, as the first Permanent Secretary in charge of the Next Steps programme wrote, the departmental permanent secretaries were not in favour of a distanced model and agencies remained part of the administration of the civil service (Kemp, 1990).

A specific issue for the NSA was their accountability and reporting. This was and remains complex, as these agencies report both to their departments and to Parliament as recognised through the double accounting officer mechanism (Theakston, 1995; Haddon, 2012). The NSA worked within quasi-contractual framework agreements with their departments that stretched over five-year periods (Talbot and Talbot, 2019). There was an assumption that this operating system would lead to more internal efficiency (Kemp, 1990). The use of agencies might also assist government departments in making their own budget savings while protecting the central, policy-making activities that form a smaller proportion of the departmental budget. However, Hyndman and Anderson (1995) could find little or no reference to efficiency and effectiveness in the annual reports provided by the NSA. The NSA chief executives had some autonomy and acted as accounting officers but the permanent secretaries of the sponsoring departments were also accounting officers for the agencies, meaning that both could be summoned to Parliament to give evidence about their activities but the outcome was less accountability (Black, 1993). The agencies were institutionally but not culturally prepared for outsourcing.

The NSA led to some fracturing of the civil service as agencies were given their own powers to set pay and conditions (Theakston, 1995). The agencies operate in a 'revolving doors' system for staff moving back and forth from the civil service (David-Barrett, 2011). While the revolving doors practices are primarily regarded as part of the relationship with the private sector, at the most senior level this has been an operational model between the civil service, agencies and major charities (OECD, 2009). It is also seen as a civil service objective to place its former senior officials in leading roles in the public, private and voluntary sectors. In part, this has increased since there has been a requirement of those taking most senior roles in the civil service to have external experience (Greer and Jarman, 2010). This provides experience for a fixed period and a safe path back to the centre of government, operating in both directions (Parry, 2004). At the end of their careers, civil servants frequently move on to run charities or other public bodies (González-Bailon et al, 2013). This makes the continuing relationship strong, ensuring there will be no overt criticisms of government policy as former civil servants' awards and honours will be dependent on compliant behaviour.

After 1997, the Labour government had a greater understanding of what was required in the GATS. It was also clear that there were two major government sectors, health and education, that had very little competition, while introducing it would provide policy and public acceptability challenges. This was to be a major focus of Labour Party policy through their term in office to 2010, starting with schools and then moving on to health (Baldwin, 1999; Cribb, 2008). Elsewhere in government, agencies were re-absorbed into departments and there were still approximately 40 in 2013, although by 2018 only 25 per cent of civil servants were employed in agencies (Talbot and Talbot, 2019). However, there had also been a considerable increase in the use of private sector management consultants for policy support in central government (Saint-Martin, 2012). While these were not in agencies, they were also not part of the civil service, demonstrating private sector access to government markets, through the use of major service companies such as PWC, Accenture, Deloitte, Serco, Capita and Carillion (NAO, 2006b, 2019c).

Citizen's Charter

The Citizen's Charter was introduced by Major in 1991 and worked alongside the Next Steps team and the Efficiency Unit in the Cabinet Office (Haddon, 2012). It was also a mechanism to develop readiness for privatisation in the civil service (Theakston, 1995). The Citizen's Charter was said to mirror much of the management thinking in the 1980s, which was becoming more customer focussed (Osborne and Gaebler, 1993). It was also designed to assist users of outsourced services in understanding what they could expect and how to achieve redress for failures. The Citizen's Charter initiative extended the same approach into the public sector 'to use the mechanisms of privatisation, contracting-out and competition to provide more consumer choice' (Theakston, 1995, p 146). By 1993, over 30 citizen's charters had been published.

However, the approaches to preparing citizen's charters were criticised because they did not offer any legal guarantees of service levels or redress to a service user that might be expected in contracted services (Stewart and Walsh, 1992; Pollitt, 1994). Further, there was no additional funding to ensure that the charters were the basis of improvement. As Theakston (1995) points out, there was a second agenda for the introduction of the Citizen's Charter, which was the potential to create more marketisation within those services not already exposed to competition. The government announced its intention to open more central services to competition and to introduce market testing for others (Milne, 1997).

Market testing

The introduction of market testing was a further step in the preparation for the implementation of the GATS across central government (Rittenberg and Covaleski, 1999). The application of efficiencies through the creation of NSA and the departmental outsourcing of cleaning and catering were indications of the expected limits of the GPA and GATS in Whitehall. In 1991, in *Competing for Quality*, the Treasury proposed extending competition to the core of Whitehall for professional and specialist services, and in 1992, all departments were required to come forward with proposals for privatisation (Theakston, 1995). Many activities had been regarded as being outside the privatisation remit and it was assumed that by using NSA approaches civil servants could effectively bypass them (Pliatzky, 1988). In practice, they had been lured into a sense of security that they would not be faced with further competition.

In the market testing initiative, each government department was required to identify 25 per cent of their activities and staff that could be opened to competition before the next general election (Gains, 1999). The focus of this approach was seen to be cost cutting or dismantling the civil service rather than meeting the GATS agreement (Rhodes, 2001). The results were less than anticipated but still significant (Newman et al, 1998). There were 389 market tests. In some cases, the civil service was allowed to bid for the work, and in 68 per cent of such cases its bids were successful. In 113 other market testing exercises, the civil service was not permitted to bid for the work and these services were privatised. Even those bids that were won in-house demonstrated that their work could be more efficient and led to a reduction of 14,000 jobs (Theakston, 1995). A second target for market testing of 35,000 civil service jobs was announced and to be completed within a year (Pilkington, 1999). This was a major transfer of jobs to the private sector, and while 73 per cent of in-house bids were successful, the government claimed that there had been a reduction of 26,000 jobs; of the £2bn worth of work that had been reviewed, £1bn had been transferred to the private sector. There was an expectation that at least 25 per cent of departmental work would be transferred to external bodies. This privatisation of services was described as a 'one-way street' (Theakston, 1995, p 151) and services would not re-enter the civil service again. At the same time, the core executive services became more distanced from the rest (Gains, 1999), as sensitive government policy was protected from the provisions of these liberalisation agreements.

Procurement

In addition to institutional restructuring in government to prepare for liberalisation, there was also recognition that procurement capacity should be strengthened (Audet, 2003). GPA and GATS procurement rules were applied through EU regulations and directives, which had greater powers of intervention for failure to comply and significant remedies through the European Court of Justice (Bovis, 2019). These changes in wider international policy were reflected in UK domestic policy reviews that would support the implementation of these changes once finalised (Erridge and Greer, 2000). All international agreements have a long tail of negotiation and discussion that afford government core departments time to prepare (Wallace, 1988; Dudley and Richardson, 2004). The Cabinet Office and Treasury manage the domestic policy agenda and use these negotiation periods to change the expectations of public services towards embracing the private sector more widely.

In 1995, a White Paper, *Setting New Standards* (HMT, 1995, Cm 2840), was published. The paper recognised recent developments, such as outsourcing. It set out a new strategy by defining procurement and emphasising standards, in particular: fair competition; whole life costing; a step change in professionalism; benchmarking and a new statement of best practices. Implementation of this approach was supported through a policy network across Whitehall. However, the initiatives for procurement were promoted from the top down and there was little ownership of them by the officials involved in their delivery (Erridge and Greer, 2000). Further, the issue of procurement was not considered to be of sufficient importance to be a top tier management issue by the permanent secretaries and boards of individual departments (Rhodes, 2001). Procurement was regarded as an instrument of administration and delivery whereas the highest status issues for the boards were policy advice. Support for procurement was not a way to obtain career advancement in a policy-dominated world.

While the recognition of procurement as a mechanism for efficiency and effectiveness was generally welcomed, the manner in which it was operated served to alienate senior management of the departments (Dowding, 1995). The Treasury control of procurement was also reinforced through the link with the spending review, which departments relied upon for funding their preferred initiatives. Procurement was harnessed to policy delivery, now directed from the centre of government rather than being led by implementing departments as before (Gershon, 1999). There was also more focus on how projects would be hitting specific targets and a greater use of data to demonstrate cost benefits or performance (Erridge and Greer, 2000).

The procurement approach of the incoming Labour government in 1997 was to implement the GPA while aligning it with wider policy objectives for joined up government, modernisation and e-government, which were major priorities in the first and second terms of the Labour government (Erridge and Greer, 2000; Morphet, 2008). Sir Peter Gershon, formerly of Marconi Industries, was commissioned by the Treasury to lead a review of the government's procurement policy (Gershon, 1999). The Treasury used policy Tsar reviews as a mechanism to implement change (Levitt and Solesbury, 2012; Uyarra et al, 2014). Unlike the previous attempts by both Conservative and Labour governments, Gershon developed his review using a more inclusive approach with a range of departmental views captured through meetings and interviews (Micheli et al, 2005). The review was intended to consider all types of government procurement, which, at the time, was estimated to be valued at £13bn per annum.

Gershon also included the Prime Minister's focus on modernisation and joined up government (Morphet, 2008). He recognised the extent to which the government was increasingly using 'purchased services, e.g. outsourced facilities management, provision of turn-key systems and the use of third parties to deliver public services' (Gershon, 1999, p 1). Until this review, procurement responsibilities had been managed within departments, which led, in Gershon's view, to a failure of the government to gain the benefits of aggregation and size of contract with suppliers. Instead he proposed to introduce a common procurement framework across government through the establishment of the Office of Government Commerce (OGC) with a supervisory board led by a minister. Gershon also recommended there should be a single process across government where projects would be managed from start to finish with defined points for gateway reviews before the projects could proceed to the next stage of implementation (Fawcett and Marsh, 2012). He also considered other support measures such as procurement cards, skills and benchmarked pricing. Gershon identified the consistent use of lowest price tender processes, and while he found that some criteria-based value approaches were included within tenders, there was no indication of how these would be scored nor was there any evidence that they had been used in practice. In the whole review there is only one mention of the operating framework provided for government procurement by the EU and no mention of the GPA or GATS.

Following the publication of the review, Gershon became the head of the newly formed OGC that created a new way of conducting business (Fawcett and Marsh, 2012). The gateway review process was used for implementing government projects such as the use of a single identified number for children, safeguarding, single approaches to working with older people and school admissions (Erridge, 2005). Here the tension between the need to adhere to the review process frequently came up against the political imperative to implement commitments quickly. The review process meant more expenditure for consultants, and where gateway review boards found that projects were not ready to proceed, there was frequently an approach of forming a new board to assess the project rather than deal with the issues that had been identified. In the same way as evidence-based policy making, the government and departmental pressures for implementation triumphed over the commitment to improve the project (Sanderson, 2002). The procurement process could also be overcome by the requirements for a specific or special approach being used to bypass procedures. In some cases, more elaborate and centralised approaches to procuring specific types of services such as IT systems were expected to be filtered through another central government agency, again delaying and frustrating the original intentions of the promoting department.

By 2009, central government was still of the view that public procurement within central government was inefficient (Uyarra et al, 2014). The Transforming Government Procurement Strategy (HMT, 2007), launched as part of the 2007 Comprehensive Spending Review, also sought to raise procurement standards, develop the skills of procurement professionals, drive value for money through collaborative procurement and improve the delivery of major projects. Following the publication of this strategy, the OGC kick-started a series of Procurement Capability Reviews in central government departments (Waterman, 2008) Each department subsequently developed and implemented an Improvement Plan. Finally, the Operational Efficiency Programme aimed to further achieve efficiency savings through collaborative procurement and improvement in other areas such as property asset management (HMT, 2009).

The OGC started to assemble the government's property assets on a single database, ePIMS (Saxby, 2006). This was initially confined to assets owned by central government departments that were not operational, thus excluding much of the land owned by the Ministry of Defence. However, gradually 'joined up' government has continued to prevail and ePIMS survived the demise of the OGC through Total Place (Bovaird, 2010) and then One Public Estate (OPE) programmes (Local Government Association et al, 2018). OPE is now primarily run by the Local Government Association and has made a significant advance in identifying any publicly owned land in an area on a Geographical Information System (GIS). Although devised to support disposals and community accountability, OPE has had a greater effect demonstrating the scale of their land ownership to local authorities. This in turn has offered many local authorities the opportunity to use smaller sites, not identified previously as being suitable for housing (Morphet and Clifford, 2020).

5

Local Government: Compulsory Competition and Best Value

Introduction

The wider liberalisation of local authority services started once negotiations began to extend the Government Procurement Agreement (GPA) to local government in 1988 and inclusion in the emerging General Agreement on Trade in Services (GATS) through the GATT Uruguay Round that started in 1986. This had a significant effect on the outsourcing of local government services that had hitherto been delivered by directly employed staff. Margaret Thatcher's government anticipated this through the application of Compulsory Competitive Tendering (CCT) in 1988 and it was continued by the Labour government's approach through the best value regime (Wilson, 1999). The policy approaches adopted by successive governments were framed in an immediate ideological construct of New Public Management (NPM), which diverted the public sector away from the underlying international agreements that the UK had entered into (Dunleavy and Hood, 1994). However, the wider role of performance culture supported the establishment of local authorities as more credible institutions than other parts of the UK state by 2010.

The expansion of the GPA, together with the application of GATS to sub-national government, introduced some mechanisms for implementation (Audet, 2002). In order to ensure that states complied, an international system of single national accounts (SNAs), initially agreed in 1968, was updated through a UN agreement in 1992 as the World Trade Organization was coming into being (Preeg, 2012). While not mandatory within the WTO, in 2002 the EU agreed that each member state should prepare the SNA. In the UK, these were introduced in 2007 following the

Atkinson Review (Atkinson, 2005a, 2005b). SNAs established the system of assessing the scale of public expenditure by sectors and how much of the budget is to be exposed to competition as a consequence. They also support assessments of national and regional productivity and the Treasury commissioned specific reports to accompany these assessments (HMT, 2001, 2004).

In preparing the SNA, governments were required to assess all public expenditure. This was then used to ensure that a sufficient portion has been exposed to competition across all sectors so that none was protected. The role of local government is significant in the SNA. It has been estimated that the expenditure of local government represents 65 per cent of all state expenditure in the Organisation for Economic Co-operation and Development (OECD) although this varies between states (Audet, 2002). While there has been a focus on the transparency afforded by the publication of the SNA (Bastida and Benito, 2007), there has been less indication of the SNA's role in determining the levels of public sector market liberalisation.

The implementation of performance management as preparation for public sector market liberalisation for local authorities across the whole of OECD was carried out by discussions and policy transfer (Pollitt and Bouckaert, 2000; Sanderson, 2001). While neoliberal ideology was at the heart of public sector liberalisation from the early 1970s, it was also becoming clear that the practices of delivery could be managed in different ways, through social value tender processes. In France, there was a shift to use a concessions model, which offered contracts to the market to run services while maintaining control and flexibility within public bodies (Bel and Foote, 2009). This was also extensively used by Sweden and other EU member states (Audet, 2003).

In the UK, liberalisation was used to reshape local authorities in more fundamental ways. It was aligned with a second new policy, which was agreed in the EU in 1992 and was the extension of subsidiarity (Duff, 1993). UK core government departments considered how the role of market liberalisation could be used to change local authority power and autonomy in service delivery (Wilson, 1999). Local authorities could have more power but less to control.

From direct provision to competition in local government

In the period before the Thatcher government, many councils had been providing services to each other or had joint arrangements (Tomkinson,

2007). The 1972 Local Government Act permitted councils to set up joint committees to run services and many pursued this approach particularly for IT, cemeteries and sports facilities (Parker, 1990). Councils also used the 1970 Local Authorities Goods and Services Act to provide services to each other. As soon as Thatcher came to power, she started to implement the GPA with particular focus on local government. While not part of the agreements of the Tokyo Round in 1980 there was a recommendation that this should quickly be extended to sub-state government (Croome, 1996). In the UK, local government is not part of the constitution, unlike most other countries (Scott et al, 1994). This means that local authorities are controlled by powers conferred on them through specific legislation (Copus, 2006; Bailey and Davidson 1999). This is particularly manifest in any local authority official report where the power to execute any decision is cited with reference to specific legislation.

There were major presentational difficulties for the government in preparing for local government liberalisation. While the Thatcher narrative of efficiency and cost cutting had some traction with the public, there was no general embrace of a competitive approach to public service delivery from local authorities, professionals or the electorate (Gyford, 1991). While the use of compulsion was one mechanism for delivering market liberalisation more rapidly, there was also a need to promote these changes in a softer way to the public. In the 1980 Local Government, Planning and Land Act, there was provision for competition in local government services for highways work and housing maintenance (Smith, 1988; Walsh, 1989). This was not compulsory at the time, although a few Conservative local authorities such as Southend on Sea and Wandsworth undertook outsourcing of some of their services including refuse collection, cleaning, street cleansing, housing maintenance and caretaking (Parker, 1990). The financial savings reported from both councils were significant and became the basis of a low council tax regime in Wandsworth that was rewarded by central government financial support (Jacobs, 1988; Stoker, 1989). However, while the savings were achieved, by early 1985 only 41 of 456 councils in England and Wales had taken up this approach (*The Guardian*, 5 March 1985, p 32, quoted in Parker, 1990).

Compulsory Competitive Tendering (CCT) for blue-collar services in local government was introduced in the Local Government Act 1988 coinciding with the extension of the GPA to sub-national government. The introduction of the compulsory element into legislation was new and reflected the UK government's requirement to demonstrate that a range of public services were open to competition. In order to comply with the GPA, a significant and abrupt shift in policy signals and practice was necessary. Responses to the 1980 Local Government, Planning and Land Act demonstrated that it was unlikely that such approaches would be adopted by local authorities on a voluntary basis. While the government's narrative for imposing CCT in blue-collar services was about cost cutting and efficiency, there was no evidence that introducing private sector contractors to undertake the same services would be any cheaper in the long run, as demonstrated in other liberalised sectors (Price, 2005). Although service efficiencies could be found through preparatory processes for competition, savings also related to reductions in services provided (Chaundy and Uttley, 1993; Wilson, 1999). This argument was used by local authorities, but external pressures to meet international obligations prevailed although this was not acknowledged. As Bulmer and Burch (2005) have indicated, central government's approach to meeting these agreements was frequently clandestine. CCT was also promoted by the government as a mechanism for reducing costs to poll taxpayers (Parker, 1990; Painter, 1991). While the 1988 Act focused on blue-collar services, there was also an indication that white-collar professional services such as accountancy would be added, although this never occurred in practice (Walsh, 1995; Wilson, 1999).

The arguments that were used to introduce CCT were concerned with the performance of public service delivery. This was a particular issue where local authorities had their own Direct Labour Organisations (DLOs) and later Direct Service Organisations (DSOs) established through the 1980 and 1988 Acts. The government considered that there were few incentives for councils to be more efficient (Flynn, 1981; Ruddock, 1994). There was also a government assumption that occasional market testing could ensure that councils would achieve value for money by benchmarking against the private sector (Helgason, 1997). However, many council services, such as refuse collection, were not operated by the private sector and there were no comparisons available. Service specifications were also changed in an attempt to support in-house bids to maintain existing direct service providers. The same issues occurred in Scandinavia when implementing competition to win public refuse collection contracts (Gustafsson and Saksvik, 2005; Busck, 2007). For other services, such as cleaning in buildings, or later for white-collar services, there were comparisons that could be made although they were for different types of activity (Rittenberg and Covaleski, 1999).

The third argument used was that CCT could introduce better performance management into the delivery of services and provide value for money. It is this component that particularly engaged those interested in NPM as a mechanism to explain changes in public service delivery focus towards performance management (Hood, 1991; Dunleavy and Hood, 1994). After John Major became Prime Minister in 1990, there was an opportunity to consider the level of service delivery the public expected and their ability to engage in service delivery specifications, through the Citizen's Charter. However, this did not appear to have much effect, with service improvements being attributed to other reforms (Pollitt, 1994; Sanderson, 2001).

There was also a view in Whitehall, which mirrored the civil service view of central public service delivery, that local authorities could focus on higher level professional matters if they were not directly engaged in service delivery (Parker, 1990). However, this centralised view failed to recognise the role of councillors, the importance of local public service delivery and their control over it (APSE, 2006). When housing and highways maintenance failed, it was possible for councillors to complain about the quality of delivery and then for some immediate action (Gyford, 1991; Stewart and Walsh, 1992). When services were contracted out, a service default depended on the wording of the original specification, and if this issue was not included, then the council would have to pay for the actions required. In some services, such as refuse collection, this made changes to the contracts for increasing recycling costly or impossible until the contract was concluded or terminated (Boyne, 1998). There were also concerns about collusion on price between contractors and there was some evidence of this in road building (Parker, 1990). Finally, there were concerns about local authorities' skills to draft contract specifications and then examine tenders to assess whether contractors could deliver them. An element of collusion was found between councils and contractors where outsourcing was favoured, although elsewhere contract packaging and detailed specifications were used to discourage external bidders for services (Shaw et al, 1994). There were also additional costs for councils, as contract managers and inspectors were needed to assess the quality of the contractor's work, defaults and penalties.

The 1988 Act included specific uses of the word competition, stating that local authorities should only undertake services if they can do so competitively. It made six conditions under which local authorities could deliver services, which were based, albeit anonymously, on the GPA and EU approach to implementing competition of goods and services. These included having a specific advertisement for the contract and also setting limits for work values that were required to implement EU single market and GPA provisions. Where the local authority was small, then the *de minimis* rule was applied and local authorities were not required to open their services. The Act also required the establishment of trading accounts for services so that the private sector could have some indication of the relative costs of the services and how they were operating. The Act also required that local authorities not consider 'non-commercial' criteria, that is contracts should only be awarded on the lowest price. This was in direct contravention of the GPA, GATS and Single European Market (SEM) agreements where contracts could be awarded on public/ social value criteria that were established and published at the outset. It took over 20 years before local authorities routinely used this approach to tendering for their services and is now frequently used (LGA, 2019). It has also been included in the Public Services (Social Value Act) 2012. In central government, tenders are still primarily assessed on the lowest price, although in 2018, it introduced social value principles into procurement. The selection of contracts using the lowest price has led to the loss of numerous contracts for UK public services and goods being successfully tendered by other EU member state companies (Topham, 2017). It has been ascribed to EU procurement rules but evidence from other EU and WTO member states demonstrate that other practices have always been possible (Badstuber, 2018).

The process of applying CCT within local authorities was introduced over a five-year period with the first round launched in 1989. When CCT was implemented, local authorities had to expose their services to competition in tranches (Wilson, 1999). This meant that the local authorities had time to establish the costs of services and contract processes and also allowed a contractor market to develop to bid for this work. At the same time, potential contractors lobbied the government to prioritise competition for their preferred sectors (Milne, 1997). When shifting any service from in-house to market provision through the CCT process, it was necessary for local authorities to draw up a specification so that potential contractors could tender for the work. This specification was required to be reasonable and not written in such a way that would deter potential contractors from bidding. In order to go through this tender process, local authorities had to understand their existing specifications and costs including the productivity of the labour force (Painter, 1991). One consideration was the extent to which any one contractor would have access to the details of existing staff (Seal, 1999).

The range of services included within the 1988 Local Government Act subject to CCT included refuse collection, building cleaning, street cleaning, schools and welfare catering, grounds maintenance and vehicle maintenance and these were frequently strongly unionised (Marsh, 1992). Most local authorities employed refuse collection staff as part of a DLO (Szymanski and Wilkins, 1993) and offering the opportunity to compete for this work by third-party organisations would require details of their work design to be shared. Where councils employed direct labour through a DLO, it was allowed to compete although within specific guidelines that were regularly extended by the government (Flynn, 1981).

There were both political and economic objections to the introduction of CCT (Shaw et al, 1994). The political objections were frequently from Conservative councils in rural areas that were of the view that such drastic changes in the provision of services were not aimed at their type of council and were really meant to reform larger Labour councils that they considered to be inefficient (Boyne, 1997). More generally, Stewart and Walsh (1992) argued that marketisation was not appropriate for the public sector as it would change the nature of the relationship between the council and its electorate. Others argued that the introduction of CCT would not be cost effective and would require the introduction of client managers in addition to those running the services as an overhead to these services and added to the price offered by the market contractors (Seal, 1999).

The role of public choice theory in supporting the basis of CCT was strong (Boyne, 1998). It assumed that public officials would need to be forced to deliver services in ways that were focused on the customer, consumer or citizen rather than satisfying their own interests. CCT not only externalised the delivery of services but made transparent the decision making about how service standards were set, how service delivery was equalised across a whole local authority area and what were the outcomes of service delivery when considered against wider political and policy objectives (Wilson, 1999). These savings might be used to offer other services that have been awaiting funding. However, public officials are also budget maximisers and do not willingly wish to give up any savings made through contracting efficiencies.

Once services had started to be put out to contract, there were differences between the ways in which local authorities responded. Painter (1991) undertook a survey after the first year of CCT and found that in many councils DSOs were not only bidding for the work but also winning (Parker, 1990). This pattern was mainly shown in metropolitan areas and Scotland. In London, more external contractors were successful and Painter (1991) ascribes this to the pro-Thatcher Conservative councils. In his work, Painter found that local authorities expressed their willingness to implement CCT in four main groups – the first he called the new right who were keen to reduce services, staffs and budgets. The second were non-committal who were neither for it nor against it and were content to let CCT take its course. These local authorities were also likely to be Conservative. The third group were those in favour of in-house delivery but were not averse to cutting costs. These councils were both Labour and Conservative. The fourth group of councils were committed to in-house provision without cutting services. These were Labour councils that were committed to the public sector ethos and their own labour force. Overall, in the first year, Painter found that three quarters of contracts were retained in-house. However, this position changed with the establishment and closer inspection of tendering processes by the Audit Commission (Kelly, 2003), after which more contracts were awarded to the private sector. A similar survey to Painter's was undertaken in the North of England by Shaw et al (1994), where five local authority responses to CCT were recorded – hostility, fear, pragmatism, neutrality and enthusiasm, with three quarters falling between pragmatic and neutral.

At the point of transfer of the service from direct employees to external organisations, the employees were protected for a short time by the EU Acquired Rights Memorandum (CEC, 1997), also known as TUPE (Transfer of Undertakings (Public Employment)). The government's arm's length approach to EU legislation meant that the people in the UK were not well informed about it (Morphet, 2013). The government attempted to downplay the legality of TUPE to support the private sector on the transfer of public services and this created uncertainty (Kerr and Radford, 1994). The role of TUPE in CCT was not understood by local authorities, their labour forces or trades unions. Further, Adnett and Hardy (1998) demonstrate how confusion about TUPE's applicability was spread by the government. This had a significant effect on local authorities and their employees during CCT processes. In their survey of councils in the North of England, Shaw et al (1994) found that only one trades union representative mentioned that it may be possible to claim rights at the point of staff transfer.

Although CCT was abolished by the Labour government, there was some evidence that the practices of competitive tendering of services continued (Gómez-Lobo and Szymanski, 2001). The introduction of CCT began changing the culture of local authorities, and some political commitment, community expectations and investment in competition occurred. In some services, CCT improved the level of service and costs reduced (Boyne et al, 2010). Where refuse collection was privatised, after initial hiccups on handover, frequently householders experienced no major differences and satisfaction ratings as measured by the Audit Commission increased (Chaundy and Uttley, 1993; Szymanski, 1996). In some cases, local authorities employed those with experience of contracting although there was also some 'producer capture' and less formal relationships between council and contractors developed (Walsh, 1995). In some councils, contractors did not perform well and systems were not in place to manage them, regardless of the overarching performance framework. There was also evidence that improving service standards and reducing costs through revised working methods were frequently the result of changes made before outsourcing so that in-house teams could retain the contract.

Some councils anticipated the extension of CCT to white-collar services. Where local authorities decided to outsource professional services such as Berkshire County Council to Babtie, there was uncertainty about how contracted and permanent staff could work together (Wingfield, 1995). There were concerns about the ways in which information may be used and shared by contracted staff for commercial gain within their companies. There was also little understanding of the responsibilities of contractors to their clients from their staff. The introduction of more commercial awareness in councils, coupled with the economic downturn in the early 1990s, started to change employment practices (Harris, 2008). Where there were recruitment freezes for full-time permanent employees, councils started to employ contract, temporary and part-time staff to help overcome organisation-wide bans on recruitment. On the other hand, the threats of introducing external competition was used to change labour practices (Shaw et al, 1994). The effects of CCT had started to change councils and public expectations.

The arguments put forward for the implementation of both the 1980 and 1988 Acts were taken to be ideological and there was no reference to meeting the GPA as one of the key drivers of this legislation (Parker, 1991, 2009). Rather it was seen as part of the Thatcher government's cost cutting measures, her wish to reduce the size of the state and the power of the trades unions (Marsh, 1991). There was also a view that the implementation of the 1980 and 1988 Acts was a mechanism to reduce the power of local authorities (Painter, 1991). This failure to appreciate the role of the state and its obligations for its own procurement was significant in understanding the way in which competition policy was being implemented. It overlooked the extent to which central government was using powers over local government to meet target percentages of public services exposed to competition while protecting its own position from liberalisation. There was some consideration of these issues in a major research programme on the central–local relations funded by the Economic and Social Research Council between 1978 and 1984 (Goldsmith and Newton, 1983), which examined how power relations were being changed particularly through central control of finance and the way central government was embedding local government within its control, reducing its autonomy. While some considered this relationship to be synergistic (Keohane and Nye, 1989) others argued that local authorities still had powers and could act to support their local communities (Barrett and Hill, 1986). Whatever the drivers behind this major central–local relations project, it embodied the *zeitgeist* of change and the ways in which the government was preparing to use legislation and powers to require local authorities to open their services to competition. This broke the post-war consensus of central and local governments being co-producers of the national and local welfare state and moved to the creation of oppositional cultures.

New Public Management

The New Public Management (NPM) narrative was convenient as a tool of statecraft, diverting attention for the policy change to immediate political ideology rather than the longer term commitments to the application of the GPA and forthcoming GATS. There was also little connection with the preparatory approaches being taken in central government through agencification and quangos. While central government created arm's length bodies that they could control by continuing to apply direct management (Lewis, 1997; Audet, 2002), local government was required to take a different approach through compulsory competition.

As the government's approach to the implementation of the international trade agreements did not feature in public discourse, it was left to others to project political theories on to competition policy to explain its provenance. The introduction of performance management had a central role in the introduction of liberalisation in specifying services and costs of delivery. The focus on performance management, particularly in local government through the umbrella term of NPM, included a range of approaches. These encompassed the principal–agent theories of clients and contractors (Ward, 2007; Mills et al, 2019), public choice theories of rational decision making (Dunleavy, 1994; Gruening, 2001) and the role of benchmarking in service delivery (Bovaird and Löffler, 2002; Kuhlmann and Jäkel, 2013). These approaches to managing public service outputs, which could be measured in a variety of ways, took over from public service ethos although there was no reason why these new methods should specifically remove this approach to public service delivery. It ensured that the public services moved to a user-centred rather than producer-centred approach – a culture that lasted until 2010 in the UK.

The UK approach to public service delivery was also found in other OECD countries such as the US, Sweden and New Zealand (Boyne, 1998) with the coincidences of changes in central government purpose and culture for public services attributed to policy transfer (Common, 1998). NPM, as a framework for public sector liberalisation, was considered across a range of countries but little or none of this was related to the GPA and GATS agreements. For those countries that were members of the WTO and also members of the OECD, support for implementation of these international agreements was provided by

PUMA, a public management advice service. The PUMA approach indicated that there should be a framework for public service performance that would be associated with understanding costs and delivery criteria. The OECD operated PUMA by undertaking international benchmarking reviews (Helgason, 1997; Barzelay, 1997). Benchmarking provided a mechanism to prepare public services for competition while allowing states to place them within understandable and comparative bands. This allowed examination of competitive processes that were being applied. This benchmarking method also ensured that assessment of public services could not be avoided within OECD member states (Sanderson, 2001).

Would there have been a different view about the provenance of NPM if governments had been more transparent about their international commitments to introduce the GPA and GATS into local government? In the UK, local authorities could grasp the issues of implementation of EU procurement rules and how they should be applied. This differed from any public discourse on wider international agreement on liberalisation. One consideration for the government may have been that more transparency about requirements to implement the international agreements would have provided a context that opened other questions about the way in which these agreements were being interpreted in practice and how long they had been influencing public policy. The role of the core executive in applying public sector liberalisation as a tool of institutional reform was a continuation of government practices for change and followed the approach adopted when the UK joined the EU (Wallace, 1973; Morphet, 2013). However, while the role of the SEM and its associated procurement regime was understood by local government, the introduction of compulsory competition was not, and scalecraft offered few choices other than to associate this orphan policy with statecraft using political ideology (Morphet, 2017).

The use of NPM theories to explain the preparation of neoliberal competition was correct but in projecting contemporaneous political ideology on to the implementation of competition it overlooked the underlying dynamics of these international trade agreements (Lamer, 2009). It should have been no surprise that the Labour government continued competition as an operational norm for local authorities in 1997. If there had been more transparency about the context for these Labour policies, there might have been a recognition that the requirement for compulsory competition for public services had been dropped to be replaced by a softer, more nuanced but wider regime of best value. However, if there had not been the period of CCT before 1997, would the incoming Labour government have been able to continue on this path? Was this change of government a convenient use of statecraft to reset the local government competition narrative?

Best value

As local authorities had started to meet the GPA target percentages for opening up services, it was possible to ease, although not remove, these requirements (De Graaf and King, 1995). By the time that the Labour government came to power in 1997, the effects of CCT in the outsourcing of local government activities together with council housing right to buy sales had already served to deliver much of the competition in local government services that the GPA/GATS agreement required when it came into force (Woolcock and Hodges, 1996). There could now be a de-escalation and rowing back on the sectoral compulsion that had been part of the CCT regime, but at the same time, it was not possible to remove the requirements. There had also been a focus on the price of contracts in the Conservative government approach to CCT up to 1997, but it was becoming clear that the lowest price was not the only method offered for the selection of contractors through competition. There could be a social value approach, provided that it had been set out as part of the contract specification and the criteria were clear. The election of a new Labour government in 1997 meant that there was a strong expectation, particularly in local government, that CCT would be abolished and not replaced by any similar regime (Morphet, 2008) but the international agreements on public sector liberalisation still had to be met. The size of the local government market was a considerable proportion of the total available for competition (Audet, 2002). Once again, the introduction of some aspects of new international trading agreement for local public services in 1996 coincided with a change in Prime Minister.

The incoming Labour government in 1997 therefore had to continue the competition regime for local public services but was able to use compulsion in a different way. The best value regime, which was implemented through the 1999 Local Government Act, required that all local authorities had a programme of market testing for their services. Although not explicitly stated, this now incorporated elements of social value principles and was set out in the 'improvement' narrative (Boyne, 1999; Rashman and Radnor, 2005). This wider approach, based on the 4 'Cs' – challenge, compare, consult and compete – would be tested by the District Audit and Audit Commission both taking an interventionist approach (Kelly, 2003). However, again there was no explanation from the government about the international agreements made for opening competition in local government services. As Boyne (1998) stated, the CCT contracts that had been entered into by local authorities would lapse and there would be no compulsion to re-tender them to the market but the cultural change had been made. Local authorities would be expected to show how they would obtain best value for their service delivery using a range of methods and increasingly through encouragement for strategic partnerships and shared delivery with other local authorities (Morphet, 2008).

In local government, the introduction of best value as a replacement for CCT was unexpected in 1997. Many in local government considered that the incoming government was reneging on its pre-election promises but the government's commitment to introduce it came soon after its election (Armstrong, 1997). Further, the best value regime extended competition to include all services operated by local authorities and these were to be reviewed with an examination of the potential for their delivery through competitive means. This meant that it could now include the government's responsibilities for the implementation of GATS through the inclusion of services. However, unlike CCT, the mechanisms and processes for establishing best value were based on a wider platform of public service principles and not totally dependent on lowest price contract selection. The role of best value was included within a commitment to working together between central and local governments through a nod to post-Treaty on the Functioning of the European Union subsidiarity and multi-level government and enshrined in the government's signature of the Local Government Charter of Self-Government, many years after it was first invited to do so (Wilson, 1999). The incoming Prime Minister, Tony Blair, was also concerned about local government being a potential Achilles heel for the future re-election of a Labour government. Immediately before the 1997 general election there had been a major councillor corruption case in Doncaster, which was an important issue of public trust in Labour-run local government (Morphet, 2008). This was also after nearly 20 years of the oppositional undermining of local authorities by successive Conservative governments. Some were of the view that the Labour Party had espoused the approaches of NPM and neoliberalism and incorporated them within their approaches to managing public services (Hutton, 1996). This was the case but not the whole picture. The Labour government had taken on international agreements to liberalise the public sector but had radically changed the approach adopted from the previous ten years of compulsion to one that allowed a wider approach to setting standards and expanding the type of organisations that could provide local services (Haugh and Kitson, 2007), in an approach that could be continued into the next government (Alcock, 2010).

While the competition aspects of the best value regime had some similarities with CCT, there were important differences (Wilson, 1999). Services were not expected to return to the 1970s direct delivery model but there was a much closer alignment to WTO and EU contracting principles that allowed a range of delivery models with partners and voluntary organisations and were not dependent on contractor selection based on the lowest price (Demirkaya, 2006). It applied in England and Wales. The operation of best value was set out in the 1999 Local Government Act, which included a number of duties for local authorities implementing best value. These were the need to meet the requirements for the 4 'Cs'. The introduction of consultation with communities on the type of service to be delivered was a reference back to the Citizen's Charter implemented by Major in 1991 (Pollitt, 1994). In order to apply the best value process on a manageable basis, each council was required to prepare a Best Value Performance Plan that set targets, benchmarks and a programme for applying a best value review process for all services within a defined time period (Boyne, 1999). This plan and the processes applied to deliver it were subject to the assessment and agreement of the council's auditors, drawn primarily but not exclusively from the public sector. While important, best value was also set within a wider range of local government reforms including the organisation of their democratic government arrangements, which ended committee government and moved to an executive and scrutiny model, with the option of directly elected mayors (Morphet, 2008). The council reforms also included external relationships that were embedded in Local Strategic Partnership that councils were expected to form and the adoption of the legally required Sustainable Community Strategy. These together provided the mechanism for working with the community and private sector partners and achieving the environmental commitments made in Local Agenda 21 as part of the UN Rio Earth Summit in 1992 (Lambert, 2006).

The origins of the best value regime and subsequent approach were never discussed before the 1997 general election and appeared as a fully formed policy immediately after (Milne, 1997). The relationship to GPA/GATS was never made publicly, submerged in statecraft. As Demirkaya (2006) commented, there were similarities with the Australian approach and it should be noted that there was considerable exchange between officials at the time (Morphet, 2008). In the US, there were also similarities to the statecraft that was used to introduce public service liberalisation in 1993 through Clinton's Government Performance and Results Act. Here, the approaches set out by Osborne and Gaebler (1993) for reinventing government narrative by 'steering not rowing' were in practice, masking the client–contractor relationship within a more distanced approach to government delivery. The OECD (1997) also stressed the importance of connections between the legitimacy of the government and its performance in service delivery.

The commentary on the introduction of best value was mostly focused on the continuation of neoliberalism and the role of markets. Much of the discussion was about the implementation of control over local government (Boyne, 1999; Wilson, 1999). In retrospect, with government commitments to implement the GPA and GATS across the sector as a whole, this view can be supported, at least at the outset between 1986 and 1997. It is also important to note that the UK, like other members of the WTO applying the GPA, has always been required to make an annual return about the volume of 'contestable' expenditure that has been open to competition (Audet, 2003).

The 1999 Local Government Act abolished the need to apply CCT but did incorporate all local government activities within the best value framework and could be seen as a part of a wider reformist agenda. The requirements for GATS had been incorporated within the modernisation of local government (DETR, 1998). It was another example of the way in which the civil service was able to use statecraft, at the point of a change in political leadership to apply and introduce these newly agreed rules by associating them with institutional reform. By requiring best value review of all council services, the government could demonstrate compliance with the GATS regime. However, the preceding scale of outsourcing achieved under CCT meant that there was less pressure on local government, to place their services externally, than in 1986 when the GPA was implemented. It introduced public management regimes that allowed councils to compare with others through benchmarking and local authorities were placed into audit 'families' of councils with similar demographic and geographic features (Boyne, 1997). This enabled more reasonable comparisons rather than a crude costs basis. There was also the opportunity to make a year-on-year comparison for internal improvement (Sanderson, 2001) and move towards an assumption of improvement and change.

The OECD (1997) considered that outsourcing offered less control to the state, as the service standards and those reviewing delivery on the basis of criteria by third parties could be more local and less producer driven. In the UK, it introduced more central control over the local. If citizens were involved in defining service standards, this could legitimate the size and expenditure of local government, so they had to be moderated. The OECD (1997; Barzelay, 1997) reviewed the performance management approach of ten countries and their direct links to meeting the terms of the GPA. The results showed some variation. The UK was most similar to New Zealand, where a market-orientated process was enforced. Other countries, such as Sweden, Canada, Australia and the US, achieved improvement through performance management systems. This may be because they already had some private sector delivery at the local level.

This agenda also worked with the expected increase in subsidiarity for local authorities arising from the agreements made by the UK within the EU in 1992 (Duff, 1993) and its expected extension as part of the discussion of the EU's Governance White Paper (CEC, 2001). Devolution in Scotland, Wales and London together with the Good Friday Agreement in Northern Ireland (1998) had implemented the 1992 agreements for subsidiarity. In England, the civil service response was of generating confusion through an inconsistent approach. This included local government review, and the insertion of a quasi-devolved regional layer of government offices, regional development agencies and advisory regional assemblies run from the centre was not going to be enough to meet the extended subsidiarity requirement in the longer term. The initial approach to subsidiarity in England through regional devolution in 2004 was quickly replaced by new localism (Corry and Stoker, 2002) and double devolution (Miliband, 2006) to fit wider economic policy transfer to functional economic areas (Krugman, 1980; Dijkstra and Poelman, 2012). However, if local authorities were to have more control as subsidiarity increased, then there was also a problem of changing public opinion about the competence of local government. After 20 years of vilification of local authorities, the government declared that they were to be given more powers (Raynsford, 2006). The development of new devolved structures, a demonstration of value for money and working with communities could provide a better basis for public confidence when these moves finally had to be implemented, as agreed through the Lisbon Treaty in 2007 but not applied until 2009. By 2005, local authorities had better levels of performance and public confidence than central government (OECD, 2013a). Best value was part of the process of both this preparation for greater local control and re-establishing public confidence in local authorities.

6

Creating the Public Services Market

Introduction

A key challenge for central government in implementing the General Agreement on Trade in Services (GATS) to liberalise public services when it came into effect in 1996 was to find a way of market making. It would be difficult to open public services to competition where there had been no private sector engagement before. In some public services, there had been little external provision. Introducing change and potential for opening internal processes to competition meant that private sector contractors would have to be attracted to establishing a capability to bid for this work (Walsh, 1995; Héritier, 2001). This was particularly in relation to professional and specialist functions in local and central government such as building control, finance, legal services and planning. In some services, it was possible to transfer skills between the public and private sectors very readily, such as human resources, although there continued to be differences in the cultural context of the public sector (Harris, 2008). In other local authority services, the development of private sector markets was encouraged through changes in regulation such as planning (Adams and Tiesdell, 2010; RTPI, 2019).

There were also challenges about the ways public bodies defined their activities, attributed costs and were managed. The role of performance management regimes was central to creating these markets in specifying what should be done and how it would be delivered, priced and measured (Bovaird and Gregory, 1996). In many cases, there was a need for new market making such as in building control. The deregulation of building control was common across a number of Organisation for Economic

Co-operation and Development (OECD) countries including in the EU, Australia and Canada (Meijer and Visscher, 2006; Van der Heijden, 2010). In the UK, following the Building Act 1984, an independent provider of building control regulators, the National Housing and Building Council (NHBC), established a subsidiary company in 1985 to employ 'approved inspectors'. Up to this point all building control had been undertaken by professional qualified inspectors employed by local authorities. The NHBC building control professionals became the preferred inspectors for many private sector development companies and their role was highlighted in the Grenfell Fire tragedy (Hodkinson, 2019).

In order to prepare public services for the application of GATS, the government chose to progress this through a narrative of efficiency and effectiveness – first on government procurement (Gershon, 1999) and then on a wider range of services focused on productivity (HMT, 2001, 2004; Gershon, 2004). In central government, procurement was not primarily focused on buying other than supplies and travel together with some consultancy. However, if larger parts of government processes were to be outsourced, or at least opened to competition, then it was important to ensure that procurement processes were fit for purpose. This was followed by reviews of efficiencies that then allowed the Treasury to set performance targets and transformation outcomes for internal delivery through the Comprehensive Spending Review (CSR). The CSR has been used to realign the UK government's programmes and priorities to those it had agreed within the EU and provided seven-year programmes of change (Gamble, 2015). However, the processes could also be used to achieve government objectives. While the UK was proud of its civil service and democratic processes, it was also the case that the EU's seven-year programmes included administrative and bureaucratic reforms within them (Patz and Goetz, 2015). Research on measuring the size of the public services market including issues about the modes of supply (Chang et al, 1999) has demonstrated how this has influenced institutional structures within the government (Armingeon, 2004) and work design (Parker, 1990; Painter, 1991; Shaw et al, 1994).

A central government challenge in introducing competition and outsourcing services into local government was having adequate numbers of suppliers willing to bid for work in an unknown market. While competition for the delivery of capital projects and maintenance, refuse collection and cleaning became established following the introduction of compulsory competitive tendering (CCT) in 1988, the opportunities for competition in back office services were slower to develop. There was already the opportunity to purchase 'off the shelf' payroll systems that could be used by individual authorities to share between them.

Initially the Treasury assumed that having a common payroll system across local government would provide most of the efficiency savings that the government was seeking for e-government investment (Morphet, 2008). However, payroll systems were relatively inexpensive as their features for local government were no different from those of other employers. For financial systems, there were differences between public and private sector accounting systems and it was not possible to use the same ones. Local authorities were providing housing benefits on behalf of central government and there could be multiple rule changes each week. Some firms, particularly Capita founded by a former local authority accountant, had established a service to operate these financial systems and other providers were offering specific housing payments services. However, these were sporadic in their take up by local authorities and only covered a small part of the potential market in local government services (ODPM, 2004a, 2004b, 2004c). Preparation for outsourcing services was promoted through a range of specific initiatives that each supported the internationally agreed processes of liberalisation.

Preparation for outsourcing public services 1990–1997

The narrative of public service reform changed in 1990 after John Major took over as Prime Minister. The application of statecraft shifted the focus in public services to effectiveness and public choice and away from efficiency and finance. For local government, this approach was not so confrontational as in Margaret Thatcher's period as Prime Minister, but the government maintained the narrative that local authorities were inefficient and profligate with funding (Stoker, 1989; Wilson and Game, 2011). The narrative also suggested that the public should have more control over what local authorities were delivering. At the same time the government was increasingly exercising control on their behalf through performance management (Boyne, 1997; Sanderson, 2001). The effectiveness narrative was based on the notion that the private sector was more efficient despite the difference in service types and risks (NAO, 2020b). Further, the private sector could always decline to serve a customer whereas local authorities remained providers of last resort. As a transition to private sector involvement in public sector service delivery, the government introduced a range of new initiatives. These had the benefit of providing a soft introduction for the private sector to the public sector services and also making public bodies more accepting that the private sector could deliver services on their behalf.

Public–private partnerships

The introduction of public–private partnerships (PPP) provided a mechanism to introduce competition into public services while maintaining a public-facing narrative of public ownership. In practice, these PPP were fully contracted services, as the risks in the partnership were borne by the client (OECD, 2008). Even where the contract was structured to share the risk and reward, the client side was still expected to bear the final costs in service failures (NAO, 2020b). The role of the UK's international agreements on GATS implemented in 1996 and through the application of the Single European Market (SEM) in 1992 was never part of the public discussion of the introduction of PPP (Flinders, 2005). Instead, the government's narrative, like that of other countries, was primarily focused on injecting additional private sector funds into the public sector and improving public sector efficiency and effectiveness through the application of private sector principles and working methods (OECD, 2008). The use of the term 'partnership' was a distraction from the contracted relationship that would inevitably result. The term 'contracting' was most frequently used for capital projects but extended to the use of the term 'partnership' when this was introduced for services. PPP were undertaken for a variety of public services and many were for services of general public interest that included additional regulatory compliance. These included PPP for addiction management (Knai et al, 2015) and air traffic control services (Goodliffe, 2002). PPP have also been used by many other countries including the Netherlands (Klijn and Teisman, 2003) and Singapore (Hwang et al, 2013) and for international development programmes (Samii et al, 2002). Some PPP have been grouped together in major national foreign policy initiatives such as China's belt and road programme in Asia, Africa and now extended to Europe with a Memorandum of Understanding with the government in Italy (Huang, 2016; Amighini, 2019).

PPP were a popular format for construction projects, and by 2017, the UK government had concluded over 700 projects with private sector capital of £56bn funding (HMT, 2019). The UK, together with Australia, was one of the first countries to use PPP but this practice has now expanded to a range of countries, where it has been described as an 'alluring' initiative (OECD, 2008, p 12) although a number of issues associated with the use of PPP remain. The extent to which PPP projects can bring efficiency gains depends on the operation of public services in each country. There are also considerations of the use of statecraft in framing public policy narratives for their introduction and use, which is influenced by the extent of public acceptability. In focussing on construction and operational services, PPP can be kept in the background of the public's interaction with these elements of the contract. However, when there are problems or crises, the lack of manoeuvrability within the PPP can lead to both organisational and public frustration (Wettenhall, 2003).

Of greater consideration, initially overlooked when PPP were introduced as the main source of funding and delivery, is the issue of project governance and the influence that PPP have on government and political agendas (Flinders, 2005; OECD, 2012). The language of partnership can confuse the nature of contractual relationships, reducing levels of contract management applied. It also reduces understanding of ownership, responsibility and risk. The partnership is a contract even where risks are shared. When PPP fail, the responsibility lies with the public sector and the partnership concept disappears. While the private sector partners will bear some of the risk, which is priced into the contract, if they fail, the public sector will have to take on the service or complete the contract as shown in the failure of Carillion (Demirag, 2018; Loxley, 2018; NAO, 2020b) and the probation service (Robinson et al, 2016; NAO, 2019a).

The issues that beset PPP, through a range of examples in the NHS and government departments (Grimshaw et al, 2002), demonstrate the same characteristics of concern and little evidence that lessons have been learned through these processes (Broadbent et al, 2003). There are issues about potential skills being lost to the client organisation and then failure to adequately manage the contractor (McKee et al, 2006). The balance of power is with the client in the contract specification and default mechanisms if these are strong enough and then applied in practice (Wettenhall, 2003). In some government services, where outsourcing has been used to offload what are perceived to be low status, marginal or poorly run services, there is little interest in maintaining any in-house knowledge to manage the contract. When problems arise and appear in the media, officials have moved on. Ministers will then call in more private sector consultants to find out what has gone wrong, as they are the only organisations likely to have enough expertise in the service area from other contracts they have run (NAO, 2014a).

Private Finance Initiative

One of the forms of PPP that have been most frequently used is the private finance initiative (PFI). It was introduced in 1992 by the Conservative government to inject private sector funding into the public sector and remains in use in 2020. The intention of PFI was to move the risk of providing built facilities such as hospitals, schools and housing away from the public sector and into the private sector, which could build and run them for up to 60 years. PFI has been used by all governments since its introduction (Broadbent et al, 2003; Mizell, 2018), including projects promoted by the Labour government through Building Schools for the Future programme from 2006 onwards (Kakabadse et al, 2007) and the privatisation of the London Underground in 2003, although this was later taken back into public ownership in 2010.

In return for the construction and use of the facilities, the public sector organisation pays an annual fee for the contract period after which the facility returns to public ownership. For the government, PFI was also a mechanism to remove public expenditure from the government's balance sheet and improve the appearance of public sector accounts (NAO, 2006a). PFI could also be regarded as a mechanism for reducing public sector expenditure in any specific year or short-term period although without any assessment of the whole life costing of the project (Boussabaine and Kirkham, 2008; Meng and Harshaw, 2013). The costs repaid on any PFI project far outweigh the delivery of the project by direct public service (NAO, 2020e). PFI is also used for larger projects and takes, on average, seven years to be negotiated and commenced. The scale of risks, costs and preparation fees for PFI projects may be a barrier to entry to those seeking to use this method to provide infrastructure (Dixon et al, 2005). PFI contracts are the same as those for goods and services although they can be a hybrid in their form. In the EU, PFI contracts have to be advertised and negotiated within the WTO guidance, as set out within the EC frameworks.

A key component of the PFI negotiation is identifying risk reduction through the project as this is the public sector commissioner's priority. The risk is apportioned between the parties and the relative balance of risk is reflected in the cost of the contract to the client public body. Those engaged in bidding for the work can assess the balance of risks and prepare a contract price accordingly. The assumption in PFI is that at least some of the risks are shared or accepted by either party or reserved by the client government department (Bing et al, 2005). While some of the projects can be less risky in their building stages (Li et al, 2005) other risks emerge in their operation.

The National Health Service (NHS) has been a major user of PFI, and by 1992, there were 127 PFI projects, primarily for hospitals (NAO, 2018b). However, criticisms of the use and role of PFI in the NHS emerged after ten years of operation, suggesting that its use has been a political and ideological response rather than any evidence-based policy making about effectiveness (Thomas, 2019). It is also important to consider that the NHS was one of the last areas of government service into which the GPA and GATS were introduced. Health care services have also been an issue for the EU in the operation of the SEM (CEC, 2015b). In primary health care, general practitioner services and other smaller procedures that could be outsourced have been privatised either to external providers or to general practitioners directly. However, more specialised secondary health care had only been open to competition at the point of the purchase of services through private health insurance. There was less experience of NHS contracting services to private providers for anything other than routine procedures and non-clinical services (Confue, 2019).

The introduction of PFI meant that competition was introduced but was kept apart from direct delivery of medical services in the hospital and focused on the building and facilities management such as maintenance and cleaning. Initially there were concerns about whether the NHS trusts, which were partners to individual PFI contracts, could be held financially accountable. This uncertainty led to initial lender reluctance until the government introduced specific legislation in the NHS Residual Liabilities Act in 1996 and the NHS (Private Finance) Act in 1997 that gave lenders specific guarantees (Broadbent et al, 2003). In evaluating the outcomes for private sector partners of PFI, profit margins and returns have been found to be significantly more than would be required to cover the cost of the contract (Hellowell and Vecchi, 2012) while some of these benefits arise from PFI debt restructuring during the course of the contract (NAO, 2006a).

There have been several criticisms of the PFI approach in health management and operation, including concerns that governments are supplying political solutions to managerial responsibilities (Broadbent and Laughlin, 2003). This decoupling of day-to-day management from the main activities of the hospital may be expedient, not least as third-party contractors can be attributed with blame for service failures (Bowman et al, 2015). However, the PFI failures that have occurred demonstrated that accountability remains with the public sector organisation (NAO, 2020b). This accountability cannot be outsourced. A second issue is the way in which the business case and value for money assessments are made and whether they are likely to result in cost savings over time as required for any PFI agreement (Broadbent et al, 2003). As the cost of funding for capital projects through the Public Works Loans Board is always lower than the market rate, when considering value for money and business cases, the potential savings have to come from other parts of the contract evaluation including the reduction of risk or efficiency savings in operation (Bing et al, 2005). The risk assessment savings are more difficult to assess and these areas within the business case could be manipulated in order to produce a positive outcome for PFI (OECD, 2008).

The new Labour approach

Creation of service delivery companies

When the liberalisation of public services was introduced, the market responded by establishing service delivery companies that grew over time through amalgamations and takeovers. These service companies were formed in different ways. Capita was founded by a former local authority director of finance (Aldridge and Stoker, 2002) whereas others such as Amey and Mouchel expanded their activities into the service sector from an engineering base. However, there were still statecraft challenges of introducing more liberalisation into the public sector including local government in the mid-1990s when most local authorities were being selective in their use of contracted services (Painter, 1991; Shaw et al, 1994). Councils had experience of these services working in some areas such as waste collection and housing, but with increased pressure on performance and funding, local authorities were often returning services to in-house delivery at the end of their contracts (Shaw et al, 1994). There was a focus on increasing efficiency and reducing back office costs. There were also additional costs as a client, including managing and maintaining contract compliance procedures, establishing and instigating default mechanisms and penalties and making changes to long-term contracts that may be obliged by new legislation (Warner and Hefetz, 2008). Without change being included in contract specifications, contracts can fail or result in additional costs of handling service complaints and disputes about resolving them.

In order to help change this view, Rod Aldridge, who founded Capita, engaged the New Local Government Network (NLGN), a Labour government supporting think tank, to embrace the service contracting model. The approach, espoused by Aldridge, focussed on public service performance that would help to achieve the public service reforms that the Labour government was seeking through partnership with the private sector (Clarke, 2002). Working with the Labour government, the NLGN and academic Gerry Stoker made an explicit attempt to incorporate public values into private delivery methods (Aldridge and Stoker, 2002). In a report, they indicated that markets in public services did not exist and had to be made through government encouragement. Aldridge also suggested that the private sector shared the same ethos as the public sector and it was wrong to denigrate its priorities, not least when the private sector had recruited so many public sector staff to run its services. He also defended profits and suggested that they were important in the public sector. He stated that the accountability that existed in the private sector was greater than that in the public sector because profit margins were used for performance management. Aldridge and Stoker argued that the public would be better served if private sector contractors were responsible for more public services and these would be better than those managed internally. They recommended the establishment of a charter for public services and their delivery, rather than focusing on contracts and their obligations to clients.

e-government

An important element of the efficiency programme, developed as part of the EU SEM for service integration, was that for e-government, which was included in the EU programme 2000–2006 (CEC, 2000, 2001). In order to support cross-border transactions and to reduce the effects of non-tariff barriers to trading services within the EU, online methods of regulatory permits and procurement could be a means of accelerating these changes (Torres and Pina, 2002). Once in practice they could reduce the effects of borders for goods and people and promote the four freedoms espoused in the single market – for goods, people, services and capital.

In the UK, the CSR for the period 2000–2004 included £2bn to support the implementation of e-government in central and local governments (Morphet, 2008). The allocation of UK funding in England was given to both central and local governments, with central government receiving two thirds of the £2bn budget, appointing an e-envoy and a supporting office. It was focused on changing the ways central government conducted its business both internally and with citizens. In addition, with a separate budget, there was a major project for e-health including patient records (Martin et al, 2007) and new ways of undertaking the transfer and use of data between different parts of the secondary health system.

Local government in England was provided with one third of the e-government budget and this was put under the general management and delivery of a central government team recruited from local government. Local government focused on improvements to service users through increasing the range of channels open to citizens to request and use services through web delivery and one-stop shops for personal and telephone use. This was unlike approaches taken elsewhere, for example in the US, which focused on the back office (Carter and Weerakkody, 2008; Morphet et al, 2019). UK central government projects were primarily focused on major reforms of back office services including benefits. There were some exceptions in the customer-facing services provided by the government such as those introduced by the Driver and Vehicle Licensing Agency for driver and vehicle licensing and by the Home Office for passports. Other projects such as that for courts and justice were brought into the programme. Some of the initiatives that were evolved were based on linking systems between local and central governments.

While it might be expected that such investment in technology and take-up would be the subject of business cases before investment (Irani et al, 2005), this was not the case in local government. Here the focus was on increasing the proportion of services available online and their transactional fulfilment of the request rather than being merely informational. The success of this local authority reorientation, towards a user-focus linked into the back office, was blind-tested each year for specific services. Local authority league tables were published through SOCITM's Better Connected reports from 2000 onwards.

The same approach was not adopted by central government (Kuzma, 2010), and over time, it has removed all individual departmental websites together with their informational structures. Instead there is a single gov.uk presence that can only be accessed via specific online queries and search engines. In central government, e-government has been used to reduce information access while hiding it in plain sight.

The e-government changes in local government shifted relationships between local authorities and their electorates who became clients, customers and citizens. While there has been criticism of the introduction of the use of the term 'customer' into the development of e-government (Mosse and Whitley, 2009), it changed the perspective and relationship focus within local authorities. While using these approaches to become more efficient and effective, by reducing face-to-face and telephone enquiry costs, it also meant that local authorities had to understand the experience of those applying for or using these services, so that their application and fulfilment processes could be mapped and measured. The front-facing channel strategies and e-services approach in local government enabled a number of local authority services to be shifted online including planning applications, schools' admissions, payments, missed service complaints, libraries and booking systems (Morphet, 2008). Some local authorities started to offer account systems such as those used by Amazon in the private sector (Vize, 2019; Naylor and Wellings, 2019).

Local government was offered incentive payments by central government in return for achieving levels of delivery across a range of ten transactions types (Morphet, 2008). This approach was successful in embedding efficiencies in delivery in local government, and in 2016, the UK was at the top of the UN's list of e-enabled countries for local service delivery. The availability of e-government is considered to be popular and well used (Kolsaker and Lee-Kelley, 2008) with local authorities such as Wigan, with an older population, having 70,000 citizens with local accounts in 2019 (Vize, 2019; Naylor and Wellings, 2019). This is despite the older age group being regarded as a specific challenge in achieving channel switching for service delivery (Choudrie et al, 2013).

Gershon efficiency review

The review of public sector efficiency conducted by Sir Peter Gershon (Gershon, 2004) was undertaken after reviewing government procurement for the Treasury and accompanied that on productivity in health (HMT, 2004). This preceded the 2006 Health Act, which introduced further competition into the NHS. The Atkinson Review of productivity was also published (Atkinson, 2005a, 2005b). The Gershon review focussed on efficiencies in front-line government services and, again, was in support of delivering the GATS. The work on e-government was beginning to demonstrate, in local government at least, that there was considerable progress in efficiency by moving to online service access through channel switching. Back office systems were also being brought together by local authorities working on common standards, taxonomies and service mapping (Morphet, 2008).

Gershon used a targeted level of savings to be achieved by 2008 that was a mechanism to drive change. In local government, it was assumed this would be achieved through best value (Demirkaya, 2006), e-government, changing work design through business process re-engineering (Weerakkody and Dhillon, 2008) and working in partnerships with other public organisations together with the private sector. However, there were doubts whether this level of savings could be found (*The Guardian*, 7 March 2005). This scepticism was rooted in the failure of local authorities to meet the £6.75bn savings target set in 2000, when 5 per cent of best value efficiency target had been achieved. Following the Gershon efficiency review, the government supported the development of Regional Efficiency and Improvement Partnerships (RIEPs) to stimulate and incentivise productivity improvements in local government through joint working (Tomkinson, 2007).

Using 'lean' working in central government services (Radnor and Johnston, 2013) was also an effort to change working cultures and use private sector expertise to support service redesign. While 'lean' approaches were developed for manufacturing, they have also been used to reduce the costs of back office administration. Despite the focus in the government on the role of the customer, citizen or user of services (HMT, 2007) the purpose of 'lean' approaches has been to improve internal processes. While the initial focus was on the reduction in waiting times for services or in service delivery errors, this was shifted to back office improvements (Seddon and Brand, 2008). Following the review of the 'lean' approach in two central government services – Her Majesty's Revenue and Customs and the court service, Radnor and Johnston (2013) found that focussing on efficiency could reduce the effectiveness of the service being transformed through lean methodologies. This removal of the customer-facing approach, which has also occurred in other government services such as benefits, has transferred the costs on to the citizens.

Aggregating demand in local government: Strategic partnering taskforce

Strategic partnering between the government and the private sector developed through construction and major transport projects (Cox and Townsend, 1998). It originated in dealing with procurement failures, particularly in the assignment of risk. In defining strategic partnering, Cox and Townsend define this as where the client has an extended relationship with a limited number of suppliers over a number of projects (Alderman and Ivory, 2007) and the incentive for suppliers of goods or services in entering into these partnering arrangements is that they can be extended to further projects without going through procurement processes. In 2000, strategic partnering was introduced by central government as a means of delivering local government services. These would be partnerships between the private sector and local authorities, sharing the risks and rewards, suggesting that the relationships between the public and private sectors were equal. This became known as Shared Strategic Partnerships (SSPs) and developed as joint ventures between local authorities and private service providers. The government identified the key objectives and benefits of SSPs (Morphet, 2008) and, in 2000, established a task force of private sector secondees to support their development and roll out. These secondees, from major private sector accounting and consulting firms, were invited to advise government and local authorities about the aggregation of the market through partnering arrangements (ODPM, 2004a). This support for aggregation was attractive to larger private sector consultancy firms as it increased the contract value but also, in taking a partnering approach, included a working method that did not define all services to be included at the start of the contract (ODPM, 2004b). This allowed contracts to include additional services that would not be subject to separate tendering processes. This approach to procurement was unusual.

In order to support the development of these new aggregated contracts, advisory support was made available through government-funded RIEPs for demonstration projects. The Audit Commission already had responsibility for the assessment of companies for CCT (1990–1997) and then the implementation and compliance with the best value regime that followed (Boyne, 1999). They had also undertaken detailed studies about how councils could improve their delivery of specific services and assets such as property, charging regimes, benefits, revenues collection and libraries. The role of the strategic partnering team, following the Gershon Review, was to insert the private sector's role into this, although without much evidence of efficiencies.

SSPs were primarily between larger companies and local authorities such as between BT and Liverpool City Council, IBM and Somerset County Council, and Capita and Blackburn with Darwen Council. These contracts were valued at £20–£30m per annum and included the establishment of call centres and back office functions for revenues and benefits and other core services such as HR and payroll (Tomkinson, 2007). These SSPs were supported and endorsed by a former chief executive of one of the local government associations (Filkin et al, 2001). Some SSPs never advanced beyond negotiation as local authorities withdrew – such as Kent CC with Capita while others have been terminated (Whitfield, 2014). Where smaller local authorities wanted to engage in these SSPs, they were encouraged to pool their requirements with other councils and seek a joint contract between them and a partner without specifying all the services to be included in the contract (ODPM, 2004a, 2004b; Tomkinson, 2007)

These SSPs were attractive to the private sector, as they had service aggregation as their core method of working (ODPM, 2004a). This aggregation could be across services in a single council or across similar services in a range of councils. It also meant that by aggregating and taking a partnering approach, there would be fewer competition processes. The concept of partnering put together organisations that had the same objective. Strategic partnering also required some common philosophy between the partners whether this was a commitment towards quality management or other objectives (Naoum, 2003). There was also an expectation that partnering would be based on improving trust between organisations working together (ODPM, 2004a; Chan et al, 2004). They were expected to be different from traditional contracts for goods and services, particularly in the ways they could change customs and cultures within the local authority organisations and it was in this way that they were expected to achieve the savings identified in their business cases (Roberts, 2004).

One of the key components in establishing a case for strategic partnering in local government was that by the creation of call centre and back office processing centres councils would be able to attract work from other companies and institutions (ODPM, 2004c). If SSPs could be developed in areas with lower employment costs, then the business case could demonstrate their attractiveness to banks and building societies and provide an alternative to offshoring. Local authority processes and methods were regarded as reliable and secure with a stronger culture of oversight that would make them attractive to third-party organisations. The inclusion of an income assessment and the potential to generate additional jobs would make an important contribution to the business case and smooth over doubts about the financial benefits of such an approach (ODPM, 2004b). In areas where there were higher wage costs, the potential for cost saving and risk sharing between the local authority and the private provider was also attractive. A further practice was the length of the contract, which was generally set at ten years and committed the local authorities to pay agreed sums annually. The way in which the contract was set out suggested that income and savings would be profiled to accrue during the life of the contract to offset costs. However, councils were also liable for underperformance in income generation of the contracts (Baker, 2012). When SSP contracts failed to make the savings that the business case had suggested, this left councils liable for these losses.

The partnering form suggested closer working relationships and less attention to the more usual forms of contractual relationships. One of the major issues in relation to SSPs was the disconnection between the contract content and detailed services to be provided. The SSP approach was based on flexibility so that the contract could be used in a variety of ways, but in reality, this risk remained with the local authority. The government acknowledged these problems and tried to build in change (ODPM, 2004c, 2004d) but in practice flexibility was difficult to include in SSP contracts of this size and scale (Watt, 2005). As partnerships, the trust element was emphasised and left local authorities later appreciating that they had agreed to fund the losses on the partnership and had accepted the risks. In many ways they proved to be like standard contracts but with local authorities distracted from placing the normal safeguards within them. This lack of specification meant that councils had difficulty in undertaking contract compliance checks and had fewer means of using penalty and default mechanisms to ensure that contractors delivered in ways agreed. This failure to be able to hold the contractor to account also meant that there were no obvious mechanisms to achieve the service improvements that the SSPs had promised at the outset (Watt, 2005). Partnering 'agreements' were not strong enough to resolve disputes, particularly to the satisfaction of the weaker parties in the relationship (Entwistle and Martin, 2005). While strategic partnering can include an inherent risk (Alderman and Ivory, 2007), in a number of projects, other objectives, particularly cost saving, became more important than the quality outcomes. In local government, in the partnering initiatives that were promoted, it seems that few of the critical factors for successful partners were present, including willingness to share resources and having a common approach (Chan et al, 2004). As Alderman and Ivory (2007) have shown, when partnering relationships start to go wrong, there is a very rapid retreat to traditional adversarial contractual relationships with a number resorting to the courts.

Local authority partnerships

While the majority of SSPs have failed, there have been some local authority partnerships, which aggregated demand, that have worked. These are particularly in finance and revenue and benefits. There are examples of where joint procurement or grouping operations have led to cost reductions and efficiencies (LGA, 2011, 2016c). Some partnerships, like the Welland, had started slightly ahead of this agenda (Tomkinson, 2007). In 1996 five co-terminus East Midlands rural authorities were seeking ways of providing services more efficiently and effectively. Through the establishment of a partnership the authorities committed to reviewing several different ways of working together, including joint procurement and delivery of services to each other. The partnership agreed at the outset that it would not be limited to taking forward only those projects that received support from all five partners and accepted that some could be progressed between the members. Others could join in later or not as they chose. The Welland partnership started by reviewing a range of services where joint working could be more efficient and included two main groups. The first was back office services such as IT and finance, including the management of benefits systems. The second was to look at service delivery over a wide rural area and examine whether services could be provided by other partnership members in the course of their work and reduce staff costs and time (Shaw et al, 1994). Here, services such as planning and building control were reviewed. While the partnership authorities were not eligible for any specific government support, their ability to demonstrate common purpose and working together meant they were able to attract pilot and specific government funding for projects. These included joint working models that other councils could also use, including community portals, customer relations management system and document management system (Tomkinson, 2007).

After the RIEP, the Coalition government introduced a local productivity programme in 2010 that was supported through Local Government Association (LGA, 2011). This programme reiterated benefits of joint working between local authorities rather than between local authorities and the private sector. These approaches included new ways of working, greater opportunities for investment and service redesign. The local productivity programme anticipated cuts in local government expenditure by central government following the economic crisis of 2008. In order to be able to respond and manage the provision of services within this austerity programme, which included the removal of the revenue support grant made to all local authorities by 2020, councils were encouraged to work together and to share their senior management teams in order to reduce staff costs (LGA, 2011, 2016c). By 2011, pairs of councils were sharing staff teams and management, including Worthing and Adur, South Oxfordshire and Vale of White Horse, and Hambleton and Richmondshire. Four councils in Suffolk joined their management teams into pairs, which developed into mergers in 2019. In Somerset, West Somerset and Taunton Deane have become a single council as West Somerset was not financially viable in an austerity context. In Dorset, where there had already been local government reorganisation in the mid-1990s, creating two unitary councils of Bournemouth and Poole leaving rural districts and the county council to operate independently, there has been further change. In 2019, all Dorset councils merged to form two new unitary councils. While some of the benefits of mergers and shared management have been identified as reducing costs, larger councils also create increased budgets for purchasing and achieving greater discounts. However, as with any use of outsourcing or institutional reform, the LGA (2011) emphasised the importance of understanding the councils' objectives if they are going to merge services or management and methods of dispute resolution if they occur. The advice also includes outsourcing and business process re-engineering as possible options for saving money.

Before considering joining up services, the LGA indicated the importance of the way performance and change are measured. This included benchmarking performance at the outset, recognising that there may be significant differences between the performance of services that are to be merged. If there is a marked difference, this may be viewed as a takeover with one council providing a service on behalf of another. The powers for these joined up services or delivery by one council on behalf of others are contained in the 1972 Local Government Act (s101 and s102) and s113 allows a council to empower an officer from another council to discharge their functions.

Local authorities have developed approaches to using the private sector within their services and learned from their experience in implementing CCT. While central government encouraged councils to purchase services from private sector service delivery partners, these approaches were not successful. However, the pressures of government austerity policies since 2010, which have been particularly severe in local government (NAO, 2019c; Morphet and Clifford, 2020), have encouraged a range of new working relationships between local authorities from combined services, managements, leadership and institutional reform. Local authorities use the private sector for specialist advice and through the establishment of joint ventures. They have incorporated liberalisation into their operations but are not dominated by it.

7

Outsourcing Central Government Services

Introduction

The requirements on central government to liberalise services as part of the implementation of the General Agreement on Trade in Services (GATS) provided an opportunity to distance the civil service from the more difficult and public-facing elements of its roles. Privatising delivery of these services enabled the introduction of performance management and cost-cutting measures that could be blamed on the contractor rather than the government. While the civil service and particularly the Home Office, often called the Ministry of the Interior in other countries, have traditionally had responsibility for police, borders, visas, migration and asylum, this has primarily been focused at a policy level. Until the late 1960s, governments had no particular interest in asylum or immigration policy as most of the post-war immigration to the UK had been from Commonwealth countries including the Caribbean and Indian sub-continent to meet employment shortfalls in UK public services (Timmins, 2001). Other migration between the UK and Commonwealth countries saw trends moving the other way as UK citizens migrated to Australia, New Zealand and South Africa.

The pressure on government departments to cut costs through the Rayner Scrutiny Reviews from 1980 onwards and then agencification through the creation of Next Steps Agencies in the late 1980s and early 1990s had generated some institutional change in the structure of the civil service (Gray and Jenkins, 1984; Dowding, 1995). While preparing to meet UK commitments for public service liberalisation through the Government Procurement Agreement (GPA) and anticipated GATS agreements, central government implemented this by prioritising nationalised industries and local government (De Graaf and King, 1995; Parker, 2009). When approaching central government services, those that were public facing, employed more staff and were not regarded as strategic were peripheralised first, in anticipation of competition requirements on the civil service. This enabled a reduction in central department employee headcounts and was expected to reduce the day-to-day management burden of these services, allowing a focus on policy issues (Theakston, 1995). These services were primarily focused on clerical tasks including tax returns, social security and pensions that employed higher numbers of low-paid staff and required most face-to-face contact. The use of agencification and then privatisation would allow the reformulation of pay bands that could lead to cost reductions in the front-line delivery services (Dowding, 1995). Separating these activities into agencies, ready for potential outsourcing, provided the civil service with a means of achieving greater financial control and performance management (Pliatzky, 1992; Haddon, 2012). These changes could help to achieve ministerial targets while removing functions from their day-to-day management responsibilities. If these services could be peripheralised and, if necessary, outsourced, then there would be greater protection to maintaining the status quo and power of civil servants at the centre (Rhodes, 2001).

Up to 1990, when Margaret Thatcher was Prime Minister, there was considered to be no role for privatisation in the public services in comparison with utilities (Seldon and Collings, 2014). However, there was also a recognition that these services employed the bulk of civil servant staff and that these were funded entirely through the public purse (Pliatzky, 1988). Within central government departments there had been a focus on outsourcing services such as cleaning, catering and messengers before moving to those services that had most people and were still directed through central policy (Ascher, 1987). It would be possible to reduce the central headcount in a dramatic way while maintaining arm's length control of policy and delivery. As Rhodes states, for the very top of the civil service in the UK, 'change affects "everyone but us"' (2001, p 112). That is while all around is changing through 'hiving off' parts of their responsibilities to obtain more efficiency and effectiveness, permanent secretaries and the civil service at the top of departments saw their continuing role as providing policy and stability and maintaining the culture of the department. The role of distancing parts of the service through agencification was about sacrificing the periphery to preserve the core. The civil service could not be seen to be resisting change so it took evasive action instead. Offering its largest and most expensive activities to the market would show intent (Talbot and Talbot, 2019). The outsourced services would allow senior civil servants to pull the command levers more readily to achieve results sought by ministers than was the case within their own direct reports (Lewis, 1997).

Within departments, there was cultural consensus against change (Theakston, 1995). Civil servants were concerned about opening the most senior appointments to competition from the private sector and other public services (Rhodes, 2001). By creating new jobs, head of agencies with higher pay bands, it would be possible to argue that organisational 'opening up' would be more attractive to those with careers in running large organisations at higher salaries (Black, 1993). If these new appointees were responsible for the agencies, they would still be accountable to the Permanent Secretary in their sponsoring department, regardless of their higher salaries. This approach would allow the status quo to prevail, and as Theakston states, it was more fruitful to view senior civil servants running departments as 'conservators' (2000, p 144) rather than managers or transformers.

A review of the functions remaining at the centre, as the implementation of the GATS approached in 1994, showed that some departments had done little. This included the Home Office and wider justice functions that were initially assessed to be out of reach to liberalisation requirements (Mennicken, 2013). However, there were considered to be opportunities for these more complex policy areas. In particular, services that had to be delivered within legally determined time limits and, where recipients of the service were of lower status and were less likely to complain to their MPs about the treatment they had received, were high priority (Lethbridge, 2017). The strategies taken to liberalise these services have been problematic (NAO, 2003, 2012, 2014a). There has been a failure to consider the issues in managing services concerned with individuals, and the increasing lack of experience of civil servants directly running them has exacerbated the potential for service failure. Increasingly distanced management has meant a constant round of service redesign and increasing costs for the public purse (Robinson et al, 2016).

These services have been through a range of changes about how liberalisation is to be introduced, the structure of contracts and the governance arrangements within government departments (Kirton and Guillaume, 2019). Some services have been changed every few years into new contracting models and some have been brought back into central government departments to be prepared for another round of privatisation (NAO, 2014a). Some services have been moved from the Home Office into the Ministry of Justice (MoJ) when it was established in 2007 with primary responsibility for justice issues within England and Wales (Mills et al, 2010). In trying to achieve these liberalisation objectives, the civil service has employed managers and leaders from the private sector and attempts have been made to change professional cultures – both of which have failed (Lewis, 1997; Robinson and Burnett, 2007). The services discussed here have been the focus of Conservative Party political agenda for crime and disorder that added issues of migration and immigration. The services have been primarily managed by the same group of service companies from the outset, and despite their specific failures in managing services and facilities, they have continued to be appointed to manage new contracts (Bowman et al, 2015). The issues being delivered through these services have also been compounded by failures to adhere to the European Convention of Human Rights (Gentleman, 2020).

Prison Service

Her Majesty's (HM) Prison Service was created as an executive agency within the organisational structure of the Home Office in 1993 and then in 2004 it was included as part of the National Offender Management System (NOMS) by bringing together HM Prisons and the National Probation Service. It is now the HM Prison and Probation Service (HMPPS) agency. The creation of the HM Prison Service Next Steps Agency came as a response to the Woolf Report on prison riots (Prison Reform Trust, 1991) and, while not delivering on its recommendations, provided an impetus for change (NAO, 2003). There was also pressure for the implementation of outsourcing from outside the government in the late 1980s by think tanks such as the Adam Smith Institute, continuing their role in changing the cultural narrative of public service delivery (Heffernan, 1996). From the private sector, G4S was seeking to expand its market in the UK at the same time as the US and Australia (Mennicken, 2013, p 209). When the HM Prison Service executive agency was formed in 1993, already half of the civil servants were employed in agencies. This new agency would be one of the largest. As an agency, it was required to undertake market testing as part of its remit, comparing the efficiencies of directly managed prisons with a few that were to be totally privatised. One pilot for a privatised facility was a remand centre and the second was a prison to be run by a US company (Black, 1993). The first private prison was the Wolds, which was to have been a remand prison, contracted to deliver this. However, once the contract had been agreed the role of the prison changed.

This approach allowed the government the opportunity to demonstrate the start of liberalisation of the prison service to meet its GATS obligations. A further degree of market testing was introduced through the outsourcing of internal services. It was expected that some of these would be outsourced to public sector providers as well as the private sector including catering, education and external court duties (Milne, 1997). The court escort duties in the East Midlands and Yorkshire and Humberside were outsourced to G4S, which was also responsible for running the privatised remand centre. The Prison Service then had to bid against the private sector to operate other prisons and initially it was announced that ten prisons would be market-tested. The Prison Service was successful in its bid to run Strangeways in Manchester, although it was expected to be redeveloped to create a prison that would be more suitable for outsourcing after this process (Black, 1993). The expectation was that all the rebuilt prisons would be offered for outsourcing, with the state retaining the older ones. There was a private finance initiative for the construction and management of prisons in 1995 (Panchamia and Gash, 2012; Robinson and Scott, 2009). There were issues about the shift of education from direct employees to a privatised service. Initially there was confusion about staff and redundancy payments, but through a case using Transfer of Undertakings (Protection of Employment) (TUPE) Regulations, it was established that staff should be transferred into any new provider on the same terms and conditions (Black, 1993).

The Prison Service Next Steps Agency was created to open up the potential for competition. In practice, the Prison Service notionally had control of its budget, while responsibility was assumed to remain at the centre in the control of civil servants within the Home Office. HM Prison Service and its director were regarded as an organisational convenience and the Home Office did not consider that this made any difference to the ways in which it operated as a government department. For civil servants, 'their first task was to design an agency which, in reality, changed as little as possible' (Landers, 1999, p 123). In its first agency form, the head of HM Prison Service reported directly to the Home Secretary and not through the Permanent Secretary of the department, although there was an expectation that the staff of the Prison Service agency headquarters would all be civil servants (Black, 1993). This staffing arrangement was never accepted by HM Prison Service, which wanted to be independent and not managed by the civil service. HM Prison Service anticipated the challenges of attempting to operate two cultures – that of the private sector and of the operational public sector within a third context of a more strategic civil service controlling resources. However, the Home Office wanted to maintain control and the framework agreement between the Home Office and Prison Service was described as a 'sham' (Landers, 1999, p 121). The approaches of ministers and civil servants were reflected in ministerial changes. As Landers (1999) states, Kenneth Clarke as Home Secretary was in favour of delegation while Michael Howard was in favour of control. However, this control was not accompanied by ministerial responsibility for failures when an arm's length 'agency' problem appeared.

While the Home Office used an agency to demonstrate organisational and operational distance, this failed in a number of ways. Firstly, the distancing was superficial and was not intended in practice. Secondly, the continued exercise of control from the Home Office led to conflicts in expectations between it and HM Prison Service. Thirdly, the arm's length approach introduced through the agencification of the service was gradually eroded. The Home Office incrementally reinstated more control as prison service inspections demonstrated that performance was not improving (Grimshaw et al, 2002). At the outset there were 8 Key Performance indicators, by 2001 there were 18 and when NOMS was formed in 2004 there were 28 (Mennicken, 2013). Where specific prison performance was poor, six months was given to improve. If this failed, then there was an expectation of closure. However, some prisons did not improve, and instead of being able to benchmark the performance of individual prisons, the contract used for each outsourcing was bespoke so that there could be no meaningful comparisons. This individualisation to the level of establishment made a convenient approach for both contractors and the civil service, which sidestepped performance assessment and accountability (NAO, 2003).

Other methods were also deployed to rein in this separation. The head of HM Prison Service was the principal policy adviser on prisons and reported directly to ministers – a unique position at the time. This role was under pressure to be limited. The civil service became more controlling of HM Prison Service. There were different trades unions in the civil service and the prison service and these started to develop arguments that staff could not be appointed to different roles (Polidano, 1999). This effectively blocked any transfer of operational staff into the civil service from the prison service but not the other way round (Lewis, 1997). The appointment of the head of HM Prison Service from outside the civil service challenged the orthodoxy of power in the relationship between the Home Secretary and the Permanent Secretary of the department. It provided some transparency of the culture of these internalised relationships made popular by the *Yes Minister* TV series (Jay and Lynn, 1980–1988; Jay, 1980). It also showed that the power relationships within the civil service and between it and the ministers depended on custom and practice and were transactional. An external appointee with different experience and expectations demonstrated that alternative worlds existed (Lewis, 1997). At the height of a row about prison escapees in 1995, the

Home Secretary sacked the head of HM Prison Service and the Home Office took back control of prison functions. The role of advice to the ministers was returned to and retained by the Home Office and was transferred to the MoJ when it was created in 2007. Once recentralised, the Home Office then had to consider a different way to introduce competition into the prison service. They did this by opening parts of prison operation to competition. However, in 2004 there was a move to integrate offender management into a single agency, bringing together both the probation and prisons services into NOMS. This allowed further distancing between the sponsoring department and the management of these services. In 2007, the responsibilities for the Prison Service were moved to the MoJ.

The practice of introducing liberalisation into prison services was also taking place in other countries that were bound by the same GATS agreements. Australia was the second country after the US to introduce privatisation into the management of prisons. The process of outsourcing prisons in Australia started in 1989 and by 1990 the first centre was open and similarly there was a major programme of prison redevelopment announced in four states (Moyle, 1992). As in the UK, there was little public debate about these changes, which were promoted as managerial rather than a key policy change. In both Australia and the US, it was asserted that privatisation of prisons would be more efficient and cheaper, although there was no evidence for this before the policy was introduced (Brown, 1994) and, as with other services being liberalised, there were no market comparators. Another reason given for the privatisation of prisons was that the process provided a greater opportunity to manage standards of delivery through a contract and that this would give governments greater accountability. By 2015, the policy was extended across eight states in Australia and prisons are now managed by three public service companies including Serco and G4S. However, in a review of the policies and provision in all states, no specific claims for the benefits of privatised prison services could be found (Andrew et al, 2016). A study in the state of Victoria, where there are more people in privatised prisons, showed that while the initial assertion about lower costs of privatised prisons was found, this was not sustained over time. Improvements have been mixed and there remains contested accountability for the service, as in the UK (Sands et al, 2019). A particular issue for studies of the performance of privatised prisons in Australia appears to be lack of data (Andrew et al, 2016). As in the UK, this approach to liberalising the operation of prisons has been taken as ideological and an example of policy communities sharing similar approaches. There are also similar concerns about the continuation of this policy without the apparent benefits being achieved.

Probation Service

The Probation Service is part of HMPPS, which is an agency of the MoJ. The Probation Service's role is to protect the public and to prevent reoffending. It was transferred to NOMS in 2004, which then became the HMPPS and is now a sub-part of an agency. However, as a range of initiatives to part-privatise the Probation Service in 2014 have demonstrated, its practical ownership, in terms of policy, management and organisation, remains with the MoJ. The MoJ has been held responsible for the failure of the part-privatised Probation Service system by the National Audit Office (2019a) and was subsequently expected to move to another round of privatisation. Instead in 2020, the Probation Service has been returned into direct MoJ management.

The privatisation of part of the Probation Service in 2014 in England and Wales followed reorganisation as part of the government's 'Transforming Rehabilitation' (MoJ, 2013). The Probation Service had already been placed into 35 trusts in 2001 as part of the NOMS reforms. The approach in 2014 placed over 54 per cent of the qualified staff employed by these trusts into Community Rehabilitation Companies (CRC) established by detailed delivery contracts to manage low risk offenders (Kirton and Guillaume, 2019). There were expectations in 2013 that the CRC would deal with 64 per cent of all cases but in practice they have dealt with 59 per cent (NAO, 2019a). These CRC were established in preparation to be sold off into the marketplace. Those probation staff not transferred to these companies were senior professional probation officers and were retained in a newly formed National Probation Service for higher risk cases. The National Probation Service staff work within the previous professional codes and models applying to the trusts whereas the CRC staff were managed within detailed performance contracts (Robinson and Burnett, 2007). The staff who were transferred to CRC were moved within the TUPE Regulations and the shares in the CRC were owned by the MoJ before they were sold through the market in 2014/15. The MoJ Secretary of State indicated that there was considerable interest for the purchase of each of these 21 trusts from the private sector organisations that had experience in criminal justice systems. It was stated that there were at least four companies interested in each CRC. Also, it was revealed that at least eight of these bids included some involvement of staff in mutually owned companies (Robinson et al, 2016).

The preparation for these successive changes to the Probation Service had occurred during John Major's administration (1990–1997). Probation officers had a professional career path that provided them with a social work qualification with specific focus on offenders (Kirton and Guillaume,

2019). In 1989, the Home Secretary decided that the Probation Service should be detached from social work and a new pathway to qualification for Probation Service officers was introduced. By 2002, the Probation Service officers with this new qualification outnumbered the probation officers with an increase of 177 per cent of Probation Service officers compared with an increase of 7 per cent of probation officers (Mills et al, 2010). The Probation Service was reformed to create a National Probation Service in 2001. After this, there were further reforms to integrate prisons and the Probation Service. During this period, probation officers were insecure about their positions and how this new system would work in practice (Robinson and Burnett, 2007).

In comparison with other government initiatives for liberalisation, even within the criminal justice field, the pathways for the Probation Service were different from the rest (Robinson et al, 2016). The approach taken for the Probation Service was that under half was kept in the public sector and the rest privatised (Kirton and Guillaume, 2019). This approach to privatisation of the Probation Service left uncertainty among its staff and professional practitioners. While groups of staff were kept together within localities when the CRC were created, the privatisation process in 2014 established an artificial difference between places with public or private organisational loyalties. In time, the commonalities in the service, whether about ethos, working methods or shared communities of practice, could be expected to be changed and undermined. In order to overcome this, the Probation Institute was formed in 2014 and this issued a standard for service and operation that should be expected across probation office staff, creating a new 'ethos' (Robinson et al, 2016).

The privatisation of the Probation Service in 2014 was not successful and so in December 2020 the government decided to terminate the contracts, 14 months early. It was anticipated that the CRCs would make £269m profits for their owners at the bid stage but by March 2018 had forecast £294 losses (NAO, 2019a). In terminating the contracts, and with other losses, the government has paid a further £467m to the CRC contractors. The approach taken – including lack of preparation, failure of internal IT systems between the CRCs and the National Probation Service and a failure to predict the volume of work (it was far less than the possible 2 per cent variation anticipated in the contract schedule) – all contributed to the breakdown of this process (NAO, 2019a). While the GATS requires that services be subject to competition, there are different ways that this might be undertaken. In the Probation Service, there was no appetite for complete outsourcing, which may have kept the integrity of the service together and allowed it to operate within one provider framework (Kirton and Guillaume, 2019). Further, there was no consideration of the opportunity for an in-house bid, which might have worked in a service that was highly specialised and professionalised. It appears that the MoJ wanted to pay lip service to the notion of privatisation without losing control of the core of the service. As in other privatisation exercises, there was an attempt by the government to outsource the lower grade work and retain that which was more complex and significant. However, it had not before undertaken the privatisation of any service that is fully professionalised.

The Probation Service differed from other agencification because it involved public service professionals rather than administrators. While the central government has a number of professionally qualified civil servants, with each profession having a single head across the government, they do not sit easily within government departmental structures and culture. The senior civil service comprises of generalists, unlike civil servants within the EU member states who are primarily lawyers and accountants before joining the civil service (Page and Jenkins, 2005; Page and Wright, 2006). There has been a long tussle between the senior civil service maintaining its generalist ethos since the Fulton Report (Fry, 1990), which the civil service did much to undermine and leave unimplemented (Fry, 1990; Lowe, 2011). There have subsequently been pressures to appoint more professionals to departmental boards and senior management teams, particularly accountants (Greer and Jarman, 2010). This cultural clash is related to the view held by senior civil servants that they should take advice from their professionals and then make recommendations to ministers after they have weighed up the considerations. This mirrors the position of the Chief Scientific Adviser in the COVID-19 pandemic management.

Senior civil servants consider that professionals have divided loyalties with primary focus on their professional code of conduct – indeed those belonging to professional bodies can only be members if they abide by these codes. This also relates to debates about civil service ethics (Chapman, 1988). This means that this adherence to a professional code may cut across the advice that is given to ministers and allows for whistle blowers or dissent where those making these objections are backed by their professional standing. Government departments have several strategies for managing the senior professionals within their departments including separating them from line management responsibilities on a day-to-day basis and not allowing them to give evidence to Parliamentary Select Committees. Further, they make their professional officers responsible to mainstream civil servants and keep them at middle levels of seniority. Even where accountants are placed on departmental boards, they are one among a group of mainstream civil servants and their advice is diluted.

The Probation Service is an outlier in the range of public services opened to competition in the UK central government. The National Health Service is managed by a professional management cadre albeit experienced in health management but not primarily trained as professional health practitioners (Confue, 2019). In its approach to liberalising the Probation Service and determining the percentage of its activities that would be outsourced, the MoJ took an approach that split these probation professionals into public and private employees and moved away from a professionally led service to one that was management led (Kirton and Guillaume, 2019). While the early action by the Home Secretary had attempted to reduce the professional standing of probation officers in 1994, by creating a new qualification and despite all the changes in the 1996, 2010 and 2014 reforms, probation officers still have a strong sense of their own professional role, ethics and experience. In other professions that were mainly in the public sector, such as planning, the evolution of professionals working in both the public and private sectors occurred over time and was not forced through any specific privatisation initiatives (Adams and Tiesdell, 2010). For probation this was different. The staff, the trades unions and the justice system were against outsourcing yet it was implemented without any pilots or testing of possible outcomes that were regarded as an 'assault on professionalism' (Kirton and Guillaume, 2019, p 940). The move from the role of probation officers in social work to criminal justice systems has changed the ways in which both professionals and their clients are regarded. The professional approach is one that helps to change behaviour, be more personal and achieve more beneficial outcomes for clients and society (Kirton and Guillaume, 2019). The deprofessionalised contractual approach in the criminal justice system prefers to describe clients as offenders with stigmatised connotations. However, both groups have been pushed into a more performance-based depersonalised approach to working, with less time to discuss cases with colleagues or have deep engagement with clients.

The successive rounds of reform and attempts at privatisation in the Probation Service have not proved to be successful (NAO, 2019a). The character of the service has been undermined and attempts have been made to deny its underlying culture by deprofessionalising it away from social work to offender management. These attempts suggest that public services that are strongly engaged with clients that may be regarded as low priority and status can continue to require more time and effort to manage than is anticipated. Senior civil servants in government departments have found that whereas the agencification and then outsourcing of services were expected to reduce their management responsibilities, the reverse is the case (Rhodes, 2001). Paying lip service to the requirements of the GATS in central government has not been easy to submerge. While permanent secretaries are responsible for agency budgets and have to appear before Parliamentary Select Committees to account for their services, the methods of outsourcing and subsequent management do not give them the levers to pull to improve services when they fail or overspend. Faced with these problems, services have to be brought back into the departments and the additional costs are not provided by the erstwhile contractors but by the public purse.

UK Border Agency

The UK Border Agency (UKBA) was established in 2008, and in 2013 it was replaced by the UK Visas and Immigration Agency, during which time its direct staff had fallen from 23,500 to 7,500 by 2020. In 2009, the UKBA stated that it was intending to reduce costs and change the way that worked through improving processes (NAO, 2012). This assumed the method chosen would be privatisation. To prepare for this, the UKBA implemented business planning and targeted approaches to improve delivery, including the creation of a value for money directorate. However, there were continuing failures in the integration of information between parts of the service, and in 2012, a second wave of transformation was instigated (NAO, 2014a). At the same time, the UKBA was reducing the headcount of its own directly employed staff to save money. In 2013, it was decided to remove the responsibility for asylum and immigration and management of the Border Force into the direct management of the Home Office and to end the role of the UKBA.

These functions formed two new directorates within the Home Office and was said to be motivated by poor culture and record within the UKBA and lack of integration between internal IT systems (NAO, 2014a). The transition to two internal directorates within the Home Office for visas and immigration was perceived to have some positive effects on staff culture but less impact on outstanding cases of asylum seekers where over 300,000 remained open in 2014 (NAO, 2014a). At the same time, as the service objectives and staffing had not been aligned it was hard to assess the performance of the new arrangements. The Home Office established a target culture for deportation of those not meeting immigration or asylum tests. The NAO stated that in 2017–18 Immigration Enforcement expected to achieve 12,800 enforced removals and broke this target down into weekly targets of around 230 to 250 removals (NAO, 2020f). In achieving these targets, the numbers were apportioned to specific teams and geographical areas. The reinforcement of the 'compliant' environment also meant that there was a sharing of information with other departments although the NAO (2018a) and other bodies had already recommended that these practices stop until data quality was of a higher standard.

The practical implementation of immigration removal through the use of centres had been privatised (Bacon, 2005). In January 2015, the Home Office had eleven designated Immigration Removal Centres (IRCs), four designated Residential and Short-Term Holding Facilities and one Non-Residential Short-Term Holding Facility. Four of the IRCs were managed by the Prison Service and the others outsourced to private companies including Mitie, GEO Group, G4S and Serco. By 2019, the numbers of centres had reduced and all but one had been outsourced, with the remaining centre managed by the Prison Service (Silverman and Griffiths, 2019). Life inside these IRCs has been described as worse than being in prison (Taylor, 2018) and heavily criticised by the Parliamentary Select Committee for Home Affairs (21 March 2019). Since then, Serco has been awarded the contracts for two centres at Gatwick, effective from May 2020 and taking over from G4S. Serco already ran another IRC. It is noticeable that the contract specification for removal of detainees places considerable emphasis on their support and physical welfare. Since 1989, there have been over 30 deaths in IRCs across the country (Silverman and Griffiths, 2019).

In 2018, the Windrush affair also demonstrated the ways the Home Office had been applying immigration legislation to longstanding Commonwealth economic migrants and their children who came to the UK before 1973 (Gentleman, 2019) . These migrants were given indefinite leave to remain as per the 1971 Immigration Act although the Home Office did not issue those affected by this legislation with any documentation or hold any records of who may be affected by it (NAO, 2018a). The migrants' position has been made insecure following the implementation of the Home Office 'hostile environment' policy (Tyler, 2018). This was later named as a 'compliant environment' particularly since 2010 and developed in the 2014 and 2016 Immigration Acts, through which the rights of migrants have been reduced including removing access to benefits, health data, driving licences and bank accounts (Hiam et al, 2018).

The approaches to migrants adopted by the Home Office focused on targets for all aspects of this policy including deportation and refusal of driving licences where the Driver and Vehicle Licensing Agency was given a target of 10,000 licence revocations in 2014/5, although there appears to be no basis for this figure (NAO, 2018a). Immigration Enforcement has had a focus on organised crime, sex trafficking and marriage abuse. In their investigations of the Windrush issue, the NAO (2018a) concluded that it was reasonable to assume that the targets would have some impact on the way in which the staff would undertake their work. While such cases take some time to come to resolution, there may be a temptation to meet targets by focusing on easier cases where the government provided little documentation as in the Windrush generation (Gentleman, 2019). Despite numerous reports indicating that the data used by the Home Office to support their actions to implement the hostile environment were flawed for the Windrush generation (NAO, 2018a) it took no action, nor did the department consider that the government principles of legal entitlements and administrative practices applied (Gentleman, 2019). Finally, there was a concern that the Home Office policy focussed on enforced removal targets above other types of case.

For the Windrush generation, there are examples of ways in which the methods of contract management, which had been learned through a range of services since 1988, have been applied for political ends. The approaches used appear to have been more strictly applied than in the management of other contracts, and the integrated focus between the Home Office and the privatised IRCs has been more effective in meeting these targets than for other contracts (NAO, 2014a). The removal of prison and probation services from the Home Office to the MoJ in 2007 has made it into a more traditional Ministry of the Interior and increased focus on immigration. In addition to the context of the Conservative Party's political agenda, there were also internal issues to consider. Since the period when these policies and programmes were put in place the then Home Secretary Theresa May was known for managing the Home Office without any major public issues but kept their activities internalised (Tyler, 2018). She was meeting a core political agenda and there was little scrutiny of her delivery. It was after she became Prime Minister in 2016 that the issues of the targeted approach appeared.

Asylum service

The UK Government has two main programmes for the management of asylum seekers within the UK. The first is detention and deportation and the second is asylum dispersal around the UK. Both programmes are privatised.

In the UK, the first privatisation of a detention centre was in Harmondsworth near Heathrow and was granted to Securicor (now G4S) following the 1971 Immigration Act. The main development of privatised services occurred after 1991, and by 2015, 80 per cent of those subject to detention and removal were managed by privatised services (Lethbridge, 2017). This is the highest level of privatisation in the services in Europe. As in other countries, the companies awarded these contracts also provided other services in the criminal justice system such as running prisons and social care. In Australia, the whole of the detention system is privatised, starting in 1996 (Mainwaring and Cook, 2019). The management of the detention centres of both G4S and Serco have been subject to investigation for sexual abuse of the detainees together with their overall mental and physical health (Gentleman, 2020).

Asylum dispersal services have been operated around the UK using private sector housing within specific local authorities. In 2010, the government privatised the provision of dispersal accommodation reception services for asylum seekers to three private sector providers. As Darling (2016) notes, this system came to public notice when the contractor responsible for housing asylum seekers in Middlesbrough started to identify the houses being used for this service by external marking, which opened residents to abuse. In the approach to asylum seeker dispersal from 2000, the Home Office initially used local authorities as their intermediary body rather than one of their own arm's length agencies but in 2012 moved from this approach to employ three service companies, G4S, Serco and Cleared, which together made up COMPASS – Commercial and Operating Managers Procuring Asylum Support. In the period 2000–2012, the approach to dispersal was criticised in several ways including the lack of support available in the dispersal locations, separation from the benefits system used by the rest of the population and delays in sourcing adequate accommodation. However, the introduction of COMPASS as a privatised service was not to address these concerns but rather as a mechanism for implementing austerity and cost cutting. While the services were costing £100m over a year, there was an intention to save £150m over seven years (Darling, 2016).

Darling (2016) argues that the UKBA targeted savings in the asylum service were relatively easy to make as asylum seekers had no votes and were unable to work. They were entirely dependent on the support the state provides and targets for demonisation in an increasingly populist agenda. The effect of transferring the contract away from local authorities to COMPASS also meant that local authorities still had to provide services but these were no longer funded as part of an integrated approach (Alonso and Andrews, 2020). Further, staff who transferred from local authorities to COMPASS did not stay long as there was a distinct change in ethos from that of supporting people to meeting contracted performance targets (Darling, 2016). There was also a loss of experience and institutional memory of the way in which people could be better supported.

As Lethbridge (2017) demonstrates, privatisation of immigration and asylum seeker removal services has been common across a range of countries, including the US, Canada and Australia in what Mainwaring and Cook (2019) describe as an 'Anglo' model. The comparison and similarities of these four countries' practices, as the largest users of this detention approach within the international community, are reinforced by the extent to which all have systems that contravene Human Rights codes. There are other similarities in these countries favouring privatisation as a mode of delivering public services and policy transfer between governments.

8

Liberalising Health
Services and Functions

Introduction

While there is an underlying view that the state has provided health
services since the creation of the National Health Service (NHS) in 1948,
the NHS Act 1946 placed an overlay on existing arrangements rather
than creating new structures and institutions (Baldwin, 1999). In the UK,
health services have always been provided through a mixed market model.
Before 1948, general practitioners (GPs) and dentists were paid by fees
sometimes covered by personal insurance schemes or charities. After 1948,
GPs and dentists remained as individual practitioners and not employees of
the NHS and primary care has remained in the mixed economy (Propper
et al, 2002). Doctors provide most services that are free to users at the
point of delivery and charging for others such as travel immunisation or
medical certificates to confirm sickness absence to employers. The NHS
is an arm's length organisation responsible directly to ministers, and since
2012, public health has been the responsibility of local authorities (DoH,
2012). Public Health England (PHE) was established as an agency in April
2013 and had had executive responsibilities for health protection primarily
through the management of its laboratories and research. It provided
advice to local authorities and directors of public health who were
appointed by local authorities when they took on these responsibilities.
PHE reported to the Secretary of State for Health and Social Care and had
some autonomous powers. The Department of Health and Social Care
(DHSC), generally referred to as the Department of Health, was founded
in 1988 and its responsibilities, apart from public health, have remained
consistent. Social care is managed through a mixed market that is in part

run by local authorities and in part by the private sector (Cunningham and James, 2014). Health is a devolved matter and managed separately in Scotland, Wales and Northern Ireland.

The application of the Government Procurement Agreement (GPA), the General Agreement on Trade in Services (GATS) and the Single European Market (SEM) within the health and social care sector has been undertaken in a variety of ways that reflect the market's involvement in different parts of the service. Early approaches to the implementation of a private finance initiative (PFI) for the provision of hospitals and the GP model included some privatisation but these were not seen as relating to the provision of secondary care in hospitals (CEC, 2015b). Where individuals have private health insurance they can be treated outside the NHS system, but if there are any difficulties in treatments then private patients are transferred to NHS provision (Williams et al, 2001; Guy, 2019). The EU had some challenges in how competition should be introduced into health care (CEC, 2015b). It has taken a lead on pharmaceutical supply and pricing and on public health advice and practice. It also established a joint procurement approach for health equipment. The introduction of the European Health Insurance Card in 2004 was used by the European Commission (EC) as one method of unifying health care provision from the user perspective as part of free movement in the SEM, but the practicalities of provision differ (Hervey, 2008).

Within EU member states, the historical development of health insurance and service provision varies as each started from a different base. In France, there is a private system where costs are then repaid to the citizen (Rodwin and Le Pen, 2004), although it has been undergoing change within its response to liberalisation, whereas in Sweden the approach is more similar to the NHS (OECD, 2017c). As in the UK, the development of an EU-wide approach to health care through the introduction of liberalisation of health care provision was also based on an efficiency narrative (Maynard, 1994). The development of a common approach within the EU to the applications of GATS did not occur immediately after the agreement came into effect in 1994. However, there were specific concerns as to how the EU could demonstrate its progress towards liberalisation in health care (CEC, 2015b). The new World Trade Organization negotiations for the Doha Round started in 2001, and as part of this, the EU had to report the extent to which its services market had been liberalised (Langhammer, 2005). This allowed the use of the agreement and subsequent reporting requirements to promote a more integrated health policy across the EU (Hervey, 2008).

In a review of the ways in which competition could be introduced into health care, the EC identified this as an issue that had to consider in the context of the existing systems in each member state (CEC, 2015b). As the main policy narrative that accompanied the introduction of competition was one of efficiency of services, this distinguished the introduction of competition from patient choice of provider at the point of use. There had previously been some separation of the different aspects in health and social care provision and the relative responsibilities for them in each member state. In line with the World Health Organization advice (WHO, 2012), public health was identified as an issue to be dealt with at the lowest practical level and was subject to the EU subsidiarity principles adopted in 1992 and 2007. In the UK, principles of cooperation and competition were introduced into the NHS through the Health Act 2006. Initially, the NHS Confederation (2009) had advised that as health services were not undertakings and were defined as supporting social solidarity they would not be subject to the same EU competition processes as other organisations. However, in 2012 Health and Social Care Act introduced competitive tendering into the NHS and, as part of this, required clinical commissioning groups, set up in local authorities, to introduce competition for the services that were offered to a range of potential providers within their responsibility (Ham, 2018).

The implementation of competition after 2012 has been diffuse and has not featured in major NHS policy papers or initiatives (Siciliani et al, 2017). Hunter (2016a) argues that the health services are a grey area as far as EU competition law is concerned and cites as evidence that no private companies have challenged UK NHS organisations about the application of competition. This can be considered within the practise of the private sector to rarely challenge failures to offer opportunities to compete across all sectors. Hunter (2016a) also draws attention to the definition of undertakings as economic entities. However, this does not appear to consider the extension of GPS and GATS to the public sector. The EU definition of a public undertaking is where the state has a dominant interest and controls the expenditure. As such, health services are included within the WTO and EU competition requirements and have been so since the Treaty on the Functioning of the European Union (1992). In this EU approach, the provision of social care was considered as a right and provision could be by the public or private sectors. Finally, the provision of all other direct health services and the support services citizens received could be subject to competition.

Context for outsourcing

The establishment of the NHS in 1948 included two major aspects of external provision within its core (Timmins, 2001). The first was the role of the GPs as independent providers of primary health care contracted to, but not employed by, the NHS. The second was through the agreement that NHS doctors could have a private practice including the direct accommodation of private practice beds within NHS hospitals (Guy, 2019). The NHS has been in public ownership since the outset in 1948, with all staff, except GPs, directly employed. Like other public services, the process of introducing competition into the NHS began in 1983 by Margaret Thatcher's government, with cleaning, catering and facilities management (Marsh, 1991). PFI was introduced into the funding of NHS buildings including operation in 1992 (Hellowell and Vecchi, 2012; NAO, 2020b) and the major changes, in support of the implementation of the GATS, began in 2000 with the NHS Plan. As Lethbridge (2012) recognises, the initial processes of GPA outsourcing in 1983 were the first stage in the implementation of exposing health services to competition, although this is generally attributed to neoliberal ideology within the UK. At the same time the EU, through the development of the SEM (1985–1992), provided the legislative scaffolding and frameworks for the application across the EU to support compliance to these international agreements (Abbott, 1990).

The development of outsourcing for health under Thatcher and John Major as Prime Ministers was a further example of the use of statecraft in the role and use of patient narratives to carry the implementation of these international agreements to liberalise public services (Bulpitt, 1986; Pollitt, 1994). This was a gradual process and one that focussed on the running of hospitals rather than direct patient provision, with Walsh (1995) describing Thatcher's approach as 'timid' and with the 1982 general election being fought on the slogan that the 'NHS is safe in our hands' (Seldon and Collings, 2014, p 15). When competition started to be introduced into the NHS, the narrative was not on efficiency, as in other public services, but on making improvements for patients. The 1989 White Paper, *Working for Patients*, separated purchasers and providers of health care, making some organisations operable as fundholders (Croxson et al, 2001). There was a softer and less pejorative language of 'commissioning' (Regan and Ball, 2010; Calovski, 2018) rather than purchasing but the practices were the same. The argument for this approach was also similar to other performance management initiatives pursued by successive governments, incorporating efficiency and effectiveness narratives (Haddon, 2012). In this White Paper, NHS trusts were proposed to be permitted to become self-governing in order to compete with private hospitals.

The proposals by the government for a Patients' Charter in 1992 continued the focus on the patient narrative by using care waiting lists as a key performance measure (Bovaird and Gregory, 1996). The moves from 1987 onwards were preparing the NHS for competition and the implementation of the GATS in the same ways as agencification in central government. The direct institutional changes into purchasers and providers would enable all NHS trusts to purchase services as well as goods from the private sector and other organisations such as charities (Kelly, 2007). The implementation of the Patients' Charter would also allow a performance management framework to be developed that could be applied in contract specifications when market liberalisation was finally agreed in 1994. The 1992 NHS and Community Care Act enabled the government to create GP fundholders, ensuring that the whole of the NHS was set within a client–contractor model.

The development of competition practices in the NHS were managed through a softer initial approach than that used within local government. The contracts were less legalistic in their character and did not have the same mechanisms for contract default. The contracts were focused on the types of services that could be purchased in bulk, by individual case type or a mixture of minimum number of cases plus additional cases (Walsh, 1995). There were also fewer provisions for contract terminations. The development of expertise in the use of procurement, specifications and contract management takes some time to evolve (Regan and Ball, 2010). As in any public services, when the market is liberalised, there has to be skill development on both sides. The purchasers have to learn to include all the services that they require and not expect additional elements of service to be implied in contracts where they are not specified. These will be subject to additional costs. Another issue arises when legal or service requirements change during the course of a contract and changes have not been included within the specification. Again, these will incur additional costs that may prohibit change. In this period, outsourcing was also used increasingly to supply contract staff for all types of roles within the NHS system including clinicians, nurses, paramedics and service workers for cleaning and catering (Confue, 2019).

The Labour government's NHS Plan 2000 introduced a range of competition measures. These included the opportunity for the private sector to undertake a range of specialist services in independent sector treatment centres such as for hip surgery and cataracts (Cribb, 2008; Guy, 2019). These were associated with meeting specified waiting list times for more frequently applied procedures. The system introduced allowed patients to be treated by a private provider if their chosen hospital could not see them within the target waiting limit (Ennew et al, 1998; Propper et al, 2002). GPs were also able to contract their 'out of hours' services to their Primary Care Trusts from 2004 onwards (Regan and Ball, 2010). Another aspect of competition between NHS providers was introduced through 'choose and book' patient choice for elective surgery (Guy, 2019). However, as the EC (CEC, 2015b) pointed out, patient choice cannot be counted as competition for the purposes of competition law, despite there being widely held views to the contrary (Hunter, 2016a).

The election of the Coalition government in 2010 was followed by another White Paper, *Equity and Excellence: Liberating the NHS* (DoH, 2012b). While continuing the approaches to competition that had been in place in health since 1980 (Regan and Ball, 2010; Bovaird, 2016), the title of this White Paper comes closer than any other to associating its proposed measures with compliance to international liberalisation commitments. This was also another example of a change in the government to reset the mechanisms for the application of the GATS – this time in the health sector. This approach was focused on patient choice and was a similar narrative to that introduced by Major through the Citizen's Charter in 1991 (Pollitt, 1994), changing the public's view on why private sector health care provision, operation and delivery within the NHS was going to be difficult just as it had been with other public services. However, the focus on the patient choice was perceived to be a mechanism that would indicate citizen advantages rather than to emphasise the introduction of outsourcing and 'the public are already incentivized out of their motivation for the common good' in personal and individualistic choices (Regan and Ball, 2010, p 504). The 2012 Health and Social Care Act introduced competition into the NHS through the newly established local Clinical Commissioning Groups. It made them funders and procurers of services, although the choice of suppliers has been limited and restricted to specific types of procedures (Ham, 2018). It also forced the introduction of rationing for particular types of procedures purchased from hospitals such as hip and knee replacements and, where there were severe budgetary pressures, no choice in providers at all.

Introducing competition into primary care

When GPs became fundholders in 1990, they entered into service purchasing or commissioning arrangements, with secondary organisations that were service providers. It was expected that these service providers would be NHS hospital trusts that would compete to provide services to the GP fundholders (Propper et al, 2002). The use of these fundholder powers allowed GP practices to choose the location of their services and encouraged them to act in a more 'entrepreneurial' way in respect of their patients, performance and budgets (Ennew et al, 1998). Not all GP practices became fundholders and there were questions asked about whether those patients obtaining services through a fundholder contract would receive swifter service than those requiring treatments through the traditional route. While there were some treatment time improvements in specialities with long waiting times, such as hip replacements and cataracts, benefits were achieved by changing the hospitals that the GPs used. These might have been achieved without any other actions. There were no other significant reductions in waiting times in other services (Propper et al, 2002).

There were also concerns that the hospital providing services may lose income if fundholders chose to find other ways of providing elective surgery or managed to provide specific services in their own premises (Croxson et al, 2001). Some services for elective surgery were provided by independent treatment centres that were introduced in 2004. Here patients could choose to use this provider if the waiting list times extended beyond those specified and they could be referred to these or other providers in order to reduce waiting lists. There were 80 centres planned to undertake elective surgery and when launched it was assumed that 10 per cent of elective surgery would be undertaken in this way (Cribb, 2008), with the majority being provided by private sector consortia. Some GPs joined purchasing consortia to reduce the additional commissioning workloads on their own practices, breaking one of the objectives of the fundholder scheme, that GPs would have greater relationships with their own local hospitals (Propper et al, 2002). Other GP practices, that were on the pathway to fundholding status, increased the extent to which they sought elective procedures in the year before they became fundholders as their future fundholding budget would depend on this. This meant that they were able to expand the practice budgets overall and then elective surgery commissioning declined in the first year of fundholding (Croxson et al, 2001). Fundholding GPs were not asked to account for their expenditure once they had moved into a commissioning role.

Some GPs started to appreciate that they could retain part of the commissioning budgets through their own direct provision of treatment (Ennew et al, 1998). They extended the services they offered in the surgery rather than referring patients to another provider and kept the funds within their own budgets. At the same time, hospital trusts became aware and concerned about these practices together with the provision of independent treatment centres (Timmins, 2005; Pollock and Godden, 2008). Some hospital trusts decided that they needed to attract more patients directly in order to keep them within their own budgetary systems, including establishing their own GP practices. GPs also opened pharmacies to provide another source of income and act as providers of vital signs testing outside the surgery. Pharmacists could also undertake diagnosis and basic treatments to keep patients out of the Accident and Emergency systems in hospitals (Butterworth et al, 2017). These different types of integration may have patient and efficiency benefits but they have been driven by market considerations.

Another issue for GP fundholders was that the size of their budget may depend on the health and demographics of their patients. Some more prosperous areas such as North Hampshire have the greatest average life expectancy in the country but also the greatest demand for healthcare from the affluent 'worried well' population. GPs are able to extend their budgets in these locations more than in other areas of the country that have higher levels of poverty and ill health (Young and Leese, 1999). Some parts of the country are 'under-doctored', having poorer access to hospital care, and GP markets have been used to attempt to address this (Wilson et al, 2006). A range of new medical schools including Staffordshire and Plymouth have been established as interventions to create nodes for health care and a cadre of medical professionals who, it is hoped, will remain in the area.

When the quasi-market was introduced into primary care through GP fundholders, not all GP fundholders wanted to behave in a market way. There were no penalties for delays in service provision or incorrect invoices being issued and most GP practices operated much in the same way as before (Ennew et al, 1998). When the practice of GP fundholding was reviewed by the Audit Commission (1993), it was found that some GP practices had accumulated large surpluses in their budgets at the end of the year. There were no sanctions or performance criteria placed on GPs in their use of these budgets (Croxson et al, 2001). In 1997, GP fundholding was abolished by the incoming Labour government but the purchaser–provider split was retained and turned into practice-based commissioning where all services could be purchased. This approach, which removed the specific use of competition by some organisations or some services but replaced it by the application of competition for all services, was similar to that used in local government through best value. These budgets were held by newly formed Primary Care Trusts and it was not compulsory for GP practices to operate in this way. However, if they did and made savings, these could be used for practice service improvements (Ennew et al, 1998).

The practices of fundholding for GPs were expanded into the creation of local authority Clinical Commissioning Groups after the 2012 Health and Social Care Act when competition was introduced more fully. In reviewing the pattern of initiatives for competition in primary care between 1990 and 2012 it is possible to see a consistent, underlying pathway to the soft introduction of markets and competition into GP practices. Initially there was no compulsion or sanctions for failure to deliver better services. There were incentives to save money through more competitive behaviour and extend the practices to provide more services. There was a diversion of patient choice that some (Guy, 2019) (but not the EU) have considered to be a competition option (NHS Confederation, 2009). However, this has led to the eventual introduction of competition. This linked set of policy initiatives demonstrate that while GPs are not directly employed by the NHS their costs and budgets are taken to be enterprises in the EC definition. This means that they have not been exempt from the introduction of competition into their use of the national resources to purchase services for patients. As the EC review indicated, the introduction of competition into health care is a 'delicate' matter (CEC, 2015a) but it has not made the NHS immune from the GATS.

Introducing competition into secondary care

The liberalisation of secondary health care in the UK was more challenging. Competition was introduced through PFI by Major in 1992 (Flinders, 2005) and then specifically targeted for use in the provision of hospitals by the Labour government through the NHS (Private Finance Act) 1997. As with other mechanisms used to apply the provisions of the GPA, GATS and SEM, there was little government narrative or evidence as to why PFI was a preferred funding method for the provision of this type of public facility. PFI is a form of public–private partnership (PPP) generally made between a public sector organisation and a private sector consortium. However, it is a contract rather than a partnership as risks are not shared (NAO, 2020b). The public sector cannot offload its responsibilities to the private sector and always retains the ultimate responsibility for services and their delivery. PFIs are delivered through a special purpose vehicle, a company constructed for the project by a consortium of suppliers. This consortium will comprise a 'topco' to manage the finance and legal/contracting issues, a 'capco' to provide the infrastructure and an 'opco' that is concerned with running the facility once it is completed. Since its introduction, PFI has been used by all governments and criticised by all oppositions. The provision of PPPs, where much of the public service expenditure remains direct rather than being subject to competition, demonstrates the extent to which the sector is meeting the GATS and GPA target percentages of funding exposed to competition. PFI project funding has shifted on and off the public balance sheet and, at times, the UK government has had to step in to fund the PFI rather than the private sector (NAO, 2018b).

Since the introduction of PFI, over 50 English hospitals have been funded in this way although not all have been completed or become operational. In 2016 a Centre of Excellence was established in the Department of Health to manage PFI contracts. The NAO has reviewed the operation of PFI on several occasions (NAO, 2006a, 2018b, 2020b, 2020e), and by 2017, there were 127 PFI NHS schemes. When Carillion collapsed in January 2018, it was undertaking a range of services for the UK government that were able to be taken on and continued within public management (NAO, 2020b). However, two major PFI construction projects for hospitals were left unfinished – the Midland Metropolitan Hospital and the Liverpool Royal University Hospital. Both hospitals were commissioned by NHS trusts and each had a company established to manage the projects that were financed by the government, with Carillion as the lead contractor and finance raised from the market (NAO, 2020b). These PFI project companies are paid for the construction and use of the hospital for a period of 30 years being paid for the hospital on its completion and availability for use. The PFI agreement is structured so that these special purpose vehicle companies had contracts with Carillion for the delivery of the hospitals and the payments for the hospital are made by the commissioning trust on a monthly basis for 30 years, after which the hospital passes into the trust's ownership and the contract ends (NAO, 2020e).

At the time of the collapse, the Liverpool hospital was nearly complete and the Midland hospital was two thirds complete. After the collapse of Carillion, it became clear that the PFI companies established to deliver the hospital could not do this using another contractor as there was insufficient funding remaining in the project. Both hospital contracts were taken over by the UK government and new contractors were found and funded outside the PFI system. As the NAO (2020b) stated, the use of the PFI approach is an incentive to the contractor to undertake the construction work on time and on budget but when there are delays and cost overruns, as in this case, the PFI system is not robust enough to ensure that the project is delivered and the risk falls back on the public sector. The hospitals will be delivered between three to five years late and the cost overrun to the public purse will be 98 per cent since the PFI contracts were signed (NAO, 2020b). The NAO has assessed this cost overrun in real terms rather than using a value for money (VFM) calculation that would have been preferred by the Department of Health and Social Care and the NHS. However, it was also discovered that the quality of the design and construction of both hospitals did not meet a range of standards and these have had to be rectified. This has particularly been an issue at the Liverpool hospital (NAO, 2020b).

PFI was first used in Australia and has also been used in Spain as well as other countries. In Australia there has been a focus on the governance of the PFI and the ways in which the specification and fulfilment of the contract both provide VFM and meet public service objectives. Here the assessment of VFM is set against the private sector comparator, a method that sets out how the project would be undertaken in the public sector and then a comparison is made. In making this comparison there also needs to be an account made of the flexibility of direct delivery in comparison with the potential rigidity of a contract (Clifton and Duffield, 2006). In Australia there has been consideration of the appointment of a regulator to manage the facility and change elements in the contracts in response to public needs. This regulator would be similar to those for utility services of general public interest in the UK. As well as considering adapting methodologies, there have also been studies that have compared the performance and outputs of Australian and UK PFI. In Australia, the most developed sectors for PFI are through the delivery of economic and social infrastructure projects. While there are similarities between the way UK and Australian PFI processes work, the UK has less focus on the construction of contracts to deal with changes throughout their existence (Lam and Javed, 2015). This is a significant issue in the UK where contracts have been required to be changed as contract processes have been found to be inadequate and the government has had to step in if the contract has failed completely.

As with other parts of public service where private sector competition has been introduced, there has been a narrative that the role of PFI has been to secure VFM and to achieve management efficiencies and benefits (Brown, 1994). Evaluation of PFI in practice, by the NAO, has shown that in some sectors, such as construction, there has been a demonstration of VFM. However, there have been other criticisms of its use (NAO, 2012) that might suggest some more fundamental changes to the system or its abandonment altogether. However, what is not certain is that if PFI is stopped whether there would be sectors of the UK economy that would not meet their GPA or GATS thresholds. If this were the case, would this bring pressure to bear for competition in other parts of these sectors? As noted in the introduction of markets within GP practices, even those who opted to be fundholders did not necessarily want to pursue a market approach and saw it as a mechanism to increase their practice budgets rather than enter into procurement engagement with different providers.

Introducing markets for health information

The publication of the government's *Information for Health: An Information Strategy for the Modern NHS 1998-2005: A National Strategy for Local Implementation* (1998) by the NHS Executive set out a programme for the management and reuse of NHS data for a variety of purposes. The strategy considered all aspects of health information gathered by the NHS and its analysis through the use of IT systems. While individual patient information has to be kept secure and private, the use of big data for use in research and for targeting specific types of health provision is also considered important (Collins, 2016). The focus of the strategy was to link the collection of local primary health data with the needs of national requirements, and after the publication of this strategy, all local health trusts had to align their formats with the national Information Management and Technology approach. The basis of the new system was the Electronic Patient Record (EPR) (Martin et al, 2007). There were also changes in the collection of qualitative data and how they can be recorded, coded and then analysed so as to ensure that they are equivalent across all practitioners and trusts. There were also issues where different specialities require different data to be collected. The EPR system was reviewed (NAO, 2011b) and abandoned by the government in 2011.

In 2006 Dr Foster, a company using NHS data as a basis for its business, was established as a joint venture company with a stake funded by the NHS. Dr Foster uses NHS data to provide analysis for the NHS and individuals. At the time of its creation, there were criticisms that there had not been an appropriate procurement process. This joint venture was subsequently investigated by the NAO (2007) and by the House of Commons Health Select Committee, which found that, while the NHS had purchased a 50 per cent share in the company, it was only worth between £10m and £15m in total and the Treasury's advice on joint ventures had been ignored. In 2015, it was sold to Telstra for a sale price between £10 and £20m.

Between 2008 and 2013, Dr Foster published individual hospital performance guides that enabled the public to examine, compare and contrast the performance of individual specialities and outcomes for each hospital (Kafetz, 2016). This was also an important source of information as part of the introduction of the 'choose and book system', which allowed patients to determine their own preferred place of treatment at the time of its commissioning from primary care (Guy, 2019). The development and access to hospital data had some significant outcomes such as the identification of high mortality rates at some hospitals, including that in Staffordshire, which have been the subject of subsequent inquiry (2013).

The Dr Foster data were also put alongside other hospital performance data provided by Capita and the BBC. However, gradually these public performance data guides have been withdrawn including the one from Dr Foster (Kafetz, 2016) on the basis that the Care Quality Commission set up by the government could provide more rigorous comparative data.

In 2019, Google acquired access to bulk NHS data (Hunter, 2016b). Initially, Google has been passed five years' worth of patient data. This followed the acquisition of patient data from a London NHS trust in 2014 by DeepMind, a company owned by Google Alphabet. This was subsequently the subject of an inquiry and the NHS trust was found to have broken the law on data management. In 2018, DeepMind was taken over and absorbed into Google so that these patients' records could be used in a more targeted way for individual diagnostic purposes. The Royal Free Trust in London was the first to have an agreement with DeepMind for transferring NHS data and it renewed the contract in 2019 after DeepMind was transferred to Google Health. Taunton and Somerset Health Trust has a five-year contract with Google for sharing live patient data. This trust is a global exemplar in information sharing and has had additional funds to develop open source application programming interfaces (APIs) from the government. This contract sends EPR data in bulk to Google together with patient encounter and diagnostic information. The contract appears to permit Google Health to pass on the information to app makers, although it is unclear if this is free or for a charge (Porteous, 2018). The work with Google has been through systems that have been developing methods of analysing patient data, with specific conditions like acute kidney injury being the first to be put into practice.

While individual Google contracts with NHS trusts may not provide the ability to link personal data with individual accounts, the data are being used to develop predictive diagnosis through the use of artificial intelligence. Despite there being an adverse finding against the action of the Royal Free Trust by the Information Commissioner's Office in 2017, further trusts have entered into agreements for data sharing with Google subsequently (Kafetz, 2016). The Royal Free states that the data are still under the trust's data controller while Google remains as a data processor. However, the contract has been established within the data protection regulations of General Data Protection Regulation (GDPR) and the trust has not yet updated its public information to reflect Brexit and the removal of the UK from this regulation and the position of patient data privacy after this (Basu and Guinchard, 2020). The GDPR has protected individual patient data within the EU. However, following the UK's decision to leave the EU being finally agreed upon in 2020, a number of tech providers including Google are transferring the hosting of all UK data they hold about individuals to US jurisdiction where the GDPR will not apply. While under DeepMind the streams approach included an independent ethics review panel, this was closed down when it was transferred to Google. All the five hospitals that have contracted with Google Health are in London. The Somerset and Taunton NHS trust decided not to go ahead after a pilot and Yeovil has decided not to go ahead at all.

9

Outsourcing in Education

Introduction

The introduction of liberalisation into education varied according to each part of the sector. Universities already had a mixed economy of state funding for fees, public and private sector research funding, spin out companies and endowments, so there was less of cultural issue to address within the institution, although academic staff were less supportive of this approach (Walford, 1988). For new universities, the removal of higher education establishments from local authority control and their transition into the same model as other universities in 1992 appeared to reflect a longstanding pathway for new universities (Stone, 1998). This was not publicly associated with the preparation for the implementation of the General Agreement on Trade in Services (GATS) in 1996, where the vast majority of public services were subject to market liberalisation. The leadership of each university within this expanded set of institutions would need to change to include private sector experience but incentivisation of competition between universities for students and funding would encourage change (Deem et al, 2007).

For younger children, the provision of pre-school care has always been a mixed market (Melhuish, 2006). Parents placed children in local authority nurseries attached to schools or run independently. Parents also used au pairs and nannies employed directly or placed their children in private day nurseries or with child minders. In this sector, there was no expectation of universal public provision and the opportunity to place a child in a school nursery related to local policy. In some local authorities such as London, there was a strong commitment to nursery places in both free-standing and school-related settings but there was no consistency across the country.

The most difficult and challenging part of education provision to introduce liberalisation was that of mainstream school education for children aged 5–18. The role of private education through public and preparatory schools had been the subject of reviews including the 1944 Education Act, which had introduced them into the state system using the 11 plus and the direct grant and voluntary aided models rather than adopt a policy of abolition but many of these returned to the private sector when comprehensive education was introduced in 1976. In the public sector, schools were directly run by local authorities or organisations with faith-based affiliations – particularly the Church of England and the Catholic Church (Cairns et al, 2004). Most private sector schools are not regarded as businesses and many are operated by foundations or charities based on historical institutions including city livery companies and local historical grammar schools founded in the fourteenth to seventeenth centuries. Another wave of public schools were founded after the 1870 Education Act, when many local authorities also founded grammar schools that gave local children access to wider educational opportunities through scholarships and bursaries to Oxbridge (Forster, 2014).

When the GATS was introduced in 1996, in secondary education, most children were in comprehensive schools although some local authorities retained the 11+ – as in Kent and Buckinghamshire (Cribb et al, 2013). Introducing market liberalisation into a predominantly local authority system, where education was provided as a right by the state and funded through taxation, was going to be difficult to manage with the general public (Amato and Farbmann, 2010). However, by 2020, this transition to liberalised school provision for most children in the secondary phase had been accomplished. Most English children are now educated in academy schools – that is schools owned and run by the private sector singly or in chains (Eyles and Machin, 2019). This is also increasingly the case with schools for 5–11-year-olds. The academy chains have been supplemented by the introduction of free schools that have government support and can be opened by local groups of parents (Hatcher, 2011). Local authorities now run the minority of secondary schools and have few powers over the quality and management of state-funded schools operated by the private sector. Local authorities are required to fund specific school places for children who are disabled or excluded or who have special needs. Further, local authorities are still placed in national league tables based on the examination results of schools mostly outside their control although the government does not publish similar rankings for academy chains (OECD, 2015c; Allen and Burgess, 2020). This chapter discusses how this transition from public direct provision of education to publicly funded education has been achieved.

GATS and Single European Market

The introduction of liberalisation into education as a response to the GATS has taken various forms. There have also been discussions about how far education is a market to which s101 of the Treaty on the Functioning of the European Union (TfEU) 1992 applies. GATS competition law applies to universities although it is deemed to be a complex issue (Sauvé, 2002; Packham, 2003). In the EU, member states have decided to use the Open Method of Coordination (Cini, 2001) or soft law to determine its approach. There was also a change in the emphasis from state responsibility for university competition policy to one that was a shared competence between the European Commission and member states (Gideon, 2012). In the UK, the push towards liberalisation and marketisation by the government was stimulated by the Browne Report (2010). In universities, teaching provided within private sector settings is regarded as subject to market rules, and given their geographical proximity and subject competition, it is unlikely that they will be exempt from competition rules and be able to rely on the Block Exemption Regulations for public services provided by the EU (Gideon, 2012). The European Commission has subsequently found that universities are hybrid organisations where teaching and research can be in different supply markets and where postgraduate and undergraduate teaching are further divided into different markets (Gideon, 2012). There have also been considerations of university mergers where they exist in competition in a single geographical market and the merger of UMIST and the Victoria University of Manchester was subject to an investigation by the Office of Fair Trading (OFT) in 2004. The operation of competition regulations has also meant that universities are required to charge full market costing for their research and consultancy activities as the free use of facilities could be construed as an economic benefit defined as state aid to any private sector organisation funding the research (Bianchi and Labory, 2006).

The provision of education through schools is provided by the state as a human right, and there was no consideration of their role as operating for a profit before the liberalisation of services (Amato and Farbmann, 2010) and their provision was considered as an approach to social solidarity (Gideon, 2012). When the World Trade Organization Doha Round commenced in 2000, all members of the WTO, including the EU, were required to demonstrate the extent to which their public services had been subject to liberalisation; this caused a greater examination of the operation of the GATS principles (WTO, 2020). As a consequence, there was a change in the EU definition of a competition within schools as set out in an EU Regulation on competition (CEC 1/2003) and which was particularly expected to affect the UK (Amato and Farbmann, 2010). This was anticipated by the Labour government in 2000, when city technology colleges were introduced and later changed to general category of academies in 2002 (Eyles and Machin, 2019). These schools introduced a competitive market for pupils using a range of inducements including types of teaching or a focus on specific subjects such as the performing arts or science and technology. This meant that academy schools became economic entities because their managers would benefit from increasing market shares of students through pupil funding or by attracting other investment or sponsorship (Greaves and Scicluna, 2010). For private schools, although many operate as charities, competition law also applies. Following a major case involving sharing information about fees by independent schools that were registered charities, the OFT deemed that there was a market operating for private schools and sharing information about their fees was contrary to competition rules (OFT, 2006).

Universities

In 1990, the government considered universities to be independent public bodies with students' fees and funds for academic staff provided by the government. All universities operated similar systems for their core activity of teaching, with students being offered places to study through a combined university entrance system after they had received their A-level results. The fee levels were the same for most courses although some in medicine and engineering were longer than others. University courses in Scotland have always been for four years. Some courses included funded sandwich years in industry. Students received grants and then loans to fund their time at university and this extended to students in polytechnics and institutes of higher education.

Since 1992, polytechnics that had been in the local authority sector became universities, and institutes of higher education have been either made into universities or merged within them. Between 1995 and 2000, UK central government funding for universities fell by 17 per cent (OECD, 2002). At the same time, the colleges within the University of London have become individual universities such as the London School of Economics and Political Science, Imperial College London and UCL while some of the University of London institutes such as that for education have merged with these newly independent individual college universities (Stone, 1998). There have been three further major reforms of university funding and fees in the UK and then in England in 1998, 2006 and 2012 (Browne, 2010). These moved tuition fees from being free at the point of use to now being funded by loans from the government that are repaid over a lifetime through the income tax system (Azmat and Simion, 2017). Competition in fee levels between universities and courses have also been introduced (Marginson, 2006). The same pathway to loans has been followed for student maintenance support. These changes do not appear to have affected the take up of university places (Azmat and Simion, 2017) but may have an influence on the university chosen. Postgraduate programmes have always been permitted more flexibility on fees charged and now the undergraduate programmes are more similar to this market.

One of the major concerns that has arisen since universities have become more liberalised is the extent to which this has been reflected in the salaries of their leaders (Deem et al, 2007). The scale of university institutions, including turnover, can be considerable and similar to a major company. Universities have recruited senior management staff from the private sector and salaries have increased. This has caused considerable concern in the government and for the relationship of salaries with research performance (De Fraja et al, 2019; Johnes and Virmani, 2020) and also within the academic staff that have not experienced similar salary increases over the same period of time.

Universities have introduced outsourcing for services that support students and staff including accommodation, cleaning, catering and personnel (Hopkins and Fairfoul, 2014). These have contractual obligations for individual universities, with some teetering on the edge of bankruptcy (Rudd and O'Brien, 2019). Further, some universities have attempted to influence the market for student choice by offering bursaries and unconditional places if students accept them before A-level results are received. This practice has increased from 9.25 per cent in 2013 to 15.1 per cent places in 2018 (Hubble and Bolton, 2019). These liberalising changes within universities have occurred in other countries such as Malaysia (Mok, 2007) and Australia, New Zealand and Canada (Thornton, 2011) and are described as creating the 'Enterprise university' (Marginson and Considine, 2000).

An important part of being more 'marketised' and competitive has been the recruitment of international students (Marginson and Considine, 2000). These students can be charged higher fees than home students and their numbers have not been capped in the same way (Azmat and Simion, 2017). International students also bring status and enhance a university's reputation globally (Marginson, 2006), making them a primary location for recruitment by global companies. While some universities seek this recognition across the whole of their institution, others have become global universities based on their specialisms such as economics, engineering or design. This standing will also serve to attract home students to university programmes and may be a significant feature. Between 2000 and 2011, the number of international students across the world doubled and Asian students from China, India and Korea made up 53 per cent students studying abroad worldwide (OECD, 2015c). In 2017, the UK was one of the countries with the highest enrolment of international students at 17.9 per cent and while the numbers of international students declined overall since 2010 it has started to increase again after 2018 (OECD, 2020b).

The international student market is also supported by an increase in demand that cannot be met in home nations. In China, for example, the change in the national economy has created a demand for more university places and many Chinese parents want their children to speak English (Marginson, 2006). Children are frequently sent to English boarding schools or their satellites in Asia so that they have knowledge of English at the beginning of their undergraduate programmes. This is followed by a university education in either the UK or US and in other countries such as the Netherlands where increasingly programmes are taught in English. Graduates of top 100 universities across the world are expected to have employment and societal advantages in home nations (Marginson, 2006). However, there are other issues that may be taken into consideration, including costs of visas and fees to study, the opportunities to stay on to work beyond graduation and the ease of the system as a whole. The effects of the COVID-19 pandemic may also change the habits within this market.

UK universities have also attracted students from the EU while some home students have moved to EU member state universities where there are no or low tuition fees and some courses are taught in English or for subjects where there is great competition for university places in the UK, such as medicine (Wilkins et al, 2013). Within the UK, EU students on undergraduate courses are counted as home students and pay the same fees. If English students choose to study in Scotland, where there are no university fees payable by Scottish students, they are required to pay fees. The classification of the source of students matters for university finances. International students are not capped by numbers or fees and their participation on a UK course will be for universities to decide. Some universities including Liverpool and UCL have over 20,000 Chinese students (Cebolla-Boado et al, 2018). The funding derived from these students is also important to universities because it is not subject to any controls.

University accommodation

Universities have always had a major impact on their host communities, even where they are largely contained within a campus setting (Hubbard, 2008). They bring additional spending to local areas, can create jobs through research and innovation, provide a range of other jobs for support staff and, for towns and cities that have experienced industrial decline, provide an injection of investment. The student population can also support the viability of public transport systems and their parents can support the tourist and visitor economy.

The expansion of university student numbers in the UK doubled between 1990 and 2019, having a significant impact on the availability and quality of purpose-built student accommodation and housing (Hubbard, 2008; Sage et al, 2012). In some places this has exacerbated existing housing shortages with landlords preferring student rents. In others, parents have been purchasing properties, paying mortgage and student fees through rents derived from other students taking rooms, thus putting pressure on the local housing market. The parents of international students have also purchased accommodation for them while studying and also for investment, which has happened in London (London School of Economics, 2017) and Australia (Paris, 2017).

The effect of student expansion within localities, including the transition of polytechnics and institutes of higher education into universities, has meant that the accommodation usually provided for students in the rental market has been under increasing pressure. For traditional universities, their existing halls of residence may not have been able to cope with rising student numbers. For those institutions that have recently become universities, there may have been a student base already living in the city – at home or in work. However, as the sector has developed, there has been more pressure to encourage wider settlement of students to diversify the university's impact on specific locations. In some cities the traditional town versus gown tensions have become significant and local authorities have stepped in to manage the situation – either by preventing more student accommodation or by reinforcing residential communities through supporting a wider retail diversity and a greater control of noise and behaviour (Morphet and Clifford, 2020). In some cities, the contribution of universities to regenerate the economy has been considered to be significant but the wider impact has not always materialised (Robinson and Adams, 2008). It also depends on whether the university is located within the town or on the periphery, where its impact may be less.

The provision of halls of residence and approved lodgings was once a direct function of universities and a service to students. This approach was to support students in their learning habits, to provide a bridge from home to university in the first year of study and to provide a serviced life for those studying for their finals. For medical students it provided accommodation so that they could be on call. However, the provision of private student accommodation by the market has grown (Mulhearn and Franco, 2018). The provision of such accommodation, which is newly built and close to universities, has had the effect of driving up costs of land acquisition for other types of housing and creating areas in cities where 'studentification' is driving out other types of uses including residential and general shops (Hubbard, 2008). The main driver of this type of investment development is its funding model that has now developed into an international investment category (Newell and Marzuki, 2018). The individual student units can be defined as 'pods' and investors can fund these individually, receiving immediate financial rates of return that have been higher than many other types of investment in this period. One major supplier of student housing, UNITE, had a range of institutional methods for providing accommodation with individual universities and the financial basis of these may vary, as they do in the private housing market. This is now regarded as a mature asset class for investors and one of the most liquid of operational property markets in the UK (Bowles and Davy, 2019). While, as an investment class, it has attracted some new entrants, it is perceived to be a tight market of a restricted number of providers and where market share is not expected to change (Newell and Marzuki, 2018). If this is such a lucrative market, have universities managed to generate income to support their own activities or has this been largely taken by private investors, primarily from the US and Europe?

How far is privatisation changing universities?

While changes within the institution have occurred, Thornton (2011) argues that they have also had effects on the curriculum and culture of learning. In a fees-based system, with employer demands for specific types of training and curriculum, universities have become focussed on instrumental knowledge rather than on discourse and critical education. Marginson and Considine have posed the question about how far universities have to mirror markets to service them (2000, p 13). These changes have also been widespread across the world in the curriculum in UK Commonwealth countries where institutional settings are similar. Further pressures on universities to support movement into employment, including in the professions, together with credit accumulation and cross-recognition systems may also have served to bring together curriculum to meet these agendas.

The universities remain mixed economies with the extension of outsourced services into the institutional heart of the organisation. While not defined as either public or private institutions as in the US, there are two private universities in the UK, Buckingham and London, which receive some public funding. What is the university's community role? Some universities are taking this as a priority, opening schools and campuses on sites, which potentially provide more access to less advantaged students (Johnston and Wells, 2020). Others focus on their international reputations and league tables are more important to them. The pressure on academic staff to produce highly rated research and to obtain research funding grants has increased since 1990. The introduction of the research assessment exercise in 1986, which had been repeated regularly, brought competition and league tables between universities and disciplines. It was replaced by the Research Excellence Framework in 2014. One of the pressures on staff to produce more research has been a reduction in teaching contact hours, particularly within arts courses. While each course has an approved programme and assessment scheme, the type of teaching can vary. In science subjects there are considerably more hours spent in laboratories and in practical teaching. However, in the humanities, more emphasis is placed on students undertaking their own research and producing essays or seminar papers. Humanities students have started to compare the number of contact hours for theirs and other courses. Staff are now also subject to assessment by students. While most university academics are expected to teach as part of their duties, those with major research contracts can buy out their time and substitute staff can be appointed frequently on a temporary basis. Research students may also replace them. Parents of students are also becoming interested in these issues, not least where they are paying the tuition fees (Wilkins et al, 2013).

Overall, universities have become more corporate and managerialist in their cultures (Marginson and Considine, 2000). Some academics have ignored this turn and continue as before but increasingly those who wish to obtain tenure or promotions have to meet the requirements set by universities for being excellent researchers, raising funds, being respected by their peers and publishing work in high impact journals that is widely cited. They have to receive reasonable teaching feedback scores and results from their classes. While teaching fellows have been introduced into the system, where there is no expectation of the research profile, they remain in the minority.

Schools

Like the introduction of competition into other public services, there has been a cumulative range of initiatives introduced by successive governments that have created a market in school provision. Of all the public services where competition had to be introduced, schools were considered to be particularly challenging by Whitehall and Westminster and less likely to be accepted by the electorate (Gideon, 2012; Eyles and Machin, 2019). Since 2000, there have been WTO discussions about new proposals for the implementation of GATS for the education sector (Amato and Farbmann, 2010) although this does not seem to have progressed further. However, as with all international obligations and policies, much of domestic government policy is used to anticipate these changes. These may bring some first mover advantages and encourage others to copy the approach taken. At the same time, this longtail policy approach allows for reforms to be located with prevailing ideologies to gain other political advantages. This longtail approach also provides a gentler introduction to delivery, which can change public attitudes and acceptance of change (Dudley and Richardson, 2004).

In most public service liberalisation, governments have used the narratives of efficiency and effectiveness to promote change, but this was more difficult in schools in the UK. Unlike some other countries where schools are owned and run by the central state, in the UK, schools have been managed by local authorities since the creation of local education authorities (LEAs) in their present form in the 1880s. State schools have had autonomous governing or managing bodies within this local authority structure that have administered appointments processes and staff have then been employed directly by the local authority of which the LEA is part. Like other parts of the public sector, liberalisation entered the management and operation of schools through outsourcing of support services, including school meals, cleaning, transport, building and grounds maintenance, caretaking and recruitment (Young, 1986; Gustafsson, 2004). Before competition was introduced in these services, they were delivered for all schools in the area by the LEA. However, many schools complained about the delays in the provision of these services, the standards of delivery and the costs (Edwards et al, 1999). Where provided by the LEAs, these support services were funded by budgets retained by them from the total funding for pupils provided by the government before the funds were passed on to schools. There was a continuing dispute between central government, through the Department for Education (DfE), LEAs and individual schools, as it was suggested that LEAs were depriving schools of a disproportionate slice of central funding for these services. The DfE was particularly concerned that the funding that it had managed to obtain for schools from the Treasury was not fully being passed on. In 1998, schools were invited to bid to become foundation schools that gave them more independence, although pupil funding was still passed from the government to the individual school through the LEA. In addition, in 1998, the DFE introduced 'golden handcuffs' into the budgetary system for schools by encouraging local authorities to commit to initiatives early in the annual budget cycle before their whole budgets were set, in return for a promise of additional education funding. However, it soon became clear that a high proportion of funding from total local authority budgets were being locked into education funding commitments and removed from other services. Local authorities could not maintain this approach without reducing funding for other major services such as social care and public transport (Smyth and Kelleher, 2012). However, local authorities were increasingly made responsible for poorer performing schools. The introduction of foundation schools in 1998 meant that local authorities had a reducing role in the delivery of school standards while continuing to be held to account for this comparative performance through school league tables (OECD, 2015c).

Academies

The introduction of liberalisation into schools was accompanied by statecraft (Wilkins, 2017). The media stories of LEAs' funding retention and failing to improve poorly performing schools were equivalent to the efficiency and effectiveness narratives that had been used to presage earlier public sector liberalisation in other sectors (Micheli et al, 2005). These messages undermined the core role of local authorities as direct providers of education and opened the way for the introduction of an outsourcing model. Instead of being alarmed at the proposed changes, the public had been prepared for the role of outsourced schools as being a major harbinger of 'beneficial change' (Eyles and Machin, 2019). This statecraft narrative was enhanced by the introduction of outsourced schools into two key parts of the sector – where schools were 'failing' and in support of education for emerging technologies. Through this means, the policy was able to attract support from aspirational parents or those who had little choice of local comprehensive schools for their children. As with prisons, the outsourced schools were to be provided with new facilities funded through the private finance initiative, Building Schools for the Future programme (Kakabadse et al, 2007; Kraftl, 2012).

Changes in the provision of school education in England began in 1998 with the introduction of city technology colleges (Eyles and Machin, 2019) and these were later extended to more schools by the introduction of city academies. This was preparation for the wider liberalisation of the school sector and was open to non-local authority providers. The academy schools programme was extended by the Coalition government from 2010 onwards, using evidence of the way in which competition had been introduced into the Swedish school system after 1992 (Björklund et al, 2005). These views were also supported by a Liberal Democrat think tank, CentreForum, which was funded by Serco, a public sector provider, and KPMG (Hatcher, 2011). This led to the introduction of the Academies Act 2010 that allowed all state schools to become academies. The 2011 Education Act included a presumption that all local authorities in need of a new school should seek proposals for an academy or free school to provide for these places. If this was not possible, then a local authority community school could be provided (Wilkins, 2017).

Free schools were also introduced in 2010 by the Coalition government as a specific type of academy and then extended to include all academy schools (Hatcher, 2011; Higham, 2014). This diversification away from local authority direct provision towards increasingly institutionalised academy chains allowed a different type of process and increased the number of schools available across the whole of the school age range (Keddie, 2015). The policy was described as being part of the approach to the Big Society (Kisby, 2010; Higham, 2014), which, it was argued, was required to reduce the size of the state's role in delivery. Free schools were modelled on charter schools in the US and established through a direct agreement between the government and the governing body of the free school trust, which is required. In 2015, there was a legal presumption that all new schools would be defined as free schools and directly agreed with the government (Hatcher, 2011). Free schools now also include studio schools where pupils learn through projects and university technical colleges, for 14–18-year-old pupils (Higham, 2014). This increased the range of providers through a greater involvement of the community and extended competition to the provision of schools to the voluntary sector. The extension, in addition to non-profit making trusts, offered a more acceptable way in which competition could be introduced into areas where state run services were still considered to be preferable and provided an opportunity to those parents unhappy with the quality of their local schools to engage in the market directly. It also supported the delivery of the European Commission's revised policy of supporting community organisations into the delivery of public services (Halloran, 2017), which can also be seen in the Public Services (Social Value) Act 2012.

Free schools have a different funding model and programmes from academies and multi-academy trusts. While free schools can be established by faith or community groups, they are subject to the same admission criteria as all other schools, and in faith schools, this means that where free schools are oversubscribed, then 50 per cent of the places must be open to pupils of other faiths. This has meant that they have not been a popular model for all faiths and the Catholics have preferred the voluntary aided model where all pupils come from Catholic families (Hatcher, 2011; Higham, 2014).

Those wanting to establish a free school, and operate within the context of being a 'challenger' of orthodox service provision, develop or acquire business skills in order to make a successful application and these are drawn from conventional sources such as consultants (Higham, 2014). The ability of free school applicants to acquire these skills also acts as a deterrent to those in poorer areas who may not have the time available to make an application. The application processes for establishing a free school are not in the public domain and it is only when the business case has been approved by the Secretary of State that some information about the proposal becomes available (Hatcher, 2011; Higham, 2014). While there have been criticisms over free school failures and closures, with schools having spare places and using unregistered teachers, this overlooks one of the main purposes of the introduction of free schools, which is to assist the UK in meeting the Government Procurement Agreement in ensuring competition in the school system.

There are free schools in other countries such as Canada and the US, in both of which they are known as charter schools, and Sweden and New Zealand (Björklund et al, 2005; Bunar, 2009; King and O'Sullivan, 2002). The evidence for the role of charter schools in improving performance is mixed (Hatcher, 2011) although they have introduced diversity into the system, particularly in lower performing areas. This indicates that where has been an alignment of policy objectives to promote the opening up of competition in school provision, this has been associated with a drive to improve poorly performing schools in poor areas (Böhlmark and Lindahl, 2008). This approach has also supported gentrification, where families wanting to move back into inner city areas may otherwise have been discouraged from doing so by the quality of schools available. However, the basis of the contract for free schools, as charter schools in the US, is that they have received more funding per pupil to ensure that the schools are attractive to parents (Hatcher, 2011; Higham, 2014).

Not all UK free schools have been successful, with 66 being closed or failed to open by April 2018 with £150m lost in start-up and capital costs (Allen and Higham, 2018). Moreover, a Swedish research study examining the claims of free schools in increasing educational standards found that they were not borne out in practice (Allen, 2010). Those locations where free schools did drive up performance were areas of a higher middle-class population and second-generation migrants who were also more likely to use free schools. In Sweden, these supply side reforms were introduced in 1992, creating a more deregulated education system that was designed to create a market (Björklund et al, 2005). When examining the evidence available on the effects of these reforms by 2009 and which might feed into an evidence base for policy making in the UK, research studies demonstrated that the introduction of competition into the education system did no harm but also had no long-lasting positive impact either (Ahlin, 2003; Bunar, 2009). What is interesting and not commented upon in this policy research is the introduction of the concepts of the market, privatisation and competition into the lexicon for school place provision in Sweden in preparation for the implementation of the GATS (Böhlmark and Lindahl, 2008). When it was helpful for the UK government to provide evidence of other national systems that supported liberalisation of school provision, Sweden provided a positive model.

The statecraft used to implement outsourcing of schools in England was based on the policy narrative of performance, particularly through an enhanced regime operated through Ofsted (Wilkins, 2017). The academy schools were associated with narratives of better performance but there was little evidence that this would be the case prior to the implementation of the policy. Subsequently, there have been research studies on whether academy schools have performed better than community schools, as local authority schools are now known. This has found that, in some cases, academies have performed better but this is attributed to the greater freedom they have over the curriculum offered to pupils (Allen and Higham, 2018). The increased performance of academies may result from fewer choices being made available to pupils who can only follow courses that are more likely to result in higher examination performance (Hatcher, 2011). Increasingly academies have been grouped into chains managed by single providers and have gradually been extending into primary provision up to year 6.

The introduction of academies to create a market in schools' provision has had to be developed and supported over time. This has also led to a secondary market of advisors and consultants to support applications for academies and free schools (Hatcher, 2011), funded from grants made available by the government. While academy trusts are expected to operate on a non-profit basis, the then education secretary Michael Gove stated that he was not against academy trusts making a profit and subsequently a former chair of Ofsted was involved in attempting to establish a 'for profit' academy chain. Opening the schools' market to competition has also met another GATS objective in that academy chains are now run by market providers from other countries. In Sweden, schools were initially run by trusts as in the UK, with providers subcontracted to them. However, they are now run directly by companies for profit and the Confederation of British Industry argued that such an approach would reduce costs (Hatcher, 2011). Academies have also been shown to be against any unionisation of staff (Moorhead, 2020).

Has liberalisation changed education?

The liberalisation of the education system has been more systematic than might have been thought possible by governments when they started to make these changes, particularly for schools. The extent and range of the introduction of academies into secondary education has been widespread and further diversity has been introduced through free schools. However, despite these changes being proposed on the promise of educational improvement, this has not been the case in all academies and some free schools have closed because of a failure to secure sufficient enrolments (Allen and Higham, 2018). The use of government policy narratives has taken public opinion on board without major local political disturbance while statecraft has managed to obfuscate the underlying drivers of change, that is through commitments to meet international agreements. In the school system there have been major changes while universities have incorporated and expanded their mixed economies. However, it seems likely that the government is set to return to control the home students in the university system as part of its Brexit preparation through the application of limits for student numbers, including capping the number of English students who can study in Wales, Scotland and Northern Ireland (Adams and Brooks, 2020). It is interesting to reflect that the UK's withdrawal from the Single European Market is reintroducing national protectionism by restricting competition between universities within the UK.

10

The Third Sector and Social Value

Introduction

The election of the Coalition government in 2010 brought contradicting ideologies of the role of the state and the way that it should be operating in relation to competition and outsourcing. Through the use of statecraft, the Labour government during 1997–2010 maintained the fulfilment of the commitments made through the World Trade Organisation agreements on the Government Procurement Agreement (GPA), the General Agreement on Trade in Services (GATS) and EU Single European Market (SEM) to liberalise the public sector. It continued to use the private finance initiative in the provision of public sector facilities and their management through projects such as Building Schools for the Future (Morphet, 2008; Mahony et al, 2011). It reduced the compulsory components of some aspects of competition for public services in local government while extending competition to all local authority services through best value (Wilson, 1999). It had introduced competition into education and health through a series of initiatives using the policy narrative of improved efficiency (Eyles and Machin, 2019; Guy, 2019). It introduced revised EU policy to support the third sector and the role of small and medium-sized enterprises (SMEs) into the competition framework through the creation of the Office of the Third Sector (Alcock, 2010).

When the Coalition government took power in 2010, its overriding ideology was for a small state (Gamble, 2015). The Prime Minister, David Cameron, continued the third sector and SME approach to providing public service delivery through his concept of a Big Society (Smith, 2010). There was some alignment to the government's ideology but this was not sufficiently developed to create an understandable political narrative. This confusion was noticed at the time by commentators (Lowndes and Pratchett, 2012) but its provenance was not investigated. Within the Conservative Party, the principle of moving towards a small state led by George Osborne, Chancellor of the Exchequer in the Coalition government, created by reducing the public sector, through funding cuts under the austerity narrative, was pre-eminent. The focus was not so much on outsourcing but on preventing the public sector from having any resource to spend. Subsequently, as in the response to COVID-19, this has been to replace central and local government delivery by outsourced contractors (Monbiot, 2020).

The driving force of small government and austerity was said to be a response to the economic crisis of 2008 together with the public expenditure levels of the previous Labour government (Gamble, 2015). However, this marked a longer-term approach to small state government driven by the populist agenda. This focused on the nation state, not a welfare state that supported individuals through democratic state norms that had been in place in the UK since 1909 (Pelling, 1979). While dismantling the state through changes in the social benefits rules, eligibility to live in council houses and cost reduction pressures on the NHS and education in England, the principle of the welfare state consensus of government remained in Scotland, Wales and Northern Ireland as well as in the rest of Europe. England became an outlier for this austerity narrative and its results have left local authority services significantly reduced (NAO, 2018c) and the UK being heavily criticised by a special UN rapporteur on poverty (Alston, 2019).

At the same time as the austerity programme was being implemented through government cuts there was also a new approach to localism and subsidiarity. While local government funding was being removed through the tapered withdrawal of the Revenue Support Grant in England, within the EU the principle of subsidiarity was taken to the next level of application in the Lisbon Treaty 2009 (Schütze, 2009). This was implemented in England through the 2011 Localism Act, which gave local authorities a general power of competence that included the powers to own and operate companies in the same way as the private sector. This allowed local authorities to return to some of the practices of trading and owning companies that they were forced to give up in 1980. While councils had less central government funding support, they were now able to offer other forms of services using municipal entrepreneurialism, particularly for housing and energy provision (Roelich and Bale, 2015; Morphet and Clifford, 2020). The EU principle of subsidiarity is also important in the UK as local authorities are not part of the Constitution and are reliant on specific powers to undertake any action. Beyond this, the UK central government did not apply the subsidiarity principle in the way that was required by the Lisbon Treaty, namely that all public services had to be subject to a subsidiarity test with funding and responsibility for these services passed to the level of government most appropriate for their operation and delivery. In France, for example a specific organisation has to be established to undertake these reviews as a matter of course for all legislation and public services.

The central state considered this extension of subsidiarity as an unwelcome approach and a potential reduction in its powers. Government departments argued that their accountability for expenditure to Parliament meant that they had to maintain central control even if made by local authorities. In order to reduce the impact of this legal requirement to apply, the government started to introduce new approaches to circumvent these requirements. These included the insertion of a 'deal' culture across the whole of UK local government, with groups of local authorities in functional economic areas having direct programme and financial agreements with the UK government (HMG, 2014, 2019a, 2019b). Even for those services and matters that had previously been devolved in Scotland, Wales and Northern Ireland, deals between local authorities and HM Treasury bypassed or marginalised the devolved governments in practice (Waite et al, 2018). After a period of austerity, local authorities in the UK could not refuse the offer of funding for their areas even if it came with controlling strings of programme priorities and project selection. In addition to this, in England, the government inserted a new institutional layer through the creation of combined authorities that it could manage through 'devolution deals', without giving them any powers and while seconding and populating the staff of these combined authorities with former civil servants from central government departments (HMG, 2015, 2017). At the same time, the central government also sought to resurrect a regional government structure in England in readiness to take on a more interventionist role at sub-state level (May, 2019; HMG, 2019a).

A further policy strand also appeared to accompany austerity and this was the transfer of services or service delivery contracts to the third sector initially through the Big Society initiative and then by the effects of austerity at the local level (Lowndes and Pratchett, 2012). The third sector could be useful in offering an alternative model for contracting, providing these organisations with support and bringing them more under state control through contract dependency (Alcock, 2010). The principle of social value in procurement had been available for the GPA, GATS and SEM from the outset, but in the UK, there had been a consistent focus on the route that restricted contractor selection to lowest price tenders.

Public bodies in the UK appreciated that there was another procurement route available used by other EU member states. Eventually, after an EU review of procurement effects on the voluntary sector and SMEs (Pirvu and Clipici, 2016) the government introduced this through the 2012 Public Services (Social Value) Act. Outsourcing had started to take on a different character with a far wider range of suppliers now available and, in some cases, preferred to the private sector. At the same time, the effects of austerity meant that many local authorities had to close libraries and restrict or ration services to a smaller number of users. In response, a new community movement evolved, to manage libraries and other services directly rather than the services being lost. In some locations, this community movement was supported through the parish councils and neighbourhood fora established following the 2011 Localism Act to prepare neighbourhood plans (Layard, 2012).

The role of the third sector in EU competition law

The role of the third sector in outsourcing had always been recognised but the European Court of Justice (ECJ) found that it was legally permissible within the EU treaties to allow local and regional administrations to restrict procurement for services to social enterprises (Hervey, 1998; Anheier, 2002). This practice had already been used by some member states including Germany and the Netherlands, where there was a view that competition in public sector services had been misapplied through these mechanisms to the third sector organisations seeking to provide services (Evers, 2001; Burger et al, 2001, pp 81–2, quoted in Kendall, 2005, p 10). In other member states, there were also third sector organisations providing services within the state such as housing cooperatives in Sweden and this type of organisation played a considerable part in public service provision in Europe (Evers and Laville, 2004). Without some recognition of these differences, it was acknowledged that third sector organisations would be disadvantaged through the application of the GPA and GATS not least as the bipartite approach to liberalisation of the market did not reflect European practices for welfare-based economies. There were concerns in EU member states that without proper recognition of the third sector in providing public services, the structure of the economy would become binary rather than reflect the pluralism that was already there changing the nature of the state.

The European Commission (EC) started to consider the role of third sector organisations within the context of services of general economic interest (SGEI) that have a more restrictive approach to the application of public sector liberalisation rules. The EU *Governance* White Paper (CEC, 2001) included the role of the third sector as part of the newly introduced Open Method of Coordination with specific roles in policy areas such as dealing with unemployment through the establishment of social enterprises. They were also included in discussions concerning tackling social exclusion (Kendall, 2005). While not an issue in the public domain in the UK, Prime Minister Tony Blair was centrally involved in the preparations and scope of the EU's *Governance* White Paper (CEC, 2001), and the role of the third sector in matters such as unemployment and social inclusion was also central to his agenda. The national action plans for combatting social exclusion explicitly included third sector organisations (Cabinet Office, 2001). The EC also included services that were traditionally supplied by the third sector in some member states to the list of SGEI, including health.

Introducing public value into UK outsourcing

The role of the third sector was also emerging in the EU as a location for service provision as it extended its consideration into the organisations that supported civil society across the member states (Kendall and Anheier, 1999). The expansion of the role of charities and third sector organisations in the UK began in the early 2000s, in the context of EU discussions on governance, associating Labour's Third Way (Giddens, 2001) with the development of the third sector (Haugh and Kitson, 2007). Up to that point, many charities had provided services for local authorities or offered services that those in receipt of national and local funding could use, for example nurseries and childcare, meals on wheels, luncheon clubs and social care (Milbourne and Cushman, 2015). However, the development and inclusion of the third sector offered a different approach to the wider provision of public services characterised by the public/ private service provision and an approach to public service delivery that was more associated with societal values.

These third sector organisations could provide community support, jobs and innovation through social enterprises and support the development of social cohesion within communities and across borders. The added dimension of social purpose also made third sector organisations more attractive as alternative public service providers where the private sector was not welcomed and resisted. They were another means of ensuring that liberalisation was occurring in the public sector but this time with an associated social purpose. These social enterprises could have alternative business structures such as cooperatives, used for traditional organisations such as John Lewis and the Cooperative Society as well as smaller institutions and could be based on more traditional models but with an overall social objective.

The role of public value in public sector liberalisation was considered by the UK government. Research was undertaken by the Cabinet Office (Kelly et al, 2002) and the Work Foundation (Horner et al, 2006) during the Labour government. There had been criticisms voiced at the effects on procurement processes for these groups as a consequence of the implementation of EC Procurement Directive 96/71/EC that did not reflect the ECJ judgement about the role of the third sector in service delivery. The expansion of the introduction of the third sector into mainstream public sector contracting and delivery was finally implemented by a change in the EU Procurement Directive (2014/25/EUC2014) that had been developed in response to these criticisms. In the UK, preparation for the increased role for third sector bodies was started through the establishment of the Office of the Third Sector in 2008 (Alcock, 2010), although it was not transparently associated with the changes in procurement being considered in the EU. However, in its role of examining the needs and organisation of the third sector, the UK government was able to review what preparations would be needed when the revised EC Procurement Directive was eventually implemented as a policy orphan. The principle of public value was noted as emerging as a new policy narrative without much preparation (Benington, 2009; Talbot, 2009).

The Conservative response – the Big Society

The introduction of Cameron's Big Society initiative in 2010 was intended to alert communities and third sector organisations to opportunities to provide services under the terms of the then proposed revisions to the EU Public Sector Procurement Directive. As with the earlier implementation of public sector liberalisation agreements, a major policy shift was introduced with a change in government and cloaked in a policy narrative that was able to receive ideological endorsement by both partners in the Coalition government. It appealed to the Conservatives who wanted a small state and to the Liberal Democrats who favoured community engagement and delivery. This had also been a major narrative in the 2010 Conservative Party's general election campaign and made a bridge to a continuation of the Labour government's policies for public services (Griffiths, 2009). In Cameron's version, it was possible for the third sector to function without being directly reliant on funding from central government, as he stated had been the case under the preceding Labour government (Kisby, 2010), and to offer their services for free or under contract. This approach to small local state and dependence on the third sector was reinforced by the 2010 Spending Review, which indicated public sector budget cuts of 27 per cent (Lowndes and Pratchett, 2012).

By the time that the austerity agenda was introduced by the Coalition government and particularly the Chancellor of the Exchequer, Osborne, much of the 'efficiency' had already been squeezed out of local government (Hood and Himaz, 2017). However, this austerity agenda was considered to be more overtly political rather than in the pursuit of financial efficiencies (Bailey et al, 2015). Firstly, there was an objective to place the responsibility for financial cuts on public bodies, particularly local authorities, and on the previous Labour government rather than the Coalition government. Osborne had no intention of making good the deficit that remained in the public finances after the 2008 financial crisis through increasing taxation. Secondly, he wanted to reshape and reduce the state, with a focus away from public services, so that it had a smaller role. This small state objective espoused the principle that individuals should be more self-reliant and forced into work if the welfare state was reduced to a minimum. Thirdly, there was a joint approach between Osborne and the Secretary of State for Communities and Local Government, Eric Pickles, that local authorities should be cut adrift from central government funding and grants to become self-financing as they are in other countries (Curtis, 2011) but with no similar tax raising powers. Increasingly, Whitehall moved away from regarding local authorities as partners in government and the welfare state to being defined as a sector of the economy to be managed and controlled like any other. In central government, departments were expected to reduce expenditure and had more limited budgets with cuts passed on to agencies and third-party providers. However, budget reductions are always problematic where services have been contracted out, such as for care home places in local authorities, as these budget reductions could not be passed on to suppliers. These budget cuts placed existing contracts as a first call on public organisations' budgets and reduced funding available for all other services (NAO, 2016).

The responses of government departments and local authorities to austerity developed over time. Initially, the smaller 'salami slicing' cuts to local public services, which had been the traditional way of dealing with budget reductions, were used (Lowndes and McCaughie, 2013). However, it quickly became clear that the scale of the budget reductions and the length of time they were likely to be in operation would be much longer than had been the case hitherto and the worst in living memory (Bailey et al, 2015). This meant more drastic cuts had to be implemented including for youth services, libraries, children's services, community and leisure approaches. While some of these cuts had an immediate community response, such as the operation of libraries by volunteers (Casselden et al, 2019), other cuts to service provision, such as that for young people, have been considered as a source of increased knife crime (Davies, 2018).

The effects of austerity on local government services were significant (NAO, 2018c). As a consequence of lower budgets for services, some of the greatest effects were on lower paid council services such as social care. Here employment conditions were eroded, with many staff moved to zero-hours contracts and council contractors were accused of passing on travel costs, including time spent travelling between clients, to employees (Cunningham and James, 2014). Of those working in care homes, the majority were paid at the minimum wage and many had to take jobs in multiple care homes to earn enough to survive. This practice of using zero-hours contracts, together with no sick pay provision for these employees, was a major issue in the spread of COVID-19 in care homes in spring 2020 (Booth, 2020). Many care workers were attracted to the UK from less well-off parts of the EU or elsewhere such as the Philippines to undertake these low-paid jobs, which were difficult to fill from the UK labour market. These jobs provided a first step for these workers to gain qualifications and bring their families to live with them in the UK. The Brexit referendum in 2016 and the subsequent lack of guarantees of personal and employment status in the UK have meant that many employed in this way returned home. This left the care home sector with 110,000 vacancies at the time of the outbreak of COVID-19 in the UK in March 2020.

The emerging roles of public value in outsourcing

One of the issues that the public sector has faced in the use of mixed economy models for service provision is that of defining the role of the 'public' interest and how public value can be defined as an outcome from procurement (Benington, 2011). While public value has always been a core function of public administration, Moore (1995) proposed that public value could be created as a positive public policy through strategic management and as part of the public service ethos. The creation of public value through service design and delivery is a positive policy approach in the same way as outsourcing and represents a choice of how services are delivered (Wensley and Moore, 2011). There has also been a debate about what liberalisation of public services cannot provide (Sandel, 2012). One approach to this is to consider the inclusion of public value provisions in contract specifications that are then used as part of the tender evaluations.

Some public bodies are going beyond this to consider how public value can be enhanced by the definition and procurement of services using local people and institutional capacity to undertake this more directly. In this way, rather than offering ideological opposition to competition to run services and provide goods, it is attempting to harness this procurement to implement change and cumulative public good. It is also challenging the assumption that some goods and services will always be provided by the private sector. A further dimension of public value is what it brings to society as a whole. This can include the role of regulation (Héritier, 2001), the use of resources and the management of land uses (Kazepov, 2005). It supports research and development that can be a platform for further innovation and product development (Mazzucato, 2013). This approach argues that public involvement and investment is a necessary component of societal value (Benington, 2011) and extends beyond providing public services to society. A final consideration of public value is the responsibility of public bodies to provide emergency support if there is a disaster or environmental event that displaces people and businesses, disrupting the functioning of society. It is the public value of last resort.

While public value is created, much of it is unrecognised and its contribution is not connected to the wider benefits of the welfare state or public provision (Sandel, 2012). For the private sector, the public sector's role in the allocation of land uses or focus on air quality over private means of transport is an inconvenience and any attempt to overcome these apparent hurdles can add commercial value to development. On the other hand, businesses and residents that may occupy these spaces have transferred costs from the private to the public sector. The introduction of public value is broadly understood to be an alternative method of providing services through competition (Ferry et al, 2019). However, many of the same processes are used to define and manage services that are being delivered, even if organisations providing them differ. Where other public bodies and third sector organisations provide services using a public value model, they have to employ managers at market rates, provide a surplus to contribute back to the core objectives of their charity or organisation and operate in a way that can be measured and managed. If this is not the case, then the benefits that are expected will transfer into costs to the community.

Translating public value into social value

The Public Services (Social Value) Act 2012 was a belated recognition by the UK government that the procurement regulations of the GPA,

GATS and SEM allowed the provision of public services by using the principles of social value and applying them in tender specifications, appraisals and selection. The Act goes beyond this and incorporates the wellbeing principles in the 2000 Local Government Act and 'requires you to consider, at the preprocurement stage, how procurement could improve the social, economic and environmental well-being of the relevant area, and also to consider how in conducting the process of procurement, the commissioner might act with a view to securing that improvement' (DCMS, 2018, p 2). The Act is also administered under the 2015 Public Contract Regulations that are in turn the UK's incorporation of the EU Public Sector Procurement Directive 2014. As a directive, this requires that each member state put the content into force by an agreed date and within the context of its own legislative framework provided that the outcome is as the directive intends. The EU Public Sector Procurement Directive incorporated a number of changes that facilitate the move towards awarding contracts to SMEs and also to mutual and social enterprises.

The directive also introduced ways in which information could be provided to support contractors bidding across member state borders using electronic procurement methods, and previous poor performance could be used as a specific mechanism for excluding contractors from consideration in a tender bidding process. Social and environmental factors, including life cycle costing, can now be considered in specifications and tender selection processes. It is also possible to consider the relevant skills of the suppliers when selecting a contract. The Public Services (Social Value) Act 2012 can be used in a variety of ways including to reduce health inequalities (PHE, 2015). The Act Guidance for England outlines the ways in which social value can be included in a specification and tender including initial consultation, the design of the work to be undertaken within the contract, the tendering process and contract monitoring post-procurement. The guidance also provides examples of how the Act can be used in practice:

Social
- Employing a diverse workforce for the delivery of the service including the employment of veterans and service spouses/partners – see the Armed Forces Covenant
- Collaborating with the voluntary and community sector, including users involved in designing and delivering the service
- Monitoring labour standards through the supply chain
- Improving skills and access to digital technology
- Approaches that encourage wellbeing and mental health

Economic
- Job creation/employing from a local community or disadvantaged groups
- Training and development opportunities/creation of apprenticeships
- Opportunities for Small and Medium Enterprises (SMEs) including Voluntary, Community and Social Enterprises (VCSEs)
- Prompt payment through the supply chain
- Advertising subcontracting opportunities to diverse supply chain
- Creating a level playing field for UK steel producers – see CCS [Crown Commercial Service] guidance
- Enhancing the UK Growth Agenda

Environmental
- Water consumption management
- Environmental policy and prevention strategies
- Monitor greenhouse gas emissions
- Reduction in waste to landfill
- Heritage protection
- Carbon reduction or offsetting

(DCMS, 2018, p 3)

While there has been guidance about how to use the Public Services (Social Value) Act 2012 there is less evidence about how it has been done in practice. Some public bodies were using the existing provisions in procurement regulations to undertake a social value approach. Social value was more likely to be used in capital and construction projects and 80 per cent of councils considered the Act would provide them with more support for procurement that could help to tackle wider issues such as worklessness and environmental issues (Jackson and Harrison, 2013). The government undertook a review of the way in which the Act was operating, finding that, where it had been implemented, it was positive but that its use was small (Cabinet Office, 2015). The review found that this was due to a lack of knowledge about the Act in local authorities and housing associations (Opoku and Guthrie, 2018). To share their experience, some local authorities have set up procurement groups to support the commissioning of services using social value principles. These consortia have also generated consultancies to support local authorities and the public sector in their procurement processes including their wider approaches to restructuring and reforms.

The development of co-production

One method of delivering public value is through co-production (OECD, 2011). While the relationship between the public and private sectors is known as a joint venture and has a strong focus on financial risk sharing, the development of co-production forms contracts on the collaboration between public and third sector bodies at different levels of organisations from local communities to international charities and focuses on services rather than goods. Co-production can be through direct participation or through the community having a role in commissioning and contract management through feedback of delivery quality (Bovaird, 2007; Durose et al, 2017). Sorrentino et al (2018) suggest that co-production has three waves, which are primarily located in traditional principles and definitions of public administration. However, the third wave of co-production is located in practices of service delivery where staff employed by the public sector and those in the community are engaged directly together for delivery. An example of this is the Wigan Deal (Vize, 2019; Naylor and Wellings, 2019).

There are a range of issues that need to be considered in the process of co-production, which are primarily based on the determination of the form of production that is envisaged. Initially, there may be some contracting of roles in the community that might be defined more as services rather than production (Alford, 2011). This might be defined by the community in receipt of the proposed services and how they can be engaged in specifying what is required, including its scope and dimensions. This will be bounded by finance available from the public body responsible for the delivery of the service. As with all approaches to public engagement, there are choices about the mechanisms and means and the extent to which those engaging in the processes reflect the communities receiving the services. Some public bodies have started to establish citizens fora or assemblies (Ireland, Birmingham and France). The role of all such community opinion in the delivery of public services is highly contested, particularly by directly elected representatives who argue that it is their role to make decisions on behalf of the communities including on service delivery. Other forms of co-production can be more direct and concern delivery particularly to communities or individuals with special needs. These can be identified as opportunities to achieve greater focus on the services provided and satisfaction in its delivery (APSE, 2013). The Local Government Association (LGA) provides examples of where co-production is being used to support those with mental health challenges (LGA, 2016a) and a local coordination system where people are living with long-term conditions (LGA, 2016b).

Has contracting for services changed the third sector?

For third sector organisations, relationships have changed as service delivery opportunities within UK local government emerged as a response to the change in EU procurement law and austerity. As service delivery by third sector bodies extended to contracting, this began to affect the way in which they were organised and managed (Cunningham and James, 2014). It also changed some of the relationships between public and third sector bodies. Whereas the relationship between the local authorities as commissioners and third sector bodies as providers started in a joint commitment to support service users in more locally determined ways, with a move away from approaches more associated with private sector practices, the implementation of austerity has led to a more distinct focus on core contractual issues such as price and cost. There have also been failures in the development of local authority contract specifications for the third sector. Local authorities have had a tendency to replicate a private sector form of contract, reliant on price, rather than to use the opportunities afforded by social value contracts to embody public sector values and expected outcomes into the contracting process and its subsequent delivery (Murray, 2011). This became apparent at points of retendering for services, although third sector organisations had become dependent on public sector contracts to both employ people directly and use contract surpluses to support their wider charitable aims and objectives. This meant that third sector contractors were in a weaker position to renegotiate their contracts if they wished to bid to continue to run the service. If cuts in services were being made because of austerity, there would also be concerns about reputational damage to third sector bodies who also depended on wider public support and donations to keep their charitable activities running.

Third sector bodies were frequently left with stark choices of losing contracts or employing their staff on less supported contracts. However, at the same time, after 2010, third sector bodies were in receipt of fewer funds from local authorities to support their work and from the other methods of fund raising that they have traditionally used, for example donations and legacies. The pressures for survival have also led to third sector bodies merging or joining with others to increase their role, capacity and influence or to rebrand as social enterprises (Milbourne and Cushman, 2015). There have also been pressures on third sector organisation managements to behave more in a command and control manner that is more frequently described as the way in which private sector organisations operate.

Has this resulted in third sector bodies becoming hybrid organisations? Harris (2010) argues that this approach was already developing after 2000, with the Labour government's focus on partnerships and collaboration at the local level through local strategic partnerships. There had already been a concern to join up government both vertically and horizontally through governance scales and across sectors and bodies. This was a major feature to ensure that people and places did not fall down between governance cracks. She also argues that the narrative of public service brought third sector organisations into the delivery of government services, relying on their focus for community service but at the same time making them hybrid organisations that partly sit within all three sectors.

The introduction of a range of public value methods of delivering public services provide another mode of outsourcing that is not fully recognised. The services that are provided by the third sector, including other anchor institutions or cooperatives, are still not delivered in-house and carry with them all the issues and processes associated with outsourcing to the private sector. The public value model requires society to recognise these issues if third sector bodies are to be successful in meeting the core delivery requirements. Taking a public value approach can have a much broader set of benefits to local communities if some of the 'anchor institutions' spend is used locally. As Stoker (2006) demonstrates, this goes beyond the practices of competition that have developed since 1980. However, in reflecting on the role and development of public administration in the last ten years, public value could be seen as a return to the understanding of public administration rather than an addition to it. In the nineteenth century, the role of public administration was to support the economy and community of any city. As Chamberlain demonstrated, a prosperous economy requires a healthy and well-educated labour force that can access their jobs easily housed in healthy secure accommodation (Marsh, 2009). The introduction of individualistic and atomised values in society has transferred costs to individuals and reduced the responsibilities of the state. Communities are attempting to rebuild their places in ways that would have been expected when local government was established.

11

Taking Back Service Delivery

Introduction

After 40 years of liberalisation of the public sector in the UK, there are now signs that a more mixed economy may be emerging, particularly in local government (LGA, 2019). There are a number of reasons for this. The first is a philosophical and ethical argument about the nature of public service, why it differs from a commercial service and how the public sector has reacted in crises and the last resort. Such arguments have increased with every public crisis that has occurred in the last 40 years, from flooding, foot and mouth disease, public health to social care. The political public policy narrative of outsourcing to improve efficiency and effectiveness has not been demonstrated in experience (for example NAO, 2012, 2014a, 2015b, 2020b). Costs for external providers have been higher and their performance has been mixed as demonstrated in the probation service (Kirton and Guillaume, 2019; NAO, 2019a). The achievement of lower prices has been based on removing working safeguards for employees and pushing back the costs for those on zero-hours contracts to the state (Brinkley, 2013; Hopkins and Fairfoul, 2014), either for income support or for care home deaths (Pollock et al, 2020). The second reason is that some of the structures of the outsourcing apparatus have not prevented failures. Some outsourced services have been unable to maintain their contract delivery over longer periods of time – for example rail franchises (NAO, 2015b), hospital private finance initiatives (NAO, 2020b), the probation service (NAO, 2019a) and the management of COVID-19 (NAO, 2020d). The third reason is that most contracting arrangements have been inflexible and difficult to change when needed (Mennicken, 2013). The cost reductions and efficiencies promised as part of liberalisation have not been found in practice across all services, and where they have, they have not always been due to outsourcing but rather work redesign and reducing eligibility (Bovaird, 2016).

There has also been a significant change in the understanding of public bodies, about the ways in which the European Commission public procurement legislation works. The Government Procurement Agreement (GPA) and the General Agreement on Trade in Services (GATS) were never intended to remove all direct public service provision but to open an agreed amount of expenditure to the competition. Many EU member states argued successfully that this discriminated against third sector bodies working with the local state. In this chapter, the concession model for the provision of public services (Crown Commercial Service, 2016) used particularly by the French, but also by the Germans and Dutch, will be considered as a mechanism for the use of external contractors, without being defined as outsourcing (Farley and Pourbaix, 2015). The legal provision for awarding contracts on the basis of quality rather than price (Gorse and Sturges, 2017) has now been accepted into local government practice and is being used across a range of services in contracts to require access for local suppliers, training and providing support for disadvantaged groups. Finally, the provisions for subsidiarity in the 2009 Lisbon Treaty, translated in England through the 2011 Localism Act, has allowed local authorities a general power of competence and the potential to directly provide services using company structures.

The pressures to move away from contracted services have been accelerated by the imposition of public sector budget cuts and austerity as a form of small state public policy in the UK from 2010 onwards (Gamble, 2015). This has led organisations such as local authorities, affected by these financial cuts, not only to spend less but also to find ways of generating more secure income streams that will provide a basis for public services over the longer term (LGA, 2019). The use of local authority company structures and changing procurement approaches have been significant in these innovations. In some cases, local authorities have returned to being suppliers and selling their services to others – for energy, procurement and transport management. Local authorities are also working together directly rather than being in a contractor–supplier relationship with third parties (LGA, 2011, 2016c). By joining forces, through sharing staff, buildings, tenders, services and consultants, local authorities have been able to save money and supply third parties. Some local authorities now provide housing services including maintenance and cleaning for housing associations and the private sector. Other councils are managing housing for partners and public organisations and establishing architectural practices that are part public and part private that will undertake internal and external design and management of housing delivery (Morphet, 2021b).

All of this suggests that a more fundamental shift in liberalisation practices is underway in a new version of a mixed economy and welfare state (Sandel, 2012). The introduction of competition and outsourcing has challenged the way in which public services are delivered. More fundamentally, the failures of outsourcing have stimulated a reconsideration of the state's role in supporting the welfare of individuals, communities and the economy. Outsourcing has not disappeared but it is mutating into more varied forms of relationships between those commissioning services and those receiving them. In some cases, it is increasingly recognised that the state is the provider of choice, after experiments with other forms of delivery. Elsewhere, local authorities are acting as providers to meet gaps that the central state has left in its small state ethos or that the market is disinclined to fill. Much of what is being introduced now is similar to the way that local authorities were acting over 100 years ago in serving their local communities.

Flexibility of contracts

One of the key benefits in direct service delivery for any organisation is that the delivery methods and funding can be changed by internal management. Changes can be determined relatively quickly and specifications can increase or reduce requirements or be stopped entirely. This flexibility is important at times of change such as major emergencies, budget cuts or changes in political priorities for service delivery. Where services have been outsourced, these are almost fossilised for the contract period unless there are specific inclusions within the contract specification for agreeing change. The pre-contract period for negotiation in contracts between the public and private sector is regarded as significant (Demirel et al, 2017). This is where flexibilities for unforeseen changes in legislation or environmental regulations can be addressed. This issue of flexibility can also occur in public–private partnership contracts for managing infrastructure or in construction contracts. If performance is poor in direct delivery, then organisations can change the management, personnel or specification immediately. If outsourced contracts are terminated, then the commissioning organisation will have to pay compensation, even where performance has been poor (NAO, 2020b).

Incorporating flexibility to allow change in contract delivery has been addressed in some ways by using a concession contract (Farley and Pourbaix, 2015; Crown Commercial Service, 2016). This is like a traditional supply contract and similar to the delivery of services by direct employees. In concession contracts, the public body retains control and the contract can be managed as flexibly as with in-house staff. It is not defined as outsourcing or privatisation of a service and it is therefore less certain as to how the use of concession contracts might meet compliance within GPA, GATS and Single European Market legal frameworks. Concession contracts were being let outside these frameworks and relying on provisions of the Treaty on the Functioning of the European Union (1992). In an assessment of the use of concession contracts within the EU, it was found that there were 10,000 concession contracts in France in 2014 and over 800 in Germany (CEC, 2014). The EU introduced a formal framework for concession contracts (CEC, 2014/23/EU) after a period of uncertainty about their use. The new directive was to overcome what was considered to be a loophole in the EU competition and procurement framework but it retained the flexibility that concession contracts provided to public organisations by allowing changes within the contract up to 10 per cent of its value without renegotiation (Burnett, 2014). This directive was transposed into UK law as the Concession Contracts Act 2016 for England, Wales and Northern Ireland. What is significant about the role of concession contracts is that assets are retained by the public body. If the organisation with the concession does not make a profit from exploiting an asset, such as a car park, then there is no compensation paid by the public body providing the concession (Crown Commercial Service, 2016, para 7). Concession contracts have not been used much in the UK. However, the Williams review of the operation of the railway system is expected to recommend moving from a franchise to concession model for railway operation in the UK in the future (Shapps, 2020).

Emerging changes in direct public service delivery

As public bodies have faced a decade of austerity, this has been particularly significant in local government (NAO, 2018c). Local authorities have started to explore and share ways in which they can return to more direct delivery while deploying mechanisms that help to generate income to support their wider responsibilities and activities.

Municipal entrepreneurialism

One response to austerity has been a revival by local authorities of municipal entrepreneurialism. When local authorities were founded in the 1880s, local authorities increasingly developed their public services to support safe local communities and generate income to expand their activities (Chandler, 2001). This was through direct provision of services such as water, energy, telephony and other commercial ventures. It included the zoning and release of more development land so that the authorities could generate more income through property taxes, known as 'rates'. By the 1970s, councils were undertaking some commercial services, including for other councils such as collecting council tax, IT or laboratory services in public health. While local authorities developed these services in response to local needs, many have subsequently been removed by central government including those for utilities and public health. However, the introduction of the GPA meant that the government had to consider how these traded and jointly provided services were to be made subject to competition. The government's response was to restrict local authorities in bidding to run their own or other council services through the Local Government Act 1980. Some powers for local authorities to operate companies for economic development through restricted provisions were included in this Act but the type of authority running these at any scale – the metropolitan county councils – were abolished by the Margaret Thatcher government in 1986 and local authority engagement in companies largely came to an end.

The Localism Act 2011 sections 1–7 allowed a wider reintroduction of municipal trading. However, this was accompanied by the reduction in council budgets. Since then, the majority of English local authorities have established companies to support and deliver housing (Morphet and Clifford, 2020) and other services such as energy and social care. Local authorities have been criticised for using this approach as behaving within neoliberal frameworks (Beswick and Penny, 2018; Christophers, 2018). However, as Christophers (2019) argues, addressing austerity through progressive innovation and action is part of a different approach rather than being in the same neoliberal mould. In some councils, this investment has been a mechanism for placing capital funding and securing an income to support the viability of the council over an extended period of time. Here councils are acting as patient investors, with an eye on the longer term. Some have developed community interest companies that are the owners of the property assets that cannot be sold on and create an 'asset lock' (Thompson et al, 2020).

The pressure of austerity has encouraged local authorities to consider again what legal powers they have to manage their procurement but also to look at soft powers through more active cooperation with other local institutions through the return to municipal entrepreneurialism. Much of the stimulus for this revival has come from the Evergreen initiative in Cleveland, Ohio, which has its foundation in seeking economic regeneration through the engagement of the city's institutions. The principle of Evergreen is to anchor the expenditure of local institutions in their location. This approach reflects in nineteenth-century provincialism, where the town and its industries frequently worked as one to support the local economy and its people. While provincialism was most frequently seen in locations associated with one industry or company, it was an operating model until the 1940s when more strategic approaches to the location of industrial production were introduced in the UK through the Barlow report on the redistribution of industry (HMG, 1940), recognising that while industrial cities may now be in decline, they have an institutional legacy of organisations that remain there. This includes universities, hospitals, public agencies and headquarters of some companies.

The Evergreen initiative has identified ways that this legacy of anchor institutions can be used to support local innovation and use purchasing power to support social ends (Howard et al, 2010). In addition to the anchor institution legacy, Evergreen has focused on investment in public transport and key worker housing that enables the city to support innovative initiatives. Evergreen is an economic cooperative that was founded in 2007 and operates in the poorer parts of the city. Its method is to build the economy from the bottom up rather than depending on trickle-down effects from more mainstream private sector or government investment. By combining the use of public procurement budgets across the anchor institutions, Evergreen is finding ways where it can be a local supplier of goods and services and ensuring that the procurement framework includes local suppliers and training within the procurement specifications. This approach has now drawn in central government funding to support a cooperatives' programme. Replicability is also an important objective of Evergreen (Rowe et al, 2017). This approach is being taken up by other cities in the US and elsewhere to develop their own models, although these may need to be bespoke to specific local institutional culture and conditions.

Evergreen is focussing on developing a target number of new economy initiatives including worker-owned cooperatives. While it is not able to tackle globalisation, Evergreen is working within the UN's sustainable development goals adopted in 2015. The focus on producing and consuming locally also fits with these longer term environmental goals (Coppola, 2014). Some of the businesses that have been established provide local services such as laundry (Alperovitz et al, 2010) while others are developing local energy provision. While the individual cooperatives start small, they have the objective of being profitable and are part of the Evergreen Cooperative Corporation that has been established. The cooperatives depended initially on the support of local institutions for funding and customers and this was followed by national funding support (Rowe et al, 2017). However, there are issues that may need to be considered as to whether this constitutes state aid when it enters the procurement agenda.

The development of Evergreen was within a city where the anchor institutions had already recognised the necessity of working together. This may be an issue where the principles of provincialism have been lost and there is primarily a global focus. Even universities drawing a high proportion of students from their local areas are ranked in league tables that incorporate international research and engagement. For other anchor institutions, such as hospitals, large schools, colleges, housing associations and utilities, their focus may be local. The positive role that the Evergreen approach offers for local communities may be important to attract staff to their organisations and to retain them. The staff shortages in teaching and hospitals are related to the attractiveness of residential areas and will be associated with the quality of life on offer including crime rates, housing, schools, environmental standards, open space and access to the countryside. Poorer areas attract fewer professional staff who are more mobile. When there are overall shortages, then areas without these perceived quality of life benefits are at the bottom of the list in a country where there are institutional rather than national appointments for health and teaching as in other countries including Sweden and Germany. In locations that are not attractive to professional staff, public sector contractors are frequently used to make up the shortfall. These are more expensive for hospitals and schools than permanent appointments and do not contribute to the local capacity building of the place. This is particularly the case in services such as social care. Budget pressures have driven down pay and working conditions and there are always multiple vacancies for staff either in care homes or in delivering domiciliary services.

Some English local authorities have been exploring the potential of introducing an Evergreen model for their own area. Knowsley and Preston have started reviewing their procurement expenditure, which is not committed through existing contracts. This is described as 'influenceable spend' (Jackson and Harrison, 2013), which, in Knowsley's case, amounts to over £100m per annum. This approach incorporates the contractual apparatus of the Public Services (Social Value) Act 2012 and extended to being able to use local suppliers and specify staff training contracts. Quality of delivery becomes a determinant of the ways in which contract specification criteria are framed and then applied after a competitive bidding process. The approach adopted by Preston Council is now frequently described as 'the Preston model' (O'Neill, 2016; Manley, 2017) based on the Evergreen approach started in 2013 when Preston City

Council and the University of Central Lancashire began to work together. They started to identify the major institutions in their area, including the hospital and Lancashire County Council, that might be able to exercise both leadership and economic power if they worked together.

These local partnerships are not new and were particularly promoted by the Labour government in 2000 as Local Strategic Partnerships and through business-led Local Enterprise Partnerships introduced by the Coalition government in 2010. However, neither of these institutional structures harnessed the power of public bodies working together through the use of their core procurement budgets. As Manley states, 'The figures are impressive. In 2012/13, out of £750m spent on goods and services by six Anchor Institutions, 5% was spent in Preston and 39% in Lancashire as a whole. By 2016/17, out of £620m spent on goods and services by the same Anchor Institutions, 19% was spent in Preston and 81% in Lancashire as a whole' (2017, p 1). This was achieved by reviewing the expenditure of the six institutions and the location of their suppliers, which showed that 60 per cent of the suppliers were outside Lancashire and only 5 per cent of procurement was from suppliers in Preston (CLES, 2017; CLES and Preston City Council, 2019; Chakrabortty, 2018a).

Since their joint work on procurement has been established, more initiatives have been adopted. In 2017, the Preston Cooperative Development Network was created by the council and university working together (Cannon and Thorpe, 2020), using a Dragon's Den approach to offer funding (Chakrabortty, 2018b). The council has worked closely with a local planning and development company, Hive, to deliver the council's housing and regeneration projects. It has been considering establishing a local bank to provide small business loans and to become an energy provider (Sheffield, 2017). There is an increase in the focus of this approach as a method of dealing with the potential effects of Brexit on the city (Jones, 2020). As in the US, other UK local authorities are considering the Preston model to examine how it might be used or adapted for their own councils (Chakrabortty, 2018b). One of the key dimensions of the Preston model has been the increase in community participation and engagement (Jones, 2020). Other councils have also been trying this approach, such as Wigan. Here they have implemented the Wigan Deal, where the council and the community work in partnership with a focus on improving the lives of local people (Vize, 2019). This has involved thinking about how to use its resources and helping council staff think differently with the help of an anthropologist. The strength of the ability to manage health improvement while dealing with financial cuts has been derived through a different kind of partnership working between the council and the National Health Service, which has focused on communities as assets.

There is a different commissioning model in the Wigan Deal that has moved away from a traditional transactional approach to one where providers are regarded as partners (Naylor and Wellings, 2019) and can be considered as a form of co-production. There is support for the development of social enterprises that are meeting local needs, and organisations are incentivised to work together using commissioning and contract conditions. If suppliers do not work together with other partners, then their contracts are terminated quickly. Another innovative approach has been to bring together health service commissioners across a range of service providers in an Integrated Care Commissioning Committee, which will have control over a combined budget of £683m (consisting of a pooled budget of £327m plus an 'aligned' budget of £356m) (Naylor and Wellings, 2019, p 57). This is a similar model to that being developed in Preston with a focus on integrated procurement rather than local procurement. In both cases, there is a commitment to working together at the local level to get more from the available funding than could be achieved by acting separately.

Local authority shared services

Local authorities have also started to develop other ways of procuring services through joining together to be more efficient and effective. In some cases, this has meant local authorities coming together to share staff and, sometimes, chief executives. Rather than procure services from third parties, councils have developed models for working together first and then may go on to procure services with combined budgets to obtain better contract pricing. Where local authorities are seeking other councils for the purposes of service provision or bundling up joint procurement, the Local Government Association (LGA) has a shared service match making service that is supported by productivity expertise and shared service adviser capacity. These provide funding for local authorities who want to explore different ways of working together and delivering services. The LGA acknowledges that there are complex issues including governance that need to be addressed in the management of shared services. While there has been a focus on liberalising public services from successive governments, the 1972 Local Government Act, which has been in operation for a longer period than the GPA and GATS, remains in force. This Act provides legal powers for local authorities to delegate their service delivery to another council (s101) and to establish a joint committee with other councils to manage services that are delivered together (s102). There are other powers that can be used including allowing officers from one local authority to be managed by another (s75) and to pool and align budgets (2006 National Health Service Act s113).

The power to share officers has been used to appoint joint chief executives between local authorities (LGA, 2012). South Hams and West Devon Councils have taken an 'organic' approach to sharing services, starting with the chief executive and continuing to legal services, revenues and benefits, HR and environmental health. In these cases, the councils retain their own decision-making processes and standards that are supported by the same group of staff. Three local authorities have established East Kent Services using the joint committee powers that will manage a range of back office services in the three councils. Similar approaches have been adopted by Wandsworth and Richmond upon Thames in London and Adur and Worthing, which demonstrates that these models can be used across different locations and sizes of authorities. In some cases, the sharing of staff has led to a merging of the decision making of two authorities as in Suffolk, where two new councils – East Suffolk and West Suffolk – were created in 2019, each by two councils joining together. In Dorset this has been developed into a further step where the county council, two unitary councils and remaining districts merged to become two unitary councils in 2019.

In addition to procuring services from third-party companies, local authorities can create their own single or joint companies to deliver their services. These company structures can provide tax benefits for local authorities that can be returned into supporting their services. Where local authorities have established companies for service delivery, it is possible for them to purchase services from their own companies using an EU exemption from EU procurement regulations known as Teckal. This exemption from competition in procurement is 'heavily circumscribed' (LGA, 2011, p 33) and resembles a concession model, where the council retains the responsibility for the service that its own wholly owned company is providing and the company must be principally providing services to the local authorities that own it (Trybus, 2010). The Teckal exemption cannot be applied where there is private sector benefit in the contract. Where local authorities jointly own a company that is supplying services to them, following a UK legal case in 2011, it has been established that joint or consortia governance arrangements are the same exercise in control over services as a single council (LGA, 2011). There are examples of where local authorities have joined together to create a company to provide them with services such as South Holland and South Lindsey, which have created Compass Point Business Services Ltd to provide back office services including IT for the two councils. The councils can give work to their company without going through procurement using the

Teckal exemption and can provide services for other local authorities, provided that this does not exceed 15 per cent of its total turnover.

Some councils have used private sector models to characterise the way in which they operate and provide services. Barnet Council has described its model as 'easyJet' or 'easyCouncil' when the services provided are basic and every additional service has to be paid for (Jones and Booth, 2009). The council has also entered into a strategic partnering arrangement with Capita where the service company has employed all the staff in a specific department such as planning and development. This model was developed as an alternative to the Labour government's approach to local government by a Conservative council before the 2010 general election. The Barnet outsource model was challenged through the courts on the basis that there was no consultation. In 2013, the High Court found that the challenge had come too late (Booth, 2013). A second approach has emerged in contrast with this and is described as the John Lewis model (Stratton, 2010). This has been adopted in LB Lambeth and the role of the John Lewis Partnership, as a mutual organisation that is owned by all its staff as partner members, was seen as a model for partnership working in the borough. Barnet Council has continued to outsource some its services to Capita and other providers but more recently has retained services in-house. The Lambeth model has been described as a post-political attempt to find new ways of working with residents (Penny, 2017, 2018) and may have more in common with the Wigan Deal.

Local authority direct provision of housing

Local authorities have been providing housing in a range of ways since their establishment in the late 1880s. For much of this time, councils have been providing social housing to improve public health as part of economic policy, on the model initially implemented by Chamberlain in Birmingham (Marsh, 2009). Much of the development of social housing has been funded or subsidised by central government, although it has been regarded as a local authority service. In this way, local government could be said to have been commissioned to provide this social housing as part of central government delivery of the welfare state both in its post-1909 and in its post-1945 forms. In the 1950s, as part of post-war economic construction, in addition to the government-led New Town programme, local authorities were providing housing in this way by using direct delivery or increasingly through contracted services from major building companies, many of which have now become national housing developers. By the end of the 1960s, there were public concerns about the scale of demolition of homes without their immediate replacement or dissatisfaction with the high-rise blocks that were built. There were also concerns about close knit community breakdown. The final pressure to change the quantity of this provision occurred in the mid-1970s when the twin pressures of the UK's International Monetary Fund (IMF) crisis and the advent of the negotiations on the GATT GPA, which were agreed in principle by the UK cabinet in 1976 and implemented in 1980. The removal of direct public service provision was one of the conditions of the UK's IMF bailout so these international agreements were in alignment. Thatcher's 1979 election manifesto did not include references to outsourcing or privatisation but did make a commitment to give council house tenants the right to buy their homes at discounted rates. This changed the nature of public housing, as despite numerous political commitments over time, those properties sold were never replaced and the social housing stock dwindled. Local authorities were also encouraged to sell their stock through transfer to other bodies, particularly existing or newly established housing associations. By 2019, 52 per cent of local authorities had no ability to use the legal mechanisms and government funding available to build social housing.

This change in housing policy marked a distinct shift away from the partnership between central and local government in providing the welfare state. The focus has increasingly been on the private sector through loosening mortgage availability and shifting the attention to home ownership. Housing associations were expanded to provide more rental tenure types, and in the 2010s, the Coalition government created fiscal opportunities that supported the small-scale acquisition of properties to create a buy to let market. This new market enabled individuals to create income streams and pension pots and much of the former local authority housing stock to return to the rental market. In the same period the opportunities to purchase homes by first time buyers became more difficult, particularly after the 2008 financial crisis and specific government incentives, such as the Help to Buy scheme, were introduced. As the rental market expanded and became the only housing available to those in their thirties, who would have been in home ownership in the past, rents increased and the lack of safeguards for tenants led to landlord terminating leases in order to increase rental yields.

After 2010, local authorities in England were faced with austerity that could not be met as before, with most services being reduced considerably over previous years (NAO, 2018c). Local authorities were facing increased duties for supporting those who were homeless through the 2017 Homelessness Reduction Act, regardless of whether they had any retained housing stock. Many councils were having to provide housing for homeless people outside their local authority area and many were using offices and factories recently converted to housing following a suspension of planning regulations (Ferm et al, 2020). While local authorities were facing these increasing housing pressures, from 2016, central government was distracted by Brexit and the government introduced White (2017) and Green (2018) Papers on the future of housing, the expected associated policy shifts did not occur. Faced with these concerns and an absence of government intervention into local authority activities, local authorities started to investigate and then implement a range of ways in which they could return to provide housing (Morphet, 2016).

In reviewing the ways in which local authorities have returned to providing housing, it is possible to see that a range of approaches have been used within existing individual council cultures. However, by 2019, 78 per cent of English local authorities had created housing, property and development companies (Morphet and Clifford, 2020). These companies have been established using a range of specific powers including for owning and developing all types of land and buildings, beginning with the 1963 Local Authorities (land) Act and then using the 2011 Localism Act that enabled them to establish companies in the same way as the private sector. The companies are being used for a range of purposes and many councils have established more than one company; 57 per cent of councils have joint venture companies with private sector partners, housing associations or other local authorities. These can range from major agreements to developing housing and other facilities such as schools and leisure centres as in Slough or to facilitate the development of a single small development as in Northern Lancashire. Some councils have companies that have been set up to purchase housing on the secondary market through estate agents, frequently to provide for homelessness, while others have been making strategic purchases of their former housing stock where the council is considering some major redevelopment in the future. Councils have set up companies for housing management and development, for private letting and for specific need groups (Morphet and Clifford, 2020).

The growth in the use of housing companies in local authorities has been fast and significant although not all companies have started to develop housing, as it takes at least two years between the legal establishment of the company and the first actions on development sites. This takes four years for a joint venture including due diligence. Local authorities are motivated to engage in direct delivery of housing for several reasons. The first is that they provide income that can be used to cross-subsidise council services and this freedom is greater than is provided through the government's housing measures. Councils also want to meet homelessness in a way that is both more beneficial to households and less costly to their budgets. The LGA estimates that more than £1bn is spent each year on homelessness by English councils. Where local authorities own their own housing, they hold an asset, receive rent and can provide better quality accommodation.

A further motivation for engaging in housing development has been the failure of the planning system to provide an adequate range and type of housing (Morphet and Clifford, 2020). Since 2010, the government has increasingly put pressure on local authorities to release more land for private sector housing through the planning system although this system does not allow land to be provided and protected for other housing tenures (DCLG, 2012; MHCLG, 2019). Social housing is expected to be provided by developers through planning gain, which is achieved through negotiation as part of a planning consent. The Community Infrastructure Levy (CIL) system, introduced in 2008, does not include housing as one of the ways in which this tax can be used. Despite housing developer profits increasing since 2008 (NAO, 2018c) there has been increased pressure on local authorities by housing developers to renegotiate these contributions downwards after planning consent has been given, thus reducing the number of affordable homes available. In response, local authorities have been developing housing directly. Councils have the powers to build housing without establishing a housing company but many use a company to provide tax benefits. Although local authorities cannot provide social rent homes through these delivery methods, it is possible to cross-subsidise rents within the developments and any low cost rented homes are then not subject to right to buy legislation.

In developing housing through their own companies, some local authorities have used social value procurement to ensure that contracts provide for apprenticeships and other training while other councils have used the Teckal provisions. Increasingly, local authorities have further expanded their delivery methods as they become more confident, and although many of the housing development skills have been lost since the 1980s, councils are finding ways of employing development surveyors and other professionals (Morphet and Clifford, 2020). Some local authorities are beginning to operate as patient investors, purchasing land with a view to its development in future decades. Others are working with the community or establishing their own community interest companies.

Local authority direct provision of energy

As with the provision of housing, local authorities have been energy providers throughout their modern history. Unlike housing, however, their role in the provision of energy was not at the government's behest but through both the need to provide energy locally and to generate income to use to operate other council services. Local authorities lost their interests in energy provision in 1948 when major energy providers were created through nationalisation. Energy remained in state hands until it was successively sold off through privatisation processes in the late 1980s, which separated the organisations generating supply and the consumer sale of energy (Parker, 2009, 2012). The National Grid, which is used to transmit supply, was also privatised. All these energy providers are services of general interest and are subject to the regulators that are concerned with the security of supply, prices charged to the consumer, maintenance and investment in new supply to support national interests. Since this system was introduced, it has been more resistant to changes to develop methods of supply and the need to provide energy in more sustainable ways. In response local authorities have started to open energy services companies to serve local authority properties (Roelich and Bale, 2015). Local authorities have also provided energy through combined heat and power systems, although this approach has not been more widely expanded. Woking BC has provided energy supply through its Thamesway project. These ideas have been taken up by other councils like the GLA, which have sought to purchase energy on a larger scale so that it can be sold at lower prices to consumers.

In returning to energy supply, local authorities have had a range of motivations that are not unlike those cited by councils returning to housing provision. These have included addressing fuel poverty, reducing carbon emissions, and improving air quality and economic motivations to create more jobs and generate more income. Other councils are using their energy initiatives to save expenditure. Local authorities have also expressed an interest in taking on the governance and ownership of energy supplies in their area. In progressing the direct provision of energy, local authorities are embarking on a number of approaches and models. The West Midlands Combined Authority has been funded by the government to develop smart energy projects using carbon neutral technologies, while Islington is converting waste into heat. Other councils, such as Exeter and Bristol, are ensuring that all homes built in their areas are energy efficient and some councils are directly building passive homes to reduce energy requirements to a minimum.

Another way in which energy has been supplied is through the creation of community interest companies (CIC), which have also been used as part of the portfolio approach to companies created by local authorities providing housing. CIC have often been created with local developers interested in providing local energy on a shared ownership basis (Saintier, 2017). This is a popular approach as there frequently exists shared experience of working together. In some of these cases a community organisation is the partner, and these organisations may have different relationships with and support of local authorities. There are only two local authority registered energy supplier companies: Bristol Energy and Nottingham's Robin Hood Energy (Vaughan, 2018), while some councils have created consortia to purchase energy, ranging between two and eighty members. These consortia are generating and supplying energy. More recent moves have been supported by councils responding to austerity and finding ways of controlling their fixed costs directly rather than through intermediate suppliers (LGA, 2019). Some councils, including Portsmouth, have not proceeded with plans to establish an energy company.

12

Conclusions

Introduction

In this concluding chapter, the major questions that arise from over 40 years of public sector liberalisation and consequent outsourcing are considered. As this book has demonstrated, the UK response to the implementation of the opening of competition across the public sector has been undertaken in a number of waves while some of the institutional restructuring in central government has been used as a mechanism to delay or prevent the introduction of any competition or external provision. Where outsourcing has been a method deployed by central government, it has been on the assumption that the operational practices required for external service delivery based on contracts and legal agreements do not apply and that control is still from the commissioning department. We have also noted that some of the attempts to apply liberalisation have not been successful and the government has had to take back major health and transport infrastructure projects to manage directly at financial and social cost to the country (NAO, 2020b; DfT, 2020). We have also noted that this detachment of the civil service from operational management has reduced its capacity to specify and manage contracts and to cope in a crisis (Dunhill and Syal, 2020). As the government's response to the COVID-19 pandemic demonstrates, it no longer appears to know which levers to pull and have turned to personal and political contacts to fill these gaps (NAO, 2020g).

At the same time, local government has managed to adapt to a mixed economy, to move services in and out of contracted delivery. The introduction of austerity in 2010 has allowed local authorities to develop and innovate further to include different forms of service provision working with each other and the community and to rediscover its role in providing housing both to meet needs and to generate income (Morphet and Clifford, 2020). For the National Health Service and education, there has been some liberalisation, although again this has not been wholly successful. In education, the introduction of free schools and academies has detached the ownership of outcomes from local authorities while they remain responsible to the government for school performance. Some free schools have failed and many academy schools have not improved outcomes for their children. Universities are now established as hybrid economies but when there are major shocks to the system, such as COVID-19, they may be less resilient to cope with such scale of financial change and need to revert to state support. In health, the failure of Carillion has led to two communities without new hospitals for a long period of time and at greater cost to the public purse. Core health functions in secondary care have been shielded against liberalisation, partly because there is already a private health care system in operation in the UK. The core executive has achieved these changes, in part, through the application of statecraft and policy metanarratives. It has optimised the change in Prime Ministers throughout the period, to reset these policy narratives as required to meet international agreements. Finally, it has used these external international agreements, the Government Procurement Agreement (GPA) and General Agreement on Trade in Services (GATS), to implement significant institutional changes within the state.

These are the responses to liberalisation in public institutions, but what have been the effects of these changes for the state as a whole? The failure of successive governments to discuss the effects of international trade agreements for these public services has led to a range of theories and explanations being projected on to these actions – whether privatisation by Margaret Thatcher or New Public Management by Tony Blair. This lack of transparency may be similar to that in other countries but the application of liberalisation has also been managed differently, where there has been a slower level of application, the inclusion of public value criteria in tender specification and more control of the transfer of public assets into international organisations. In other countries, there has also been more state control of its application. How has liberalisation and subsequent outsourcing changed the UK state, in perception and reality, and how have some parts of the state reformed in response? How do these changes differ from what might have occurred without liberalisation or if a more European model had been applied in the UK? Is the UK public sector turning towards more public value in procurement and the creation of an actively mixed economy? This chapter discusses these issues.

Was neoliberalism the driving force of the liberalisation of the public sector?

While it is assumed that it was Thatcher's neoliberalism that introduced competition into the public sector in the UK, as we have seen earlier, the inclusion of competition in public services was an effect of neoliberalism that started much earlier, in the mid-1950s. In some ways, the expectation that the market would return to manage contracts and services operated by the public sector through nationalisation or housebuilding was always recorded as a short-term response to the post-war economy. However, the approach in the UK was more ideological than in other countries and the use of statecraft enabled Whitehall to make major changes in the ways in which the state was operated and managed. As Mount (2020a) sets out, the public sector and the welfare state has always been considered as enemies of the Conservative Party's philosophy post-1945 and each successive Conservative government has sought to undermine its position as a central tenet of policy, including that of the Johnson government from 2019 onwards (Mount, 2020b).

What has been the impact of outsourcing on government policies and practices?

While there has been considerable debate about the practices of outsourcing and its impact on public services, it is also important to consider what impacts it has had on government policies and practices. The processes of outsourcing have distanced the central state from both the use of the budgets that they control and the ability to move quickly where services have been contracted out for long periods. This distance is said to be one of the motivations for processes that are at work to recentralise the state (Dahlström et al, 2011). While agencification has been a mechanism to decentralise but retain control (Audet, 2002), the UK's Parliamentary system has created accountability challenges for government departments who have control over budgets but consider that they have less control over delivery. This is an effect of management practices, specifications and contract management (Dahlström et al, 2016) rather than the legal position where the public sector is always accountable for the delivery of its responsibilities regardless of who is contracted to provide them. A second pressure to take back control at the centre is the extent to which services are perceived to be fragmented and different, thus creating confusion for the public. This was a major dilemma of the Labour government during 1997–2010, which wanted to decentralise decision making but also wanted to ensure standards of delivery (Smith, 2011). Since 2010, there has been a focus on re-centralising the state (De Vries, 2010) which Brexit is accelerating (Ward, 2020; Morphet, 2021a).

There has also been a vacuum in the span of control in central government and a potential to cast around for more power to fill it (Dahlström et al, 2011). This has had a significant impact on central–local relations. In the past, a strong centre for local government had been created through the Local Government Associations and the professional bodies that primarily operated within local authority services (Rhodes, 2018). These relationships have now dwindled as central departments have become more politicised through their advisors (Dahlström et al, 2011) and through lobbying pressures placed upon them by private sector providers and consultants. By 2020, the government has reduced its commitment to local decentralisation, creating Combined Authorities that are *sui generis* grant coalitions (Sandford, 2017) but not local authorities. Instead local authorities appear to be viewed as a collection of privatised services with a small rump of activity in areas such as planning that can be centrally controlled with little local discretion.

EU versus World Trade Organization

Was there any indication that the UK preferred the implementation of the World Trade Organization agreements to open up the public sector liberalisation in comparison with the Single European Market (SEM) approach, creating the framework of an EU-wide welfare state (Morphet, 2021b)? The implementation of the GPA and GATS appeared to be more aligned to successive Conservative government ideology. The narratives required to support their implementation, through both the privatisation agenda and subsequently John Major's Citizen's Charter approach, were easier to align with outsourcing. Within the WTO negotiations, as a founder member of the GATT, the UK could take an individual approach and consider that it had more soft power in the negotiations. It could influence negotiations directly through its longstanding international networks. When negotiating within the EU and between the EU and WTO, the UK had to learn to operate within a hierarchy, where other, longstanding member states had more influential voices. Although the UK was a powerful member of the EU as one its largest economies, it would also need to negotiate with France and Germany and find 'trade offs' for its preferred outcomes within the framework established through the member states (Meunier, 2005). Also, within the EU, size of the UK's economy did not always carry influence and the foundation member states had a commitment to each other that could override other considerations. The UK had been traditionally a colonial power, using its own hierarchy to manage its control and influence both directly over its territories and through international organisations. In the EU, the UK could no longer pull these levers in the same way. Even having its own Commissioner developing the EU's SEM did not create the sense of ownership that Jacques Delors, then President of the EU Commission, had hoped would be the outcome (Cockfield, 1994).

The application of the WTO agreements also allowed the UK civil service to put into effect the agreements in ways that would permit it to justify significant changes in the institutions that were part of the state but not part of the UK constitution such as local government. It understood the power of local government that had been growing since 1945 and Whitehall wanted to detach public support for it through establishing a contracting environment (Mount, 2020a). By introducing the right to buy for council houses, central government took the lead in obtaining public support for this policy area, taking away one of the key services of local government. Local and central governments had been partners in delivering the welfare state for nearly 100 years but public service liberalisation was used to break this relationship. Local government became as detached as the peripheralised agencies introduced to manage outsourcing in Whitehall and, like them, was managed as remaining under central control.

Why has statecraft been used to implement the UK's international liberalisation agreements?

The use of statecraft since the early 1970s in preparing and delivering this public sector liberalisation agenda had been considerable. In applying this approach, the central state has been able to control the narrative, the programme of delivery of the agreements, and also to use the commitments made by the UK to implement other forms of institutional change. Within central government, the position has been different. Here the civil service has sought to manage a change agenda through the reform of its internal structure towards more quango and non-departmental government bodies. However, in introducing this arm's length practice of institutional reform, central government departments have sought to maintain the same degree of control as was present when the services were managed directly. As noted in the prison service and by the Organisation for Economic Co-operation and Development (OECD), the civil service did not manage the outsourced or agency-wide services in a strong way and continued in the same way as before

(Audet, 2003). When outsourcing has gone wrong, the government has had to bring projects and services back into direct management, such as the probation service, the rail franchises and the failed Carillion private finance initiative (PFI) hospital projects, to a much greater public cost. The centre of government has used statecraft to increase its grip and control of agencies, public bodies and local government while giving the appearance of devolution, decentralisation and outsourcing. Those government activities that have managed outsourcing more effectively have been those operating at some distance from London such as the Driver and Vehicle Licensing Agency (DVLA). Hoverer, this is not true in every case as one of the continuing failed services of the Rural Payments Agency in the North East demonstrates (NAO, 2009).

In assessing why statecraft has been used as a mechanism to implement public service liberalisation, we have noted that it has allowed the centre to retain power and manage the flow of events and responses. However, there may also be a deeper set of issues and these relate to the sense that, in using this approach, the UK has of being in control of its own destiny. This was a strong message during the 2016 Brexit referendum debate and subsequent processes of negotiation for detachment. As the UK government negotiates separation from the EU, in order to be in charge of its own decisions a new policy narrative that can include the UK delivering on international agreements will be required. While the WTO agreements could have been made more transparent in the 1970s as they were in the US, the negotiations and then the adoption of the GPA were undertaken in a parallel process with the UK which transferred some of the leadership of its own responsibilities for negotiations to the EU with the WTO to the EU. This was then allied to the development of the SEM in 1985. Despite the SEM formation being led by a former UK Minister of State, the SEM has always been characterised as the UK being 'told' what to do by Brussels. However, statecraft is the *modus operandi* of the UK civil service and Whitehall's ability to control agendas through the work within the Cabinet Office and Treasury, including creating narratives of reform for other government departments as well as other parts of the state, has become an endemic operational practice.

Has there been an increase in corruption in public office?

While the UK has a record for one of the least corrupt countries in the world, one of the issues when there is more contracting will be the potential opportunities for corruption. This can be for a number of reasons and in a variety of ways. Firstly, the size of the contracts for public services can be significant and operate for periods of 5 to 15 years. The potential loss of a contract to a service provider will be a considerable risk not least as the costs of tendering for such bids can exceed more than £1m each time. Secondly, the relationships between the client and contractor can become well managed and neither side wishes to see any disruptive changes in this through a retendering process. Thirdly, there can be agreements or cartels between contractors to share out the work between them. This is managed through informal agreements on price to ensure that contracts are won by particular suppliers. Contract sizes can also be the subject of packaging so that an external contracting process is obviated as individual contract sizes are small despite them making up one major contract all together.

There can be corrupt practices in determining what will be outsourced, how it will be specified and the length of contracts. There can be considerable influence on government policy makers about these issues, which make contracts more attractive to the private sector and the scale of profit that can be achieved. The creation of larger long-term contracts has a more beneficial effect on share prices for those who win them. In local government there was an attempt to bring together local authorities to share services and create larger packages of work to make them more attractive to the private sector. In terms of direct payments in return for awarding contracts, this is more complex to achieve as a mechanism of corruption. Financial audit processes are in place that make this difficult although public officials and councils have been prosecuted for taking bribes or awarding contracts to specific parties known to them (Dávid-Barrett and Fazekas, 2019).

The informal side of corruption is undertaken through a range of social events where clients including councillors and officers can be entertained at sports and cultural events. These may be at some distance from a tendering exercise and therefore be outside any specific privatisation but can create informal and positive personal relationships. Some contractors recruit leading staff from central and local government. These former officials may have short contract bans before they can join these companies, but once there, they may have extensive contracts within the client organisation and may also provide confidence in and credibility to that contractor within the sector (David-Barrett, 2011).

The issue of the integrity of procurement has emerged as part of the government's management of the COVID-19 pandemic in 2020. Here, some contracts for personal protective equipment and track and trace have been issued to companies that are known to be donors of the Conservative Party (Geoghan, 2020). There have also been concerns about the appointment of two Conservative supporters to run the vaccine task force and the successor to Public Health England without any formal recruitment process. The Runneymede Trust together with the Good Law Project has issued proceedings against the government on this issue (Smulian, 2020). The Commissioner for the government's public appointments board, Peter Riddell, has also warned about the increasing influence of politics in public appointments (Dunton, 2020), while chairman of the Committee on standards in public life has used a lecture in November 2020 to ask if we are now in a 'post Nolan age', and asks if the culture of government has now significantly changed away from the standards that have been used for over 20 years (Nolan, 1995; Evans, 2020). The NAO has investigated the government's approach to managing procurement within the response to the COVID-19 pandemic , finding that the government established a 'fast lane' for suppliers recommended by members of the Conservative Party, with contracts being awarded to them without the usual procurement checks (NAO, 2020g). In his speech to the Conservative Party Conference in 2020, the Prime Minister stated that the future for public services was private sector delivery (Johnson, 2020), so the government's approach to COVID-19 may give an indication of what is to come.

What has been learned about the introduction of outsourcing into public services in the UK?

There have been several lessons arising from the introduction of public sector liberalisation and outsourcing, although not all of them have been learned and failures continue. While local authorities have managed to accommodate and develop a mixed economy that has evolved to apply social value principles, central government departments continue to repeat mistakes and reinvent methods of outsourcing while retaining central control. This state-led approach has been more successful in other EU member states where this has been achieved through social value specifications rather than lowest price contracting. The rhetoric of lowest price contracts has cost the UK in many ways and continues to be a charge on taxpayers. The failures of the central government's COVID-19 contracts for ventilators, Personal Protective Equipment (PPE), testing, tracking and provision of meals to shielded individuals all demonstrate this (Monbiot, 2020). The local systems led by primary care, local authorities and voluntary bodies, which have been used for every crisis hitherto, were ignored from the outset in dealing with the pandemic.

However, it is possible to set out the effects that the introduction of outsourcing has engendered in the UK state:

1. The government has managed to introduce competition into all the various types of public services that were not outsourced at the time the GPA and GATS were adopted;
2. There has been a variation in the levels of success in the introduction of the private sector into these services. In central government, the early privatisation of utilities was initially seen to be managed better but there have been subsequent problems including market narrowing, profits and offshore dividends;
3. In some services, where privatisation has been an alternative to improving management, the level of service provision has been poor and the political priorities have been locked into contracts such as the Home Office's 'compliant environment';
4. Central government services have been cheaper to operate in some cases but this has largely been the outcome of service redesign or reducing eligibility of users;
5. There does not seem to be much evidence that embedding professionals such as finance directors on central government departmental boards has changed the core culture of civil service control of contracts;
6. Some central government services appear to have been made more efficient through agencification without privatisation, for example DVLA;
7. In local government, the initiatives to aggregate the market for private sector service partnership contracts do not appear to have been successful and most have been closed or ended in the courts;
8. Joint ventures between local government and private sector partners appear to have been more successful although not all local authorities use them;
9. Where outsourcing of a well-run service has been successful, it has been in finance and revenues, although these contracts are also frequently returned in-house after a period of being outsourced, for example civil service pensions;
10. Some local authority service outsourcing has been more successful than others, for example waste collection, whereas others including social care have relied on liberalised employment practices;
11. Some organisations have developed hybrid approaches to outsourcing, for example housing management, using different approaches to utilise their strengths;
12. Local authorities have accommodated these changes better than larger central government bodies in part because of levels of local scrutiny by the press, social media and councillors – particularly in local authorities where elections are held three in every four years.

What roles has competition played in the provision of public services?

Through the use of statecraft, the metanarratives of public sector liberalisation have become mantras of governments prompting change. These tropes have been used in an unthinking way and been used as synecdoche, without explaining or understanding their underlying drivers. The introduction of liberalisation has driven wider scale state rescaling and institutional change than might otherwise have been the case, as exemplified in these countries. At the same time, these metanarratives have diverted attention away from the UK's international agreements and the wider opportunities within them for their application. The use of 'lowest price' contract selection still pervades many of UK central government contract awards while the level of successful contract operation has not improved. Most of the public crises facing governments are connected with contracted services as these are where the people meet the government's intentions face to face. These include passport management, Grenfell Tower, Windrush, COVID-19, rail franchises, Transport for London, PFI failures and free schools.

In the last 40 years it has been possible to see the introduction of competition and outsourcing in public services as a signal for change. In order to obtain the support of public opinion for outsourcing, the government has had to undermine and denigrate existing services to make the case for change using the policy narratives of efficiency, effectiveness, modernisation and austerity. These metanarratives have been used to undermine public confidence in the existing institutions of the state. At the same time, these changes have been accompanied by reductions in service entitlement, which has meant those reliant on services that have been subject to change are fearful of what this will mean for them. For vulnerable people, much of this change has been accompanied by reductions in hours of treatment and attendance and with poorer employment conditions. Despite these public institutions being undermined through attacks on public trust as a prelude to outsourcing, citizens have not seen the changes that have been promised for efficiency and effectiveness in the longer run. They have experienced more degradation in their services as budgets have been cut. Citizens do not wish to be addressed as customers or clients and want older values of public service to be reinstated. This was illustrated through the 'clap for carers' that occurred during the COVID-19 pandemic in 2020.

In local government, competition has been a mechanism to secure compliance to state-led changes. This has included using liberalisation to remove services, responsibilities and budgets while ensuring that local politicians are held responsible for these central state choices. Local government in the UK has fewer powers than any OECD country and is more reliant on central government funding. By reducing the core funding available to local authorities, central government has made them more reliant on bids and discretionary government 'deal' funding, which is only paid where local authorities are compliant in adopting the central government-chosen programmes that are handcuffed to them. Yet local government has proved to be resilient and innovative in responding to this scale of change. Local authorities have found ways of managing change.

The introduction of public sector liberalisation in the UK has also generated a range of market making in different areas of former public provision. These include the development of programme production companies and channels within the broadcast media and some choice in the provision of services of general interest. However, there remain issues about consumer choice, market restrictions and transparency that have become more difficult to challenge with practices such as transfer pricing and offshore registration for companies supplying public goods. While the COVID-19 pandemic introduced a range of subsidies for companies to assist their survival over the lockdown period, it is also the case that in some countries, including Denmark, Sweden, Wales and Scotland, companies not registered domestically have not been eligible to receive some of these subsidy funds. The introduction of markets has also restricted public access and choice, for example in the ability to view major national sporting fixtures on free to view television and the BBC is being nudged into a private sector funding mode and away from licence fees. All of these issues can be controlled and regulated through public sector liberalisation if the government chose to do so.

The application and use of performance management to establish service design and delivery dashboards has offered a mechanism to improve public delivery across services. However, it has also been used to reduce services offered through cuts in eligibility and entitlement. While this performance management approach has supported the development of a client role within local government, it has distanced central government officials from the public and in their understanding of the policy requirements and practical issues related to public services. There is now some recognition of the ways in which outsourcing can have some positive outcomes for public value in communities and these will continue to expand in the economic crisis that will follow the COVID-19 pandemic. Competition can be useful to stimulate change in public services by changing cultural practices and service design. However, it can also be used to undermine institutions and generate profits that represent funding being lost to the public bodies responsible for service delivery if left unchecked.

How has outsourcing changed the UK central state?

Over 40 years of the application of public sector liberalisation in the UK there has been a dominant use of metanarratives in the delivery of the statecraft applied to achieve the fulfilment of the UK's international agreement obligations. Central government has undermined the narrative of the welfare state to achieve these changes (Mount, 2020a). This has been a particularly dominant narrative in England. The welfare state has been used as a guiding narrative in Scotland, Wales and Northern Ireland after devolution in 1999. However, with the implementation of Brexit, these different welfare policy narratives may be reduced by Whitehall in its drive for post-Brexit recentralisation (Morphet and Clifford, 2020). Outsourcing has led to a concentration on the politics of central government rather than its protective delivery functions. Whitehall has categorised all other parts of the state as sectors that are to be managed through political actions. The distancing between the central state and the rest of the state's institutions has also led to the removal of their role as partners in support for the nation's wellbeing.

This concentrated focus on the politicisation of policy without any reflection on delivery is having consequences that are still being played out. The central state now regards delivery of services as contractual and post-political. Problems are the concern of the contractors and not the government as their clients and service specifiers. Whitehall retains control of contracts and contractors but does not recognise the associated accountability that accompanies this control. Outsourcing has left Whitehall detached from its central purposes. It remains to be seen whether a post-COVID-19 economy will lead to a reinvention of the welfare state.

How has outsourcing changed the UK local state?

The implementation of liberalisation in the public sector in 1980 was initially focused on central rather than local government but quickly extended to procurement of goods and services. In preparing for liberalisation, Whitehall changed the central narrative of the welfare state and this drove a wedge into the operation of multi-level government. Following the shared post-war mission of local and central state working together, the local state was cast as being oppositional and a nuisance in order to promote change. Nevertheless, local government appears to have responded to the use of competitive methods to provide services and then also to manage them in operation. Some councils have successfully created joint commissioning arrangements for specific services and there has also been the creation of procurement consortia for goods and services that support the application of social value mechanism. Local authorities may do less than before, as a consequence of budget cuts, but their innovation in delivery to maintain services has been considerable.

Brexit

What difference will Brexit make to outsourcing and competition? During the referendum debates and subsequent preparators for Brexit, there were expectations in the public sector that leaving the EU would mean the end to public procurement rules and processes (Morphet, 2017). The public sector was not aware of the role played by the EU in applying the international GPA and GATS agreements and using its regulatory frameworks to ensure compliance. Outside the EU, the UK will not only need to continue to meet its competition requirements but also be able to demonstrate this compliance. Brexit does not mean the end of state aid, although state aid rules were never the inhibitor to investment that the Whitehall considered. In addition, EU membership has meant that there have been less formal regulatory processes inside the EU, which will return with the introduction of hard borders between the UK and the EU. The UK also loses access to the trade agreements held by the EU for its member states and these need to be negotiated. This could take some time. If there are disputes within the EU, then these can be taken to the European Court of Justice and be resolved internally. In the WTO system, outside the EU, claims against unfair competition are bilateral between states and there has to be an application to dispute resolution procedures. At present the US is failing to agree to the dispute resolution procedures within the WTO.

COVID-19

The COVID-19 pandemic has led to the temporary removal of procurement and state aid rules in the public sector and in support for the private sector. The EU agreed to set these rules aside early in the pandemic although specific country schemes have to be notified and agreed. Despite some press commentary to the contrary, this removal of state aid rules by the EU occurred very quickly in the UK. The response to COVID-19 has demonstrated the extent to which there is a global supply market for all the equipment needed by any country. While some UK companies have been major suppliers for PPE to third countries, Public Health England has determined that the quality of their products does not meet UK specifications. Further, the reliance on a centralised global supply chain has hampered the sourcing and provision of PPE. Although the UK economy is primarily based on a service economy, there has been a move towards opening or repurposing existing manufacturing and clothing factories to providing equipment, clothing and other protractive equipment for both domestic supply and export. The government sought to bring in major UK companies, a number of which were Conservative party donors, to provide ventilation equipment and PPE without any understanding of the structure of existing UK suppliers or how to make contact to commission supply (Geoghan, 2020; NAO, 2020g). Numerous press reports also demonstrated that manufacturers had offered equipment and PPE to the UK government before selling it abroad but received no acknowledgement of or responses to their calls and emails.

This has been a privatised pandemic. This emphasis on centralisation within the UK state and its detachment from the local has been significant but not long lasting in practice. The centralisation of the state through outsourcing has meant that it assumed that national responses would be more easily controlled than other models. This failed to understand that public health is a local issue. In practice, local authorities had to step in and undertake these local tasks. This was the first crisis of this kind where local authorities were not mobilised from the outset as recommended by the World Health Organization. Also, a national campaign for volunteers served to remove local volunteers, and after a month, only 50,000 of the 750,000 national volunteers had been used. Local authorities also stepped in to provide food parcels for those who were isolated because of a medical vulnerability and where the national system did not work to support them after requiring this group to stay at home. Local authorities also aided small firms, managed local spaces for walking and cycling and gave general support to those who needed it.

What is the future for outsourcing?

The public sector outsourcing market remains large and offers options for all types and scales of public sector activity and it is becoming more diverse. For the private sector, outsourcing is potentially a riskier approach as both general providers and specialist companies, such as those providing services in care homes, are failing to offer satisfactory services and manage costs. Further, access to labour for lower paid service jobs, living wage requirements and any reform of zero-hours contracts are all placing pressures on these sectors. At the same time, charities and voluntary bodies are being drawn into the delivery of public services to maintain their charitable activities while local authorities are now returning services in-house to reduce externalised costs that are associated with outsourcing and to have a greater control of the quality of delivery. They are also establishing companies to manage and extend their assets through property acquisition and the provision of housing.

However, it is also possible to see other changes occurring in the public sector. The introduction of George Osborne's austerity mantra in 2010 together with its associated practices of reduced budgets has gone a further step in outsourcing services – in this case, not to the private sector but to the voluntary sector. The pressure to reduce public service costs and benefits through this austerity drive has led to some public organisations such as local authorities starting to deliver directly again in ways that may not have been possible ten years earlier. Further, the extent of this detached central state, together with austerity, has been identified as one of the causes of the rise in populism. The Brexit vote has served as a means of demonstrating the way in which the state is now perceived in England and is seen as not providing a safety net for its people. Outsourcing has been the means through which the UK central state has become detached from its role and responsibilities. As other countries have shown, outsourcing can be used as a servant of the state and not an excuse to dismantle it.

References

Abbott, F. M. (1990) 'GATT and the European Community: a formula for peaceful coexistence', *Michigan Journal of International Law*, 12: 1–58.

Adams, D. and Tiesdell, S. (2010) 'Planners as market actors: rethinking state–market relations in land and property', *Planning Theory & Practice*, 11(2): 187–207.

Adams, R. and Brooks, L. (2020) 'Scottish and Welsh universities criticise UK cap on student numbers'. *The Guardian*. 31 May. https://www.theguardian.com/education/2020/may/31/uk-university-leaders-angry-over-plans-to-cap-student-numbers (accessed 18 November 2020).

Addison, P. (2011) *The Road to 1945: British Politics and the Second World War* (rev. edn), London: Random House.

Adnett, N. and Hardy, S. (1998) 'The impact of TUPE on compulsory competitive tendering: evidence from employers', *Local Government Studies*, 24(3): 36–50.

Ahlin, Å. (2003) 'Does school competition matter? Effects of a large-scale school choice reform on student performance', Department of Economics, Uppsala University Working Paper No. 2. Available from: https://www.econstor.eu/bitstream/10419/82869/1/wp2003-002.pdf (accessed 14 December 2020).

Alcock, P. (2010) 'Building the Big Society: a new policy environment for the third sector in England', *Voluntary Sector Review*, 1(3): 379–90.

Alderman, N. and Ivory, C. (2007) 'Partnering in major contracts: paradox and metaphor', *International Journal of Project Management*, 25(4): 386–93.

Aldridge, R. and Stoker, G. (2002) *Advancing a New Public Service Ethos*, London: New Local Government Network.

Alford, J. (2011) 'Public value form co-production by clients', in J. Benington and M. Moore (eds) *Public Value: Theory and Practice*, Basingstoke: Palgrave Macmillan, pp 144–57.

Allen, D. (1996) 'Competition policy: policing the single market', in H. Wallace and W. Wallace (eds) *Policy Making in the European Union*, Oxford: Oxford University Press, pp 157–83.

Allen, R. (2010) 'Replicating Swedish "free school" reforms in England', *Research in Public Policy*, 10(summer): 4–7.

Allen, R. and Burgess, S. (2020) 'The future of competition and accountability in education', Report to the Public Services Trust. Available from: http://www.2020publicservicestrust.org/downloads/9_The_Future_of_Competition_and_Accountability_in%20Education.pdf (accessed 14 December 2020).

Allen, R. and Higham, R. (2018) 'Quasi-markets, school diversity and social selection: analysing the case of free schools in England, five years on', *London Review of Education*, 16(2): 191–213.

Alonso, J. M. and Andrews, R. (2020) 'Privatization, power and place: the distributive politics of asylum dispersal in England', *Regional Studies*, 1–13.

Alperovitz, G., Howard, T. and Williamson, T. (2010) 'The Cleveland model', *The Nation*, 1: 21–4.

Alston, P. (2019) 'Report of the Special Rapporteur on extreme poverty and human rights', Report to UN General Assembly, 24 June–12 July. A/HRC/41/39.

Amato, F. and Farbmann, K. (2010) 'Applying EU competition law in the education sector', *International Journal of Education Law and Policy*, 7(1–2): 7–13.

Amighini, A. (2019) 'Italy in the Belt and Road Initiative', *GeoProgress Journal*, 6(1): 53–61. http://www.geoprogress.eu/wp-content/uploads/2020/04/GeoJ2019-I1-Amighini.pdf (accessed 17 November 2020).

Anderson, K. (2005) *The WTO and Agriculture*, Cheltenham: Edward Elgar.

Andrew, J., Barker, M. and Roberts, P. (2016) *Prison Privatisation in Australia: The State of the Nation*, Sydney, Australia: University of Sydney Press.

Anheier, H. K. (2002) 'The Third Sector in Europe: Five Theses', Civil Society Working Paper 12, London: LSE.

APSE (2006) 'Public bodies for the purposes of the Local Authorities (Goods and Services) Act 1970'. https://www.apse.org.uk/apse/index.cfm/members-area/special-interest-portals/trading-and-charging/trading/ (accessed 18 November 2020).

APSE (2013) *Making Co-production Work – Lessons from Local Government*, London: Trades Union Congress.

Armingeon, K. (2004) 'Institutional change in OECD democracies, 1970–2000', *Comparative European Politics*, 2(2): 212–38.

Armstrong, H. (1997) 'Five sides to a new leaf', *Municipal Journal*, 4 July, 18–19.

Aron, R. and Singh, J. V. (2005) 'Getting offshoring right', *Harvard Business Review*, 83(12): 135–43.

Ascher, K. (1987) *The Politics of Privatisation: Contracting Out Public Services*, Basingstoke: Palgrave Macmillan.

Ashford, N. (1990) *Reaganomics and Thatcherism: From Ideas to Policy*, Washington DC: Heritage Foundation.

Ashton, T. and Press, D. (1997) 'Market concentration in secondary health services under a purchaser–provider split: the New Zealand experience', *Health Economics*, 6(1): 43–56.

Atkinson, A. (2005a) *The Atkinson Review: Final Report. Measurement of Government Output and Productivity for the National Accounts*, Basingstoke: Palgrave Macmillan.

Atkinson, A. (2005b) 'Measurement of UK government output and productivity for national accounts', *Journal of the Statistical and Social Inquiry Society of Ireland*, 34: 152–60.

Audet, D. (2002) *The Size of Government Procurement Markets Substate and Local Government*, Paris: OECD. http://www.oecd.org/newsroom/archives/1845927.pdf (accessed 18 November 2020).

Audet, D. (2003) 'Government procurement', *OECD Journal on Budgeting*, 2(3): 149–94.

Aust, A. (2013) *Modern Treaty Law and Practice*, Cambridge: Cambridge University Press.

Aveyard, S., Corthorn, P. and O'Connell, S. (2018) *The Politics of Consumer Credit in the UK, 1938–1992*, Oxford: Oxford University Press.

Azmat, G. and Simion, S. (2017) *Higher Education Funding Reforms: A Comprehensive Analysis of Educational and Labor Market Outcomes in England*, Bonn: IZA – Institute of Labor Economics.

Bacon, C. (2005) 'The evolution of immigration detention in the UK: the involvement of private prison companies', Refugee Studies Centre Working Paper No. 27, Oxford: University of Oxford.

Badstuber, N. (2018) 'Renationalising Britain's railways – EU law not a barrier', *The Conversation*. https://theconversation.com/renationalising-britains-railways-eu-law-not-a-barrier-96759 (accessed 18 November 2020).

Bailey, N., Bramley, G. and Hastings, A. (2015) 'Symposium introduction: local responses to "austerity"', *Local Government Studies*, 41(4): 571–81.

Bailey, S. J. and Davidson, C. (1999) 'The purchaser–provider split: theory and UK evidence', *Environment and Planning C: Government and Policy*, 17(2): 161–75.

Baker, K. (2012) 'Understanding strategic service partnerships', *Public Performance & Management Review*, 35(4): 660–78.

Baldwin, P. (1999) 'A National Health Service in Quangoland', in M. Flinders and M. Smith (eds) *Quangos, Accountability and Reform: The Politics of Quasi-Government*, London: Palgrave Macmillan, pp 152–61.

Baldwin, R. E. (1994) *Towards an Integrated Europe* (Vol. 25, No. 234), London: Centre for Economic Policy Research. Available from: http://citeseerx.ist.psu.edu/viewdoc/download?doi=10.1.1.114.1928&rep=rep1&type=pdf (accessed 14 December 2020).

Ball, M. (1983) *Housing Policy and Economic Power: The Political Economy of Owner Occupation* (Vol. 828), London: Routledge.

Banister, D., Akerman, J., Nijkamp, P., Stead, D., Dreborg, K., Steen, P. and Schleicher-Tappeser, R. (2000) *European Transport Policy and Sustainable Mobility*, Abingdon: Taylor & Francis.

Barrett, S. and Hill, M. (1986) 'Policy bargaining and structure in implementation theory: towards an integrated perspective', in M. Goldsmith (ed.) *New Research in Central-Local Relations*, Aldershot: Gower, pp 34–59.

Barzelay, M. (1997) 'Central audit institutions and performance auditing: a comparative analysis of organizational strategies in the OECD', *Governance*, 10(3): 235–60.

Bastida, F. and Benito, B. (2007) 'Central government budget practices and transparency: an international comparison', *Public Administration*, 85(3): 667–716.

Basu, S. and Guinchard, A. (2020) 'Restoring trust into the NHS: promoting data protection as an "architecture of custody" for the sharing of data in direct care', *International Journal of Law and Information Technology*, 28(3): 243–72

Baumgartner F. and Jones, B. (1993) *Agendas and instability in American Politics*, Chicago: Chicago University Press.

Beesley, B. (1983) 'The Rayner Scrutinies', in A. G. Gray and W. I. Jenkins (eds) *Policy Analysis and Evaluation in British Government*, London: RIPA, pp 33–4.

Bel, G. and Foote, J. (2009) 'Tolls, terms and public interest in road concessions privatization: a comparative analysis of recent transactions in the USA and France', *Transport Reviews*, 29(3): 397–413.

Benington, J. (2009) 'Creating the public in order to create public value?', *International Journal of Public Administration*, 32(3–4): 232–49.

Benington, J. (2011) 'From private choice to public value', in J. Benington and M. Moore (eds) *Public Value: Theory and Practice*, Basingstoke: Palgrave Macmillan, pp 31–49.

Bercow, J. (2019) 'Speakers statement', *Hansard*, 18 March, volume 656.

Beswick, J. and Penny, J. (2018) 'Demolishing the present to sell off the future? The financialisation of public housing in London', *International Journal for Urban and Regional Research*, 42(4): 612–32.

Bianchi, P. and Labory, S. (2006) 'Empirical evidence on industrial policy using state aid data', *International Review of Applied Economics*, 20(5): 603–21.

Bing, L., Akintoye, A., Edwards, P. J. and Hardcastle, C. (2005) 'The allocation of risk in PPP/PFI construction projects in the UK', *International Journal of Project Management*, 23(1): 25–35.

Björklund, A., Clark, M., Edin, P.-A., Fredriksson, P. and Krueger, A. (2005) *The Market Comes to Education in Sweden: An Evaluation of Sweden's Surprising School Reforms*, New York: Russell Sage Foundation.

Black, J. (1993) 'The Prison Service and executive agency status — HM Prisons plc?', *International Journal of Public Sector Management*, 6(6): 27–41.

Blauberger, M. (2009) 'Compliance with rules of negative integration: European state aid control in the new member states', *Journal of European Public Policy*, 16(7): 1030–46.

Blitz, B. K. (1999) 'Professional mobility and the mutual recognition of qualifications in the European Union: two institutional approaches', *Comparative Education Review*, 43(3): 311–31.

Blomqvist, P. (2004) 'The choice revolution: privatization of Swedish welfare services in the 1990s', *Social Policy & Administration*, 38(2): 139–55.

Bockman, J. (2011) *Markets in the Name of Socialism: The Left-Wing Origins of Neoliberalism*, Redwood City, CA: Stanford University Press.

Boffey, D. (2015) 'Virgin Care among firms with lucrative NHS deals and a tax haven status', *The Guardian*, 21 March.

Böhlmark, A. and Lindahl, M. (2008) 'Does school privatization improve educational achievement? Evidence from Sweden's voucher reform', IZA Discussion Paper No. 3691.

Booker, A. (1999) 'Balancing the scales – the growth, role and future of the regulators', in M. Flinders and M. Smith (eds) *Quangos, Accountability and Reform: The Politics of Quasi-Government*, London: Palgrave Macmillan, pp 180–90.

Booth, R. (2013) 'High court rejects legal challenge to Barnet's "easyCouncil" plans', *The Guardian*, 29 April.

Booth, R. (2020) 'Agency staff were spreading Covid-19 between care homes, PHE found in April', *The Guardian*, 18 May. https://www.theguardian.com/world/2020/may/18/agency-staff-were-spreading-covid-19-between-care-homes-phe-found-in-april (accessed 18 November 2020).

Born, G. (2011) *Uncertain Vision: Birt, Dyke and the Reinvention of the BBC*, London: Random House.

Boussabaine, A. and Kirkham, R. (2008) *Whole Life-Cycle Costing: Risk and Risk Responses*, Hoboken, NJ: John Wiley.

Bovaird, A. G. and Gregory, D. (1996) 'Performance indicators: the British experience', in A. Halachmi and G. Bouckaert (eds) *Organizational Performance and Measurement in the Public Sector*, Westport, CT: Quorum Books, pp 239–73.

Bovaird, T. (2007) 'Beyond engagement and participation: user and community coproduction of public services', *Public Administration Review*, 67(5): 846–60.

Bovaird, T. (2010) *Model of Public Outcomes and Cost Implications: Thinkpiece for Birmingham Total Place Initiative*, Birmingham: INLOGOV.

Bovaird, T. (2016) 'The ins and outs of outsourcing and insourcing: what have we learnt from the past 30 years?', *Public Money & Management*, 36(1): 67–74.

Bovaird, T. and Löffler, E. (2002) 'Moving from excellence models of local service delivery to benchmarking "good local governance"', *International Review of Administrative Sciences*, 68(1): 9–24.

Bovis, C. (2015) 'Building social value in public procurement', *European Procurement & Public Private Partnership Law Review*, 10(4): 227–30.

Bovis, C. (2019) *The Liberalisation of Public Procurement and Its Effects on the Common Market*, Abingdon: Routledge.

Bowles, L. and Davy, J. (2019) 'Student accommodation', Research Article, 20 June. https://www.savills.co.uk/research_articles/229130/283706-0 (accessed 6 January 2020).

Bowman, A., Ertürk, I., Folkman, P., Froud, J., Haslam, C., Johal, S., Leaver, A., Moran, M., Tsitsianis, N., and Williams, K. (2015) *What a Waste: Outsourcing and How It Goes Wrong*, Manchester: Manchester University Press.

Bown, C. P. (2004) 'Trade disputes and the implementation of protection under the GATT: an empirical assessment', *Journal of International Economics*, 62(2): 263–94.

Boycko, M., Shleifer, A. and Vishny, R. W. (1996) 'A theory of privatisation', *The Economic Journal*, 106(435): 309–19.

Boyne, G. (1997) 'Comparing the performance of local authorities: an evaluation of the Audit Commission indicators', *Local Government Studies*, 23(4): 17–43.

Boyne, G. (1998) 'Competitive tendering in local government: a review of theory and evidence', *Public Administration*, 76(4): 695–712.

Boyne, G. A. (1999) 'Introduction: processes, performance and best value in local government', *Local Government Studies*, 25(2): 1–15.

Boyne, G., James, O., John, P. and Petrovsky, P. (2010) 'What if public management reform actually works? The paradoxical success of performance management in English local government', in H. Margetts, P. 6 and C. Hood (eds) *Paradoxes of Modernization: Unintended Consequences of Public Policy Reform*, Oxford: Oxford University Press, pp 203–20.

Brinkley, I. (2013) *Flexibility or Insecurity? Exploring the Rise of Zero Hours Contracts*, London: Work Foundation.

Broadbent, J. and Laughlin, R. (2003) 'Control and legitimation in government accountability processes: the private finance initiative in the UK', *Critical Perspectives on Accounting*, 14(1–2): 23–48.

Broadbent, J., Gill, J. and Laughlin, R. (2003) 'Evaluating the private finance initiative in the National Health Service in the UK', *Accounting, Auditing & Accountability Journal*, 16(3): 422–45.

Brown, A. (1994) 'Economic aspects of prison privatisation: the Queensland experience', in D. Biles and J. Vernon (eds) *Private Sector and Community Involvement in the Criminal Justice System*, Canberra: Australian Institute of Criminology, pp 103–17.

Browne, J. (2010) *The Browne Report: Higher Education Funding and Student Finance*, London: DBIS.

Buller, J. (1995) 'Britain as an awkward partner: reassessing Britain's relationship with the EU', *Politics*, 15(1): 33–42.

Buller, J. (1999) 'A critical appraisal of the statecraft interpretation', *Public Administration*, 77(4): 691–712.

Bulmer, S. and Burch, M. (2005) 'The Europeanization of UK government: from quiet revolution to explicit step-change?', *Public Administration*, 83(4): 861–90.

Bulpitt, J. (1982) 'Conservatism, unionism and the problem of territorial management', in P. Madgwick and R. Rose (eds) *The Territorial Dimension in United Kingdom Politics*, Basingstoke: Macmillan, pp 139–76.

Bulpitt, J. (1986) 'The discipline of the new democracy: Mrs Thatcher's domestic statecraft', *Political studies*, 34(1): 19–39.

Bunar, N. (2009) 'Can multicultural urban schools in Sweden survive the freedom of choice policy?', Stockholm University Linnaeus Center for Integration Studies Working Paper No. 3.

Burk, K. and Cairncross, A. (1992) *Goodbye, Great Britain: The 1976 IMF Crisis*, London: Yale University Press.

Burnett, M. (2014) 'The New European Directive on the award of concession contracts – promoting value for money in PPP contracts?', *European Procurement & Public Private Partnership Law Review*, 9(2): 86–103.

Burton, J. (1987) 'Privatization: the Thatcher case', *Managerial and Decision Economics*, 8(1): 21–9.

Busck, O. (2007) 'Marketization of refuse collection in Denmark: social and environmental quality jeopardized', *Waste management & research*, 25(4): 384–91.

Butterworth, J., Sansom, A., Sims, L., Healey, M., Kingsland, E. and Campbell, J. (2017) 'Pharmacists' perceptions of their emerging general practice roles in UK primary care: a qualitative interview study', *British Journal of General Practice*, 67(662): e650–8.

Cabinet Office (2001) *Preventing Social Exclusion*, London: Cabinet Office.

Cabinet Office (2015) *Social Value Act Review*, London: Cabinet Office.

Cabinet Office (2017) *National Risk Register of Civil Emergencies: 2017 Edition*, London: Cabinet Office.

Cairns, J., Gardner, R. and Lawton, D. (eds) (2004) *Faith Schools: Consensus or Conflict?*, Abingdon: Routledge.

Calovski, V. (2018) 'The New NHS in England: exploring the implications of decision making by Clinical Commissioning Groups and their effect on the selection of private providers', Doctoral dissertation, University of Kent.

Campbell, J. (1994) *Edward Heath: A Biography*, London: Pimlico.

Cannon, M. and Thorpe, J. (2020) 'Preston Model: community wealth generation and a local cooperative economy', Participatory Economic Alternatives Case Summary No. 20. https://opendocs.ids.ac.uk/opendocs/bitstream/handle/20.500.12413/15219/Case_20_Preston_Model_FINAL.pdf?sequence=1 (accessed 17 November 2020).

Caputo, J. S., Wynyard, R. and Alfino, M. (1998) *McDonaldization Revisited: Critical Essays on Consumer Culture*, Westport: ABC-CLIO.

Carozzi, F., Hilber, C. A. and Yu, X. (2019) 'The economic impacts of help to buy', UCL Working Paper.

Carter, B., Danford, A., Howcroft, D., Richardson, H., Smith, A. and Taylor, P. (2012) '"Nothing gets done and no one knows why": PCS and workplace control of Lean in HM Revenue and Customs', *Industrial Relations Journal*, 43(5): 416–32.

Carter, L. and Weerakkody, V. (2008) 'E-government adoption: a cultural comparison', *Information Systems Frontiers*, 10(4): 473–82.

Casselden, B., Pickard, A., Walton, G. and McLeod, J. (2019) 'Keeping the doors open in an age of austerity? Qualitative analysis of stakeholder views on volunteers in public libraries', *Journal of Librarianship and Information Science*, 51(4): 869–83.

Cave, M. (2011) *Competition and Innovation in the Water Markets (Cave Review)*, London: DEFRA.

Cavusgil, S. T. (1993) 'Globalization of markets and its impact on domestic institutions', *Indiana Journal of Global Legal Studies*, 1(1): 83–99.

Cebolla-Boado, H., Hu, Y. and Soysal, Y. N. (2018) 'Why study abroad? Sorting of Chinese students across British universities', *British Journal of Sociology of Education*, 39(3): 365–80.

CEC (Commission of the European Communities) (1997) *Transfer of Undertakings: Commission adopts a Memorandum explaining the acquired rights of workers*, 11 March. Available from: https://ec.europa.eu/commission/presscorner/detail/en/IP_97_199 (accessed 14 December 2020).

CEC (Commission of the European Communities) (2000) Cohesion Programme Guidelines 2000-2006. https://ec.europa.eu/regional_policy/en/information/legislation/guidance/2000-2006/ (accessed 17 November 2020).

CEC (Commission of the European Communities) (2001) *European Governance: A White Paper*, Brussels: CEC.

CEC (Commission of the European Communities) (2014) Award of Concession Contracts Directive 2014/23/EU, Brussels: CEC.

CEC (Commission of the European Communities) (2015a) *State Aid Manual of Procedures: Internal DG Competition Working Documents on Procedures for the Application of Articles 107 and 108 TFEU*, Brussels: CEC.

CEC (Commission of the European Communities) (2015b) *Competition Among Health Care Providers Investigating Policy Options in the European Union*, Brussels: CEC.

CLES (Centre for Local Economic Strategies) (2017) *Updating the Spend Analysis Baseline: Summary Report Presented to Preston City Council*, Manchester: Centre for Local Economic Strategies.

CLES (Centre for Local Economic Strategies) and Preston City Council (2019) *How We Built Community Wealth in Preston: Achievements and Lessons*, Preston: CLES and Preston City Council.

Chakrabortty, A. (2018a) 'In 2011 Preston hit rock bottom. Then it took back control', *The Guardian*, 31 January, Available from: https://www.theguardian.com/commentisfree/2018/jan/31/preston-hit-rock-bottom-took-back-control (accessed 17 November 2020).

Chakrabortty, A. (2018b) 'In an era of brutal cuts, one ordinary place has the imagination to fight back', *The Guardian*, 6 March, Available from: https://www.theguardian.com/commentisfree/2019/mar/06/brutal-cuts-fight-back-preston-dragons-den (accessed 17 November 2020).

Chan, A. P., Chan, D. W., Chiang, Y. H., Tang, B. S., Chan, E. H. and Ho, K. S. (2004) 'Exploring critical success factors for partnering in construction projects', *Journal of Construction Engineering and Management*, 130(2): 188–98.

Chandler, J. A. (2001) *Local Government Today*, Manchester: Manchester University Press.

Chang, P., Karsenty, G., Mattoo, A. and Richtering, J. (1999) 'GATS, the modes of supply and statistics on trade in services', *Journal of World Trade*, 33(3): 93–115.

Chapman, C. (2011) *Selling the Family Silver: Has Privatization Worked?*, London: Random House.

Chapman, R. A. (1988) *Ethics in the British Civil Service*, London: Routledge.

Charmley, J. (1998) 'Selsdon man and Grantham woman', in *A History of Conservative Politics, 1900–1996*, London: Palgrave Macmillan, pp 181–200.

Chaundy, D. and Uttley, M. (1993) 'The economics of compulsory competitive tendering: issues, evidence and the case of municipal refuse collection', *Public Policy and Administration*, 8(2): 25–41.

Choudrie, J., Ghinea, G. and Songonuga, V. N. (2013) 'Silver surfers, e-government and the digital divide: an exploratory study of UK local authority websites and older citizens', *Interacting with Computers*, 25(6): 417–42.

Christophers, B. (2018) *The New Enclosure: The Appropriation of Public Land in Neoliberal Britain*, London: Verso.

Christophers, B. (2019) 'Putting financialisation in its financial context: transformations in local government-led urban development in post-financial crisis England', *Transactions of the Institute of British Geographers*, 44(3): 571–86.

Cini, M. (2001) 'The soft law approach: Commission rule-making in the EU's state aid regime', *Journal of European Public Policy*, 8(2): 192–207.

Clarke, C. (2002) 'Foreword', in R. Aldridge and G. Stoker (eds) *Advancing a New Public Service Ethos*, London: New Local Government Network, pp 6–7.

Clifton, C. and Duffield, C. F. (2006) 'Improved PFI/PPP service outcomes through the integration of Alliance principles', *International Journal of Project Management*, 24(7): 573–86.

Cockfield, A. (1994) *The European Union: Creating the Single Market*, Colorado Springs: Wiley.

Collins, B. (2016) 'Big data and health economics: strengths, weaknesses, opportunities and threats', *Pharmacoeconomics*, 34(2): 101–6.

Common, R. K. (1998) 'Convergence and transfer: a review of the globalisation of new public management', *International Journal of Public Sector Management*, 11(6): 440–50.

Confue, P. (2019) 'Outsourcing non-clinical services in NHS organisations in England', *British Journal of Healthcare Management*, 25(11): 331–6.

Convery, A. (2014) 'Devolution and the limits of Tory statecraft: the Conservative Party in coalition and Scotland and Wales', *Parliamentary Affairs*, 67(1): 25–44.

Coppens, D. (2014) *WTO Disciplines on Subsidies and Countervailing Measures: Balancing Policy Space and Legal Constraints* (vol. 12), Cambridge: Cambridge University Press.

Coppola, A. (2014) 'A Cleveland model? Experiments in alternative urbanism in the Rustbelt', *Métropoles* (online), 15. https://doi.org/10.4000/metropoles.4950 (accessed 20 November 2020).

Copus, C. (2006) 'British local government: a case for a new constitutional settlement', *Public Policy and Administration*, 21(2): 4–21.

Corry, D. and Stoker, G. (2002) *New Localism: Refashioning the Centre-Local Relationship*, London: New Local Government Network.

Cowie, J. (2002) 'Acquisition, efficiency and scale economies: an analysis of the British bus industry', *Transport Reviews*, 22(2): 147–57.

Cox, A. and Townsend, M. (1998) *Strategic Procurement in Construction*, London: Thomas Telford.

Cribb, A. (2008) 'Organizational reform and health-care goods: concerns about marketization in the UK NHS', *Journal of Medicine and Philosophy*, 33(3): 221–40.

Cribb, J., Sibieta, L. and Vignoles, A. (2013) *Entry into Grammar Schools in England*, London: Institute for Fiscal Studies.

Croome, J. (1996) *Reshaping the World Trading System: A History of the Uruguay Round*, Geneva: WTO.

Crosland, A. (1956) *The Future of Socialism*, London: Jonathan Cape.

Crown Commercial Service (2016) *A Brief Guide to the 2014 EU Public Procurement Directives*. https://assets.publishing.service.gov.uk/government/uploads/system/uploads/attachment_data/file/560261/Brief_Guide_to_the_2014_Directives_Oct_16.pdf (accessed 17 November 2020).

Croxson, B., Propper, C. and Perkins, A. (2001) 'Do doctors respond to financial incentives? UK family doctors and the GP fundholder scheme', *Journal of Public Economics*, 79(2): 375–98.

Cunningham, I. and James, P. (2014) 'Public service outsourcing and its employment implications in an era of austerity: the case of British social care', *Competition & Change*, 18(1): 1–19.

Curtis, M. (2011) 'Localism and local government finance', *Local Economy*, 26(8): 684–9.

Dahlström, C., Peters, B. G. and Pierre, J. (2011) Steering for the centre strengthening political control in Western democracies. Toronto: University of Toronto Press.

Dahlström, C., Nistotskaya, M. and Tyrberg, M. (2016) 'Is the quality of the outsourced public services contingent on the quality of bureaucracy?', Working Paper Series 2016:10, QOG: The Quality of Government Institute, Department of Political Science, University of Gothenburg.

Darling, J. (2016) 'Privatising asylum: neoliberalisation, depoliticisation and the governance of forced migration', *Transactions of the Institute of British Geographers*, 41(3): 230–43.

Dávid-Barrett, E. and Fazekas, M. (2019) 'Grand corruption and government change: an analysis of partisan favoritism in public procurement', *European Journal on Criminal Policy and Research*, 1–20.

David-Barrett, L. (2011) *Cabs for Hire? Fixing the Revolving Door Between Government and Business*, London: Transparency International.

Davies, A. (2013) '"Right to buy": the development of a Conservative housing policy, 1945–1980', *Contemporary British History*, 27(4): 421–44.

Davies, B. (2018) *Austerity, Youth Policy and the Deconstruction of the Youth Service in England*, Heidelberg: Springer.

Davies, W. (2013) 'When is a market not a market? "Exemption", "externality" and "exception" in the case of European state aid rules', *Theory, Culture & Society*, 30(2): 32–59.

DBIS (Department for Business, Innovation and Skills) (2015a) *State Aid: The Basics Guide*, London: DBIS.

DBIS (Department for Business, Innovation and Skills) (2015b) *The State Aid Manual*, London: DBIS.

DCLG (Department for Communities and Local Government) (2012) National Planning Policy Framework London: DCLG,

DCMS (Department for Digital, Culture, Media and Sport) (2018) *The Public Services (Social Value) Act 2012: An Introductory Guide to the Social Value Act*, London: DCMS.

Deem, R., Hillyard, S. and Reed, M. (2007) *Knowledge, Higher Education, and the New Managerialism: The Changing Management of UK Universities*, Oxford: Oxford University Press.

De Fraja, G., Facchini, G. and Gathergood, J. (2019) 'Academic salaries and public evaluation of university research: evidence from the UK Research Excellence Framework', *Economic Policy*, 34(99): 523–83.

De Graaf, G. and King, M. (1995) 'Towards a more global government procurement market: the expansion of the GATT Government Procurement Agreement in the context of the Uruguay Round', *The International Lawyer*, 29(2): 435–52.

Demirag, I. (2018) 'Sourcing public services: lessons learned from the collapse of Carillion inquiry', Evidence given to the Public Administration and Constitutional Affairs Committee, UK Parliament. Available from: https://www.tuc.org.uk/sites/default/files/PACACinquiry.pdf (accessed 14 December 2020).

Demirel, H., Leendertse, W., Volker, L. and Hertogh, M. (2017) 'Flexibility in PPP contracts – dealing with potential change in the pre-contract phase of a construction project', *Construction Management and Economics*, 35(4): 196–206,

Demirkaya, Y. (2006) 'The changing management of local government under New Labour in England: best value policy', *Public Administration and Management*, 11(2): 44–74.

Denham, A. and Garnett, M. (2014) *Keith Joseph*, London: Routledge.

DoH (Department of Health) (1998) *Information for Health: An Information Strategy for the Modern NHS 1998–2005: A National Strategy for Local Implementation*, London: DoH.

DoH (Department of Health) (2012) *The New Public Health Role of Local Authorities*, London: DoH

DoH (Department of Health) (2012b) *Equity and Excellence: Liberating the NHS*, London: DoH.

DETR (Department of Employment, Training and Rehabilitation) (1998) Modern local Government in touch with the community, London: DETR.

De Vries, J. (2010) 'Is New Public Management really dead?', *OECD Journal on Budgeting*, 10(1), 1–5.

DfT (Department for Transport) (2020) Rail franchising reaches the terminus as a new railway takes shape. 21 September. https://www.gov.uk/government/news/rail-franchising-reaches-the-terminus-as-a-new-railway-takes-shape (accessed 18 November 2020).

Diamond, P., Richards, D. and Smith, M. (2016) 'Re-centring the British political tradition: explaining contingency in New Labour and the Coalition's governance statecraft', in N. Turnbull (ed) *Interpreting Governance, High Politics and Public Policy: Essays Commemorating Interpreting British Governance*, New York: Routledge, pp 19–38.

Dijkstra, L. and Poelman, H. (2012) 'Cities in Europe: the new OECD-EU definition'. Regional Focus RF01/2010.

Dixon, T., Pottinger, G. and Jordan, A. (2005) 'Lessons from the private finance initiative in the UK: benefits, problems and critical success factors', *Journal of Property Investment & Finance*, 23(5): 412–23.

Dobek, M. M. (1993) 'Privatization as a political priority: the British experience', *Political Studies*, 41(1): 24–40.

Dore, M. H., Kushner, J. and Zumer, K. (2004) 'Privatization of water in the UK and France—what can we learn?', *Utilities Policy*, 12(1): 41–50.

Dowding, K. (1995) *The Civil Service*, London: Routledge.

Dudley, G. and Richardson, J. (2004) *Why Does Policy Change? Lessons from British Transport Policy 1945–99* (vol. 3), London: Routledge.

Duff, A. (1993) *Subsidiarity Within the European Community: A Federal Trust Report*, London: Federal Trust for Education and Research.

Dunhill, L. and Syal, R. (2020) 'Whitehall "infantilised" by reliance on consultants, minister claims', *The Guardian*, 29 September.

Dunleavy, P. (1994) 'The globalization of public services production: can government be "best in world"?', *Public Policy and Administration*, 9(2): 36–64.

Dunleavy, P. and Hood, C. (1994) 'From old public administration to new public management', *Public Money & Management*, 14(3): 9–16.

Dunlop, C. A. and Radaelli, C. M. (2013) 'Systematising policy learning: from monolith to dimensions', *Political Studies*, 61(3): 599–619.

Dunton, J. (2020) Watchdog sounds alarm over rising political bias in public appointments, Civil Service World, 5 November. https://www.civilserviceworld.com/news/article/watchdog-sounds-alarm-over-rising-political-bias-in-public-appointments (accessed 12 November 2020).

Durose, C., Needham, C., Mangan, C. and Rees, J. (2017) 'Generating "good enough" evidence for co-production', *Evidence & Policy: A Journal of Research, Debate and Practice*, 13(1): 135–51.

Edelman, B. G. and Geradin, D. (2015) 'Efficiencies and regulatory shortcuts: how should we regulate companies like Airbnb and Uber', *Stanford Technology Law Review*, 19, 293–328.

Edwards, P., Ezzamel, M. and Robson, K. (1999) 'Connecting accounting and education in the UK: discourses and rationalities of education reform', *Critical Perspectives on Accounting*, 10(4): 469–500.

Ehlermann, C. D. and Goyette, M. (2006) 'The interface between EU state aid control and the WTO disciplines on subsidies', *European State Aid Law Quarterly*, 5(4): 695–718.

Ennew, C., Whynes, D., Jolleys, J. and Robinson, P. (1998) 'Entrepreneurship and innovation among GP fundholders', *Public Money and Management*, 18(1): 59–64.

Entwistle, T. and Martin, S. (2005) 'From competition to collaboration in public service delivery: a new agenda for research', *Public Administration*, 83(1): 233–42.

Erridge, A. (2005) 'UK public procurement policy and the delivery of public value', in K. Thai (ed) *Challenges in Public Procurement: An International Perspective*, PrAcademics Press, pp 335–52.

Erridge, A. and Greer, J. (2000) 'Policy network analysis of UK central government civil procurement', *Public Policy and Administration*, 15(4): 25–49.

Evans, Lord (2020) 'The Hugh Kay Lecture: Are we in a post-Nolan age?', 12 November. https://www.gov.uk/government/speeches/the-hugh-kay-lecture-are-we-in-a-post-nolan-age (accessed 18 November 2020).

Evers, A. (2001) 'Will sector matter? Welfare dynamics, the third sector and social quality', in W. Beck, C. van der Maesen, F. Thomese and A. Walker (eds) *Questioning the Social Quality of Europe*, London: Kluwer, pp 296–311.

Evers, A. and Laville, J. L. (2004) 'Defining the third sector in Europe', in A. Evers and J. L. Laville (eds) *The Third Sector in Europe*, Cheltenham: Edward Elgar, pp 11–42.

Eyles, A. and Machin, S. (2019) 'The introduction of academy schools to England's education', *Journal of the European Economic Association*, 17(4): 1107–46.

Fairclough, I. (2016) 'Evaluating policy as argument: the public debate over the first UK austerity budget', *Critical Discourse Studies*, 13(1): 57–77.

Farley, M. and Pourbaix, N. (2015) 'The EU concessions directive: building (toll) bridges between competition law and public procurement?', *Journal of European Competition Law & Practice*, 6(1): 15–25.

Fawcett, P. and Marsh, D. (2012) 'Policy transfer and policy success: the case of the gateway review process (2001–10)', *Government and Opposition*, 47(2): 162–85.

Ferm, J., Clifford, B., Canelas, P. and Livingstone, N. (2020) 'Emerging problematics of deregulating the urban: the case of permitted development in England', *Urban Studies*. https://journals.sagepub.com/doi/full/10.1177/0042098020936966 (accessed 12 November 2020).

Ferry, L., Ahrens, T. and Khalifa, R. (2019) 'Public value, institutional logics and practice variation during austerity localism at Newcastle City Council', *Public Management Review*, 21(1): 96–115.

Filkin, G., Allen, E. and Williams, J. (2001) *Strategic Partnering for Local Service Delivery: A Practical Guide*, London: New Local Government Network.

Flinders, M. (1999a) 'Setting the scene: Quangos in context', in M. Flinders and M. Smith (eds) *Quangos, Accountability and Reform: The Politics of Quasi-Government*, London: Palgrave Macmillan, pp 3–16.

Flinders, M. (1999b) 'Quangos: why do governments love them?', in M. Flinders and M. Smith (eds) *Quangos, Accountability and Reform: The Politics of Quasi-Government*, London: Palgrave Macmillan, pp 26–39.

Flinders, M. (2005) 'The politics of public–private partnerships', *The British Journal of Politics and International Relations*, 7(2): 215–39.

Florio, M. (2003) 'Does privatisation matter? The long-term performance of British Telecom over 40 years', *Fiscal Studies*, 24(2): 197–234.

Flynn, N. (1981) 'Direct labour organisations', *Local Government Studies*, 7(2): 56–9.

Forster, M. (2014) *My Life in Houses*, London: Chatto & Windus.

Foy, G. (1992) 'Towards extension of the GATT standards code to production processes', *Journal of World Trade*, 26(6): 121–31.

Franklin, B. (2003) 'A good day to bury bad news? Journalists, sources and the packaging of politics', in S. Cottle (ed) *News, Public Relations and Power*, London: SAGE, pp 45–61.

Friedman, M. (1962) *Capitalism and Freedom*, Chicago, IL: University of Chicago Press.

Fry, G. K. (1988) 'The Thatcher government, the financial management initiative, and the "new cml service"', *Public Administration*, 66(1): 1–20.

Fry, G. K. (1990) 'The Fulton Committee and the preference for relevance issue', *Public Administration*, 68(2): 175–90.

Gains, F. (1999) 'Implementing privatization policies in "next steps" agencies', *Public Administration*, 77(4): 713–30.

Gamble, A. (1989) 'Privatization, Thatcherism, and the British state', *Journal of Law and Society*, 16(1): 1–20.

Gamble, A. (2015) 'Austerity as statecraft', *Parliamentary Affairs*, 68(1): 42–57.

Gentleman, A. (2019) *The Windrush Betrayal: Exposing the Hostile Environment*, London: Guardian Faber.

Gentleman, A. (2020) 'Kate Eves: the abuse of detainees at Brook House was truly shocking', *The Guardian*, 28 April.

Geoghan, P. (2020) 'Cronyism and clientelism', *London Review of Books*, 42(21), 5 November.

Gershon, P. (1999) 'Review of civil procurement in central government', London: HMT. https://www.toronto.ca/ext/digital_comm/inquiry/inquiry_site/cd/gg/add_pdf/77/Procurement/Electronic_Documents/UK/U.K._Gershon_Report.pdf (accessed 12 October 2020).

Gershon, P. (2004) 'Review of efficiency', London: HMT.

Giddens, A. (2001) *The Third Way and Its Critics*, Cambridge: Polity.

Gideon, A. K. (2012) 'Higher education institutions and EU competition law', *Competition Law Review*, 8(2): 169–84.

Gilardi, F. (2001) 'Principal-agent models go to Europe: independent regulatory agencies as ultimate step of delegation', Paper presented at ECPR General Conference, Canterbury (UK). http://citeseerx.ist.psu.edu/viewdoc/download?doi=10.1.1.202.2258&rep=rep1&type=pdf (accessed 29 September 2019).

Gingrich, J. R. (2011) *Making Markets in the Welfare State: The Politics of Varying Market Reforms*, Cambridge: Cambridge University Press.

Glasson, J. and Marshall, T. (2007) *Regional Planning*, Abingdon: Routledge.

Goe, W. R. (1991) 'The growth of producer services industries: sorting through the externalization debate', *Growth and Change*, 22(4): 118–41.

Goetz, K. H. and Meyer-Sahling, J. H. (2009) 'Political time in the EU: dimensions, perspectives, theories', *Journal of European Public Policy*, 16(2): 180–201.

Goldsmith, M. and Newton, K. (1983) 'Central-local government relations: the irresistible rise of centralised power', *West European Politics*, 6(4), 216–33.

Gómez-Lobo, A. and Szymanski, S. (2001) 'A law of large numbers: bidding and compulsory competitive tendering for refuse collection contracts', *Review of Industrial Organization*, 18(1): 105–13.

González-Bailon, S., Jennings, W. and Lodge, M. (2013) 'Politics in the boardroom: corporate pay, networks and recruitment of former parliamentarians, ministers and civil servants in Britain', *Political Studies*, 61(4): 850–73.

Goodliffe, M. (2002) 'The new UK model for air traffic services—a public private partnership under economic regulation', *Journal of Air Transport Management*, 8(1): 13–18.

Gorse, C. and Sturges, J. (2017) 'Not what anyone wanted: observations on regulations, standards, quality and experience in the wake of Grenfell', *Construction Research and Innovation*, 8(3): 72–5.

Graham, C. (1995) 'Privatization–the United Kingdom experience', *Brooklyn Journal of International Law*, 21(1): 185–211.

Graham, S. (1997) 'Liberalized utilities, new technologies and urban social polarization: the UK experience', *European Urban and Regional Studies*, 4(2): 135–50.

Gray, A. and Jenkins, B. (1984) 'Lasting reforms in civil service management?', *The Political Quarterly*, 55(4): 418–27.

Gray, A. and Jenkins, W. I. (1986) 'Accountable management in British central government: some reflections on the financial management initiative', *Financial Accountability & Management*, 2(3): 171–86.

Greaves, R., and Scicluna, A. (2010) 'Commercialization and competition and in the education services sector', *International Journal for Education Law and Policy*, 6(1–2): 13–26.

Green, D. (1978) 'What does Red Bologna mean for Britain?', *Marxism Today*, pp 195–8.

Greenwood, R., Hinings, C. R. and Ranson, S. (1975) 'Contingency theory and the organization of local authorities. Part I: differentiation and integration', *Public Administration*, 53(1): 1–23.

Greer, S. L. and Jarman, H. (2010) 'What Whitehall? Definitions, demographics and the changing home civil service', *Public Policy and Administration*, 25(3): 251–70.

Griffiths, S. (2009) Cameron's Conservatives and the public services. In S. Lee and M. Beech (eds) *The Conservatives under David Cameron*, London: Palgrave Macmillan, pp 97–108.

Grimshaw, D., Vincent, S. and Willmott, H. (2002) 'Going privately: partnership and outsourcing in UK public services', *Public Administration*, 80(3): 475–502.

Grossman, G. M. and Helpman, E. (2005) 'Outsourcing in a global economy', *The Review of Economic Studies*, 72(1): 135–59.

Gruening, G. (2001) 'Origin and theoretical basis of New Public Management', *International Public Management Journal*, 4(1): 1–25.

Gustafsson, O. and Saksvik, P. Ø. (2005) 'Outsourcing in the public refuse collection sector: exploiting old certainties or exploring new possibilities?', *Work*, 25(2): 91–7.

Gustafsson, U. (2004) 'The privatisation of risk in school meals policies', *Health, Risk & Society*, 6(1): 53–65.

Guy, M. (2019) 'Between "going private" and "NHS privatisation": patient choice, competition reforms and the relationship between the NHS and private healthcare in England', *Legal Studies*, 39(3): 479–98.

Gyford, J. (1991) *Citizens, Consumers and Councils*, Basingstoke: Palgrave Macmillan.

Haddon, C. (2012) *Reforming the Civil Service: The Efficiency Unit in the Early 1980s and the 1987 Next Steps Report*, London: Institute for Government Report.

Haigh, N. (1996) 'Climate change policies and politics in the European community', in T. O'Riordan and J. Jäger (eds) *Politics of Climate Change: A European Perspective*, London and New York: Routledge, pp 155–85.

Halloran, D. (2017) 'The social value in social clauses: methods of measuring and evaluation in social procurement', in K. Thai (ed) *Global Public Procurement Theories and Practices*, Cham: Springer, pp 39–58.

Ham, C. (2018) *Management and Competition in the NHS*, Boca Raton, FL: CRC Press.

Hanley, D. (1996) 'France and GATT: the real politics of trade negotiations', in T. Chafer and B. Jenkins (eds) *France: From the Cold War to the New World Order*, London: Palgrave Macmillan, pp 137–51.

Hansard (1979) 'Multilateral trade negotiations', 29 June, volume 969, column 832.

Harmon, M. D. (1997) 'The 1976 UK-MF crisis: the markets, the Americans, and the IMF', *Contemporary British History*, 11(3): 1–17.

Harris, L. (2008) 'The changing nature of the HR function in UK local government and its role as "employee champion"', *Employee Relations*, 30(1): 34–47.

Harris, M. (2010) 'Third sector organizations in a contradictory policy environment', in D. Bills (ed) *Hybrid Organizations and the Third Sector: Challenges for Practice, Theory and Policy*, London: Palgrave Macmillan, pp 25–45.

Harvey, D. (2007) *A Brief History of Neoliberalism*, Oxford: Oxford University Press.

Hatcher, R. (2011) 'The conservative-liberal democrat coalition government's "free schools" in England', *Educational Review*, 63(4): 485–503.

Haugh, H. and Kitson, M. (2007) 'The Third Way and the third sector: New Labour's economic policy and the social economy', *Cambridge Journal of Economics*, 31(6): 973–94.

Haughton, G. (1998) 'Private profits–public drought: the creation of a crisis in water management for West Yorkshire', *Transactions of the Institute of British Geographers*, 23(4): 419–33.

Haughton, G. (2002) 'Market making: internationalisation and global water markets', *Environment and Planning A*, 34(5): 791–807.

Hayek, F. (1944) *Road to Serfdom*, Chicago: University of Chicago Press.

Hayek, F. A. and Hanson, C. G. (1984) *1980s Unemployment and the Unions: Essays on the Impotent Price Structure of Britain and Monopoly in the Labour Market*, London: Institute of Economic Affairs.

Heffernan, R. (1996) '"Blueprint for a revolution"? The politics of the Adam Smith institute', *Contemporary British History*, 10(1): 73–87.

Helgason, S. (1997) 'International benchmarking: experiences from OECD countries', Paper presented at International Benchmarking Conference, Copenhagen.

Hellowell, M. and Vecchi, V. (2012) 'An evaluation of the projected returns to investors on 10 PFI projects commissioned by the National Health Service', *Financial Accountability & Management*, 28(1): 77–100.

Helm, D. (1992) 'Environmental regulation: the Environment Agency proposal', *Fiscal Studies*, 13(2): 66–83.

Helm, D. (2006) 'Regulatory reform, capture, and the regulatory burden', *Oxford Review of Economic Policy*, 22(2): 169–85.

Helm, D. (2020) 'Thirty years after water privatization—is the English model the envy of the world?', *Oxford Review of Economic Policy*, 36(1): 69–85.

Hendrickson, J. M. (2001) 'The long and bumpy road to Glass-Steagall reform: a historical and evolutionary analysis of banking legislation', *American Journal of Economics and Sociology*, 60(4): 849–79.

Héritier, A. (2001) 'Market integration and social cohesion: the politics of public services in European regulation', *Journal of European Public Policy*, 8(5): 825–52.

Hervey, T. (1998) *European Social Law and Policy*, Harlow: Addison Wesley Longman.

Hervey, T. K. (2008) 'The European Union's governance of health care and the welfare modernization agenda', *Regulation & Governance*, 2(1): 103–20.

Hiam, L., Steele, S. and McKee, M. (2018) 'Creating a "hostile environment for migrants": the British government's use of health service data to restrict immigration is a very bad idea', *Health Economics, Policy and Law*, 13(2): 107–17.

Higashino, A. (2004) 'For the sake of "peace and security"? The role of security in the European Union enlargement eastwards', *Cooperation and Conflict*, 39(4): 347–68.

Higham, R. (2014) 'Free schools in the Big Society: the motivations, aims and demography of free school proposers', *Journal of Education Policy*, 29(1): 122–39.

Hindley, B. and Richardson, R. (1983) 'United Kingdom: pulling dragon's teeth—the National Enterprise Board', in B. Hindley (ed) *State Investment Companies in Western Europe*, London: Palgrave Macmillan, pp 263–81.

Hirst, P. and Thompson, G. (1999) *Globalisation in Question: The International Economy and the Possibilities of Governance*, 2nd edn, London: Polity, pp 335–53.

HMG (Her Majesty's Government) (1940) *Royal Commission on the Distribution of the Industrial Population: The Barlow Commission*, Cmnd 6513, London: HMG.

HMG (Her Majesty's Government) (1988) *Improving Management in Government: the Next Steps*, London: HMG.

HMG (Her Majesty's Government) (2014) *Glasgow and Clyde Valley City Deal*, London: HMG.

HMG (Her Majesty's Government) (2015) *West Midlands Devolution Deal*, London: HMG.

HMG (Her Majesty's Government) (2017) *Second West Midlands Devolution Deal*, London: HMG.

HMG (Her Majesty's Government) (2019a) *Belfast City Region Deal*, London: HMG.

HMG (Her Majesty's Government) (2019b) *The Dunlop Review into UK Government Union Capability*. 4 July.

HMT (Her Majesty's Treasury) (1995) White Paper, *Setting New Standards* (Cm 2840), London: HMT.

HMT (Her Majesty's Treasury) (2001) *Productivity in the UK 3 The Regional Dimension*, London: HMT.

HMT (Her Majesty's Treasury) (2004) *Productivity in the UK 4 The Local Dimension*, London: HMT.

HMT (Her Majesty's Treasury) (2007) *Transforming Government Procurement*, London: HMT.

HMT (Her Majesty's Treasury) (2019) *Private Finance Initiative and Private Finance 2 Projects: 2018 Summary Data Infrastructure and Projects Authority*, London: HMT.

Hodkinson, S. (2019) *Safe as Houses: Private Greed, Political Negligence and Housing Policy after Grenfell*, Manchester: Manchester University Press.

Hoekman, B. (1995) *Tentative First Steps: An Assessment of the Uruguay Round Agreement on Services*, Washington DC: The World Bank.

Hoekman, B. (2000) 'The next round of services negotiations: identifying priorities and options', *Review –Federal Reserve Bank of Saint Louis*, 82(4): 31–52.

Holmes, M. (2019) *The First Thatcher Government, 1979–1983: Contemporary Conservatism and Economic Change*, Abingdon: Routledge.

Hood, C. (1991) 'A public management for all seasons?', *Public Administration*, 69(1): 3–19.

Hood, C. (2011) *The Blame Game*, Oxford: Princeton University Press.

Hood, C. and Himaz, R. (2017) *A Century of Fiscal Squeeze Politics: 100 Years of Austerity, Politics, and Bureaucracy in Britain*, Oxford: Oxford University Press.

Hopkins, L. and Fairfoul, H. (2014) 'Employer perspectives on "zero hours" contracts in UK higher education', *Journal of Collective Bargaining in the Academy*, 0(9): 1–16.

Horner, L., Lekhi, R. and Blaug, R. (2006) *Deliberative Democracy and the Role of Public Managers*, London: The Work Foundation.

Howard, T., Kuri, L. and Lee, I. P. (2010) 'The Evergreen Cooperative Initiative of Cleveland, Ohio', White paper prepared for The Neighborhood Funders Group Annual Conference, Minneapolis, MN. https://staging.democracycollaborative.org/sites/clone.community-wealth.org/files/downloads/paper-howard-et-al.pdf (accessed 26 January 2020).

Huang, Y. (2016) 'Understanding China›s Belt & Road initiative: motivation, framework and assessment', *China Economic Review*, 40: 314–21.

Hubbard, P. (2008) 'Regulating the social impacts of studentification: a Loughborough case study', *Environment and Planning A*, 40(2): 323–41.

Hubble, S. and Bolton, P. (2019) 'The review of university admissions', House of Commons Library Briefing Paper: Number 8538, 10 April.

Hunter, D. (2016a) 'Does the NHS still reside in a grey area for EU competition law?', The UK in a Changing Europe, 6 April. https://ukandeu.ac.uk/does-the-nhs-still-reside-in-a-grey-area-for-eu-competition-law/ (accessed 12 November 2020).

Hunter, P. (2016b) 'The big health data sale: as the trade of personal health and medical data expands, it becomes necessary to improve legal frameworks for protecting patient anonymity, handling consent and ensuring the quality of data', EMBO Reports, 17(8): 1103–5.

Hutton, W. (1996) The State We're In, London: Random House.

Hwang, B. G., Zhao, X. and Gay, M. J. S. (2013) 'Public private partnership projects in Singapore: factors, critical risks and preferred risk allocation from the perspective of contractors', International Journal of Project Management, 31(3): 424–33.

Hyndman, N. S. and Anderson, R. (1995) 'The use of performance information in external reporting: an empirical study of UK executive agencies', Financial Accountability & Management, 11(1): 1–17.

Irani, Z., Love, P. E., Elliman, T., Jones, S. and Themistocleous, M. (2005) 'Evaluating e-government: learning from the experiences of two UK local authorities', Information Systems Journal, 15(1): 61–82.

Jackson, J. H. (1992) 'Status of treaties in domestic legal systems: a policy analysis', American Journal of International Law, 86(2): 310–40.

Jackson, J. H., Louis, J. V. and Matsushita, M. (1982) 'Implementing the Tokyo Round: legal aspects of changing international economic rules', Michigan Law Review, 81(2): 267–397.

Jackson, M. and Harrison, L. (2013) 'Responding to the Public Services (Social Value) Act 2012', CLES Bulletin, 95, 1–5.

Jacobs, M. (1988) 'Margaret Thatcher and the inner cities', Economic and Political Weekly, 1942–4.

Jäggi, M., Müller, R. and Schmid, S. (1977) Red Bologna, London: Writers and Readers.

James, T. S. (2010) 'Electoral modernisation or elite statecraft: electoral administration in the United Kingdom 1997–2007', British Politics, 5(2): 179–201.

James, T. S. (2016) 'Neo-statecraft theory, historical institutionalism and institutional change', Government and Opposition, 51(1): 84–110.

Jay, A. (1980) 'Informed sources', London Review of Books, 2(10), 22 May.

Jay, A. and Lynn, J. (1980–1988) Yes Minister, BBC TV.

Johnes, J. and Virmani, S. (2020) 'Chief executive pay in UK higher education: the role of university performance', Annals of Operations Research, 288(2): 547–76.

Johnson, B. (2020) 'Prime Minister Boris Johnson delivered his keynote speech today to wrap up Conservative Party Conference', 6 October. https://www.conservatives.com/news/boris-johnson-read-the-prime-ministers-keynote-speech-in-full (accessed 17 November 2020).

Johnston, A. and Wells, P. (2020) 'Assessing the role of universities in a place-based industrial strategy: evidence from the UK', *Local Economy: The Journal of the Local Economy Policy Unit*, 35(4): 384–402.

Jones, M. D. and McBeth, M. K. (2010) 'A narrative policy framework: clear enough to be wrong?', *Policy Studies Journal*, 38(2): 329–53.

Jones, P. (2020) 'Look to Preston for an answer to Labour's – and Britain's – woes', *The Guardian*, 13 January.

Jones, R. and Booth, R. (2009) 'Council backs radical 'easyJet' services plan', *The Guardian*, 22 October.

Joseph, K. (1975) *Why Britain Needs a Social Market Economy*, London: Centre for Policy Studies.

Kadelbach, S. (1999) 'International law and the incorporation of treaties into domestic law', *German Yearbook of International Law*, 42: 66.

Kafetz, A. (2016) 'Death of Dr Foster's hospital guide has spelt the end of proper transparency', *Health Services Journal*, 6 October. Available from: https://www.hsj.co.uk/quality-and-performance/death-of-dr-fosters-hospital-guide-has-spelt-the-end-of-proper-transparency/7011101.article (accessed 14 December 2020).

Kakabadse, N. K., Kakabadse, A. P. and Summers, N. (2007) 'Effectiveness of private finance initiatives (PFI): study of private financing for the provision of capital assets for schools', *Public Administration and Development: The International Journal of Management Research and Practice*, 27(1): 49–61.

Kazepov, Y. (2005) 'Cities of Europe: changing contexts, local arrangements, and the challenge to social cohesion', *Cities of Europe*, 1: 3–33.

Keddie, A. (2015) 'New modalities of state power: neoliberal responsibilisation and the work of academy chains', *International Journal of Inclusive Education*, 19(11): 1190–205.

Kelly, G., Mulgan, G. and Muers, S. (2002) *Creating Public Value*, London: Cabinet Office.

Kelly, J. (2003) 'The Audit Commission: guiding, steering and regulating local government', *Public Administration*, 81(3): 459–76.

Kelly, J. (2007) 'Reforming public services in the UK: bringing in the third sector', *Public Administration*, 85(4): 1003–22.

Kemp, A. (2013) *The Official History of North Sea Oil and Gas*, vol. 2: *Moderating the State's Role*, London: Routledge.

Kemp, P. (1990) 'Next steps for the British civil service', *Governance*, 3(2): 186–96.

Kendall, J. (2005) *Third Sector European Policy: Organisations Between Market and State, the Policy Process and the EU* (No. 1), London: The Centre for Civil Society, London School of Economics and Political Science.

Kendall, J. and Anheier, H. K. (1999) 'The third sector and the European Union policy process: an initial evaluation', *Journal of European Public Policy*, 6(2): 283–307.

Keohane, R. O. and Nye, J. S. (1989) *Power and Interdependence*, London: Little Brown.

Kerr, A. and Radford, M. (1994) 'TUPE or not TUPE: competitive tendering and the transfer laws', *Public Money & Management*, 14(4): 37–45.

King, A. (1985) 'Margaret Thatcher: the style of a prime minister', in A. King (ed) *The British Prime Minister*, London: Palgrave Macmillan, pp 96–140.

King, A. and Crewe, I. (2014) *The Blunders of Our Governments*, London: Oneworld.

King, R. A. and O'Sullivan, F. (2002) 'Financial management in selected community/foundation schools of the United Kingdom and charter schools of the United States', *Leadership and Policy in Schools*, 1(4): 291–316.

Kingdon, J. W. (1993) 'How do issues get on public policy agendas?', *Sociology and the Public Agenda*, 8(1): 40–53.

King's Fund (2020) 'England has highest excess death rate', 30 July. https://www.kingsfund.org.uk/press/press-release/excess-death-rate-ons-mortality-data (accessed 12 November 2020).

Kirton, G. and Guillaume, C. (2019) 'When welfare professionals encounter restructuring and privatization: the inside story of the probation service of England and Wales', *Work, Employment and Society*, 33(6): 929–47.

Kisby, B. (2010) 'The Big Society: power to the people?', *The Political Quarterly*, 81(4): 484–91.

Klijn, E. H. and Teisman, G. R. (2003) 'Institutional and strategic barriers to public–private partnership: an analysis of Dutch cases', *Public Money and Management*, 23(3): 137–46.

Knai, C., Petticrew, M., Durand, M. A., Scott, C., James, L., Mehrotra, A., Eastmure, E. and Mays, N. (2015) 'The Public Health Responsibility deal: has a public–private partnership brought about action on alcohol reduction?', *Addiction*, 110(8): 1217–25.

Kochanek, S. A. (1996) 'Liberalisation and business lobbying in India', *Journal of Commonwealth & Comparative Politics*, 34(3): 155–73.

Kolsaker, A. and Lee-Kelley, L. (2008) 'Citizens' attitudes towards e-government and e-governance: a UK study', *International Journal of Public Sector Management*, 21(7): 723–38.

Kraftl, P. (2012) 'Utopian promise or burdensome responsibility? A critical analysis of the UK government's Building Schools for the Future policy', *Antipode*, 44(3): 847–70.

Kramer, D. C. (2019) *State Capital and Private Enterprise: The Case of the UK National Enterprise Board*, London: Routledge.

Krugman, P. (1980) 'Scale economies, product differentiation, and the pattern of trade', *American Economic Review*, 70(5), 950–9.

Kuhlmann, S. and Jäkel, T. (2013) 'Competing, collaborating or controlling? Comparing benchmarking in European local government', *Public Money & Management*, 33(4): 269–76.

Kuijper, P. J. (1995) 'The conclusion and implementation of the Uruguay Round results by the European Community', *European Journal of International Law*, 6: 222–44.

Kuzma, J. M. (2010) 'Accessibility design issues with UK e-government sites', *Government Information Quarterly*, 27(2): 141–6.

Kynaston, D. (2008) *Austerity Britain*, London: Bloomsbury.

Lam, P. T. and Javed, A. A. (2015) 'Comparative study on the use of output specifications for Australian and UK PPP/PFI projects', *Journal of Performance of Constructed Facilities*, 29(2): 04014061.

Lambert, C. (2006) 'Community strategies and spatial planning in England: the challenges of integration', *Planning, Practice & Research*, 21(2): 245–55.

Lamer, W. (2009) 'Neoliberalism, Mike Moore, and the WTO', *Environment and Planning A*, 41(7): 1576–93.

Landers, B. (1999) 'Of ministers, mandarins and managers', in M. Flinders and M. Smith (eds) *Quangos, Accountability and Reform the Politics of Quasi-Government*, London: Palgrave Macmillan, pp 120–31.

Langhammer, R. J. (2005) 'The EU offer of service trade liberalization in the Doha Round: evidence of a not-yet-perfect customs union', *Journal of Common Market Studies*, 43(2): 311–25.

Larsson, B., Letell, M. and Thörn, H. (2012) 'Transformations of the Swedish welfare state: social engineering, governance and governmentality', in B. Larsson, M. Letell, M. and H. Thörn (eds) *Transformations of the Swedish Welfare State: From Social Engineering to Governance*, London: Palgrave Macmillan, pp 3–22.

Layard, A. (2012) 'The Localism Act 2011: what is 'local' and how do we (legally) construct it?', *Environmental Law Review*, 14(2): 134–44.

Lee, S. (2015) 'Why am I a Conservative? From one nation technocratic pragmatism to the developmental market', Available from: https://www.psa.ac.uk/sites/default/files/conference/papers/2015/DR%20SIMON%20LEE%20PSA%20PAPER%202015%20SHEFFIELD.pdf (accessed 17 November 2020).

Lethbridge, J. (2012) *Empty Promises: The Impact of Outsourcing on NHS Services*, London: University of Greenwich.

Lethbridge, J. (2017) *Privatisation of Migration and Refugee Services and Other Forms of State Disengagement*, London: University of Greenwich.

Levitt, R. and Solesbury, W. (2012) 'Policy tsars: here to stay but more transparency needed'. British Politics and Policy at LSE. http://blogs.lse.ac.uk/politicsandpolicy/ (accessed 17 November 2020).

Lewis, D. (1997) *Hidden Agendas: Politics, Law and Disorder*, London: Hamish Hamilton.

LGA (2011) *Shared Services and Management: A Guide for Councils*, London: LGA.

LGA (2012) *Crossing the Border: Research into Shared Chief Executives*, London: LGA.

LGA (2016a) *Case Study: Lambeth Living Well*. https://www.local.gov.uk/case-study-lambeth-living-well (accessed 12 November 2020).

LGA (2016b) *Case Study: Local Area Coordination – Derbyshire*. https://www.local.gov.uk/case-study-local-area-coordination-derbyshire (accessed 12 November 2020).

LGA (2016c) *Stronger Together: Shared Management in Local Government*, London: LGA.

LGA (2019) *Profit with a Purpose: Delivering Social Value Through Commercial Activity*, London: LGA.

Li, B., Akintoye, A., Edwards, P. J. and Hardcastle, C. (2005) 'Critical success factors for PPP/PFI projects in the UK construction industry', *Construction Management and Economics*, 23(5): 459–71.

Likierman, A. (1982) 'Management information for ministers: the MINIS system in the Department of the Environment', *Public Administration*, 60(2): 127–42.

Linder, W. (2011) 'Europe and Switzerland: Europeanization without EU membership', in C. Trampusch and A. Mach (eds) *Switzerland in Europe: Continuity and Change in the Swiss Political Economy*, London: Routledge, pp 65–82.

Linder, W. (2013) 'Switzerland and the EU: the puzzling effects of Europeanisation without institutionalisation', *Contemporary Politics*, 19(2): 190–202.

Lobina, E. and Hall, D. (2008) 'The illusions of competition in the water sector: a response to the OFWAT/Cave consultations on introducing competition in the water sector in England and Wales', PSIRU Reports.

Local Government Association, Ministry of Housing Communities and Local Government, The Cabinet Office (2018) *One Public Estate: Building a Movement Through Partnership*, London: LGA, MHCLG and Cabinet Office.

Lodge, M. and Wegrich, K. (2012) *Managing regulation: Regulatory Analysis, Politics and Policy*, London: Macmillan International Higher Education.

London School of Economics (2017) The role of foreign investors in the London residential market https://blogs.lse.ac.uk/businessreview/2017/06/17/the-role-of-foreign-investors-in-the-london-residential-market/ (accessed 12 November 2020).

Lowe, R. (2011) *The Official History of the British Civil Service: Reforming the Civil Service*, vol. 1: *The Fulton Years, 1966-81*, London: Routledge.

Lowndes, V. and Pratchett, L. (2012) 'Local governance under the coalition government: austerity, localism and the "Big Society"', *Local Government Studies*, 38(1): 21–40.

Lowndes, V. and McCaughie, K. (2013) 'Weathering the perfect storm? Austerity and institutional resilience in local government', *Policy & Politics*, 41(4): 533–49.

Loxley, J. (2018) *The Collapse of P3 Giant Carillion and Its Implications*, Ottawa, ON: Canadian Centre for Policy Alternatives.

Lu, L. (2017) 'Financial technology and challenger banks in the UK: gap fillers or real challengers?', *Journal of International Banking Law and Regulation*, 32(7): 273–82.

Lyal, R. (2015) 'Transfer pricing rules and state aid', *Fordham International Law Journal*, 38(4): 1017.

Lynk, E. L. (1993) 'Privatisation, joint production and the comparative efficiencies of private and public ownership: the UK water industry case', *Fiscal Studies*, 14(2): 98–116.

Lyons, B. and Zhu, M. (2013) 'Compensating competitors or restoring competition? EU regulation of state aid for banks during the financial crisis', *Journal of Industry, Competition and Trade*, 13(1): 39–66.

Mahony, P., Hextall, I. and Richardson, M. (2011) '"Building schools for the future": reflections on a new social architecture', *Journal of Education Policy*, 26(3): 341–60.

Mainwaring, C. and Cook, M. L. (2019) 'Immigration detention: an Anglo model', *Migration Studies*, 7(4): 455–76.

Manley, J. (2017) 'Local democracy with attitude: the Preston model and how it can reduce inequality', *British Politics and Policy Blog*, 23 November.

Marginson, S. (2006) 'Dynamics of national and global competition in higher education', *Higher Education*, 52(1): 1–39.

Marginson, S. and Considine, M. (2000) *The Enterprise University: Power, Governance and Reinvention in Australia*, Cambridge: Cambridge University Press.

Marquand, D. (1999) 'Foreword', in M. Flinders and M. Smith (eds) *Quangos, Accountability and Reform: The Politics of Quasi-Government*, London: Palgrave Macmillan, pp vii–viii.

Marsh, D. (1991) 'Privatization under Mrs. Thatcher: a review of the literature', *Public Administration*, 69(4): 459–80.

Marsh, D. (1992) *The New Politics of British Trade Unionism: Union Power and the Thatcher Legacy*, London: Macmillan International Higher Education.

Marsh, P. (2009) *Joseph Chamberlain: Entrepreneur in Politics*, London: Yale University Press.

Marshall, J. N., Alderman, N. and Thwaites, A. T. (1991) 'Civil service relocation and the English regions', *Regional Studies*, 25(6): 499–510.

Martin, D., Mariani, J. and Rouncefield, M. (2007) 'Managing integration work in an NHS electronic patient record (EPR) project', *Health Informatics Journal*, 13(1): 47–56.

Mattoo, A. (1996) 'The Government Procurement Agreement: implications of economic theory', *The World Economy*, 19(6): 695–720.

May, T. (2019) PM speech on the Union 4 July. Available from: https://www.gov.uk/government/speeches/pm-speech-on-the-union-4-july-2019 (accessed 14 December 2020).

Maynard, A. (1994) 'Can competition enhance efficiency in health care? Lessons from the reform of the UK National Health Service', *Social Science & Medicine*, 39(10): 1433–45.

Mazzucato, M. (2013) *The Entrepreneurial State: Debunking Public vs. Private Sector Myths*, London: Anthem Press.

McAfee, R. P. and McMillan, J. (1989) 'Government procurement and international trade', *Journal of International Economics*, 26(3–4): 291–308.

McCarthy, N. (1999) 'The UK Competition Act 1998', *International Business Law Journal*, 5: 521–41.

McKee, M., Edwards, N. and Atun, R. (2006) 'Public-private partnerships for hospitals', *Bulletin of the World Health Organization*, 84: 890–6.

Meijer, F. and Visscher, H. (2006) 'Deregulation and privatisation of European building-control systems?', *Environment and Planning B: Planning and Design*, 33(4): 491–501.

Melhuish, E. (2006) 'Policy and research on preschool care and education in the UK', in E. Melhuish and K. Petrogiannis (eds) *Early Childhood Care and Education: International Perspectives on Policy and Research*, London: Routledge, pp 43–64.

Meng, X. and Harshaw, F. (2013) 'The application of whole life costing in PFI/PPP projects', Proceedings 29th Annual ARCOM Conference, Reading: Association of Researchers in Construction Management.

Mennicken, A. (2013) '"Too big to fail and too big to succeed": accounting and privatisation in the Prison Service of England and Wales', *Financial Accountability & Management*, 29(2): 206–26.

Meredith, S. (2005) 'Labour Party revisionism and public expenditure: divisions of social democratic political economy in the 1970s', *Labour History Review*, 70(3): 253–73.

Meunier, S. (2005) *Trading Voices: The European Union in International Commercial Negotiations*, Princeton, NJ: Princeton University Press.

Meunier, S. and Nicolaïdis, K. (2005) 'The European Union as a trade power', *International Relations and the European Union*, 12: 247–69.

MHCLG (2019) National Planning Policy Framework London: MHCLG.

Micheli, P., Mason, S., Kennerley, M. and Wilcox, M. (2005) 'Public sector performance: efficiency or quality', *Measuring Business Excellence*, 9(2): 68–73.

Milbourne, L. and Cushman, M. (2015) 'Complying, transforming or resisting in the new austerity? Realigning social welfare and independent action among English voluntary organisations', *Journal of Social Policy*, 44(3): 463–85.

Miliband, D. (2006) 'More power to the people' text of speech to National Council for Voluntary Organisations'. https://www.theguardian.com/society/2006/feb/21/localgovernment.politics1 (accessed 18 November 2020).

Mills, D. E., Bradley, L. and Keast, R. (2019) 'NPG and Stewardship theory: remedies for NPM privatization prescriptions', *Public Management Review*, 1–22. doi.org/10.1080/14719037.2019.1695883

Mills, H., Silvestri, A. and Grimshaw, R. with Silberhorn-Armatrading, F. (2010) *Prison and Probation Expenditure 1999–2009*, London: Centre for Crime and Justice Studies.

Milne, R. G. (1997) 'Market-type mechanisms, market testing and market making: a longitudinal study of contractor interest in tendering', *Urban Studies*, 34(4): 543–59.

Mizell, L. (2018) 'Public-private partnerships at the subnational level of government: the case of PFI in the United Kingdom', in *Subnational Public-Private Partnerships: Meeting Infrastructure Challenges*, Paris: OECD, pp 75–105.

MoJ (2013) *Transforming Rehabilitation: A Strategy for Reform*, London: MoJ.

Mok, K. H. (2007) 'The search for new governance: corporatisation and privatisation of public universities in Malaysia and Thailand', *Asia Pacific Journal of Education*, 27(3): 271–90.

Monbiot, G. (2020) 'Tory privatisation is at the heart of the UK's disastrous coronavirus response', *The Guardian*, 27 May.

Moon, J., Richardson, J. J. and Smart, P. (1986) 'The privatisation of British Telecom: a case study of the extended process of legislation', *European Journal of Political Research*, 14(3): 339–55.

Mooney, G. and Wright, S. (2009) 'Introduction: social policy in the devolved Scotland: towards a Scottish welfare state?', *Social Policy and Society*, 8(3): 361–5.

Moore, M. (1995) *Creating Public Value: Strategic Management in Government*, Cambridge, MA: Harvard University Press.

Moorhead, J. (2020) 'No one questioned it': teacher's tribunal victory shines light on unfettered academy powers'. *The Guardian*, 10 November. https://www.theguardian.com/education/2020/nov/10/teachers-tribunal-victory-shines-light-on-unfettered-academy-powers (accessed 18 November 2020).

Moravcsik, A. (1994) 'Negotiating the Single European Act: national interests and conventional statecraft in the European Community', in B. F. Nelsen and A. C.-G. Stubb (eds) *The European Union*, London: Palgrave Macmillan , pp 211–33.

Morgan, K. O. (1997) *Callaghan: A Life*, Oxford: Oxford University Press.

Morphet, J. (2008) *Modern Local Government*, London: SAGE.

Morphet, J. (2013) *How Europe Shapes British Public Policy*, Bristol: Policy Press.

Morphet, J. R. (2016) 'Local authorities build housing again...', *Town and Country Planning*, 85(5), 170–7.

Morphet, J. (2017) Beyond Brexit, Bristol: Policy Press.

Morphet, J. (2021a) *The Impact of COVID-19 on Devolution: Re-centralising the British State Beyond Brexit?*, Bristol: Bristol University Press.

Morphet, J. (2021b) 'Public Value management in Brexit Britain', in J. Connolly and A. van der Zwet (eds) *Public Value Management, Governance and Reform in Britain*, Basingstoke: Palgrave Macmillan.

Morphet, J. and Clifford, B. (2020) *Reviving Local Authority Housing Delivery: Challenging Austerity Through Municipal Entrepreneurialism*, Bristol: Policy Press.

Morphet, J., Morphet, R. and Batty, J. M. (2019) *New Urban Agenda: New Urban Analytics*, London: UCL CASA.

Morris, J. and McGuinness, M. (2019) 'Liberalisation of the English water industry: what implications for consumer engagement, environmental protection, and water security?', *Utilities Policy*, 60: 100939.

Morris, M. and Kibasi, T. (2019) *State Aid Rules and Brexit*, London: IPPR.

Mosse, B. and Whitley, E. A. (2009) 'Critically classifying: UK e-government website benchmarking and the recasting of the citizen as customer', *Information Systems Journal*, 19(2): 149–73.

Mount F. (2020a) 'Après Brexit', *London Review of Books*, 20 February, 42(4).

Mount, F. (2020b) 'Superman falls to earth', *London Review of Books*, 42(13).

Moyle, P. (1992) 'Privatising prisons: the underlying issues', *Alternative Law Journal*, 17(3): 114–19.

Mulhearn, C. and Franco, M. (2018) 'If you build it will they come? The boom in purpose-built student accommodation in central Liverpool: destudentification, studentification and the future of the city', *Local Economy*, 33(5): 477–95.

Murray, J. G. (2011) 'Third sector commissioning and English local government procurement', *Public Money & Management*, 31(4): 279–86.

NAO (National Audit Office) (2001) *Inland Flood Defence*, London: NAO.

NAO (National Audit Office) (2003) *Managing the Prison Estate*, London: NAO.

NAO (National Audit Office) (2006a) *Update on PFI Debt Refinancing and the PFI Equity Market* (Vol. 1040), London: The Stationery Office.

NAO (National Audit Office) (2006b) *Central Government's Use of Consultants*, London: NAO.

NAO (National Audit Office) (2007) Dr Foster Intelligence: A joint venture between the Information Centre and Dr Foster LLP, London: NAO.

NAO (National Audit Office) (National Audit Office) (2009) Dr Foster Intelligence: A joint venture between the Information Centre and Dr Foster LLP, London: NAO.

NAO (National Audit Office) (2010) *Ofcom: The Effectiveness of Converged Regulation*, London: NAO.

NAO (National Audit Office) (2011a) *Flood Risk Management in England*, London: NAO.

NAO (National Audit Office) (2011b) *The National Programme for IT in the NHS: An Update on the Delivery of Detailed Care Records Systems*, London: NAO.

NAO (National Audit Office) (2012) *The UK Border Agency and Border Force: Progress in Cutting Costs and Improving Performance*, London: NAO.

NAO (National Audit Office) (2014a) *Reforming the UK Border and Immigration System*, London: NAO.

NAO (National Audit Office) (2014b) *Strategic Flood Risk Management*, London: NAO.

NAO (National Audit Office) (2015a) *The Economic Regulation of the Water Sector*, London: NAO.

NAO (National Audit Office) (2015b) *Reform of the Rail Franchising Programme*, London: NAO.

NAO (National Audit Office) (2015c) *Welfare Reform – Lessons Learned*, London: NAO.

NAO (National Audit Office) (2016) *Financial Sustainability of Local Authorities: Capital Expenditure and Resourcing*, London: NAO.

NAO (National Audit Office) (2018a) *Handling of the Windrush Situation*, London: NAO.

NAO (National Audit Office) (2018b) *PFI 1 and PFI 2*, London: NAO.

NAO (National Audit Office) (2018c) Financial sustainability of local authorities. London: NAO.

NAO (National Audit Office) (2019a) *Transforming Rehabilitation: Progress Review*, London: NAO.

NAO (National Audit Office) (2019b) *Regulating to Protect Consumers: Utilities, Communications and Financial Services Markets*, London: NAO.

NAO (National Audit Office) (2019c) *Departments' Use of Consultants to Support Preparations for EU Exit*, London: NAO.

NAO (National Audit Office) (2020a) *Managing Major Projects*, London: NAO.

NAO (National Audit Office) (2020b) *Investigation into the Rescue of Carillion's PFI Hospital Contracts*, London: NAO.

NAO (National Audit Office) (2020c) *Water Supply and Demand Management*, London: NAO.

NAO (National Audit Office) (2020d) *Overview of the UK Government's Response to the COVID-19 Pandemic*, London: NAO.

NAO (National Audit Office) (2020e) *Managing PFI Assets and Services as Contracts End*, London: NAO.

NAO (National Audit Office) (2020f) Immigration Enforcement London NAO.

NAO (National Audit Office) (2020g) Investigation into government procurement during the COVID-19 pandemic. London: NAO.

Naoum, S. (2003) 'An overview into the concept of partnering', *International Journal of Project Management*, 21(1): 71–6.

Naylor, C. and Wellings, D. (2019) *A Citizen-Led Approach to Health and Care: Lessons from the Wigan Deal*, London: The King's Fund.

Newell, G. and Marzuki, M. J. (2018) 'The emergence of student accommodation as an institutionalised property sector', *Journal of Property Investment & Finance*, 36(6): 523–8.

Newman, J., Richards, S. and Smith, P. (1998) 'Market testing and institutional change in the UK civil service: compliance, non-compliance and engagement', *Public Policy and Administration*, 13(4): 96–110.

NHS Confederation (2009) 'What do EU competition rules mean for the NHS?' Briefing No 4. Available from: https://www.nhsconfed. org/-/media/Confederation/Files/Publications/Documents/Euro_ Briefing_4_final.pdf?la=en&hash=B51E061C058E92B05EBC6FD3A 11C7DD1D9AC8164 (accessed 14 December 2020).

Nicholls, J. (2007) *Why Measuring and Communicating Social Value Can Help Social Enterprise Become More Competitive*, London: Cabinet Office.

Nolan, Lord (1995) The seven principles of public life. https://www. gov.uk/government/publications/the-7-principles-of-public-life/the-7-principles-of-public-life--2 (accessed 18 November 2020).

ODPM (Office of the Deputy Prime Minister) (2004a) 'Incremental partnering for public/private partnering', Strategic Partnering Taskforce, Technical Advice Note Issue 9, January, London: ODPM.

ODPM (Office of the Deputy Prime Minister) (2004b) 'Rethinking service delivery: volume four, from outline business case to contract signing', Strategic Partnering Taskforce, February, London: ODPM.

ODPM (Office of the Deputy Prime Minister) (2004c) 'Rethinking service delivery: volume five: making the partnership a success', Strategic Partnering Taskforce, February, London: ODPM.

ODPM (Office of the Deputy Prime Minister) (2004d) 'Strategic Partnering Taskforce – Final Report', March, London: ODPM.

OECD (Organisation for Economic Co-operation and Development) (1994) *Performance Management in Government: Performance Measurement and Results-Oriented Management*, Public Management Occasional Papers, No. 3, Paris: OECD.

OECD (Organisation for Economic Co-operation and Development) (1997) *In Search of Results: Performance Management Practices*, Paris: OECD.

OECD (Organisation for Economic Co-operation and Development) (2002) *United Kingdom – The Role of Competition Policy in Regulatory Reform*, Country Studies. https://www.oecd.org/daf/competition/ sectors/27068497.pdf (accessed 1 February 2020).

OECD (Organisation for Economic Co-operation and Development) (2008) *Public-Private Partnerships: In Pursuit of Risk Sharing and Value for Money*, Paris: OECD.

OECD (Organisation for Economic Co-operation and Development) (2009) *Revolving Doors, Accountability and Transparency: Emerging Regulatory Concerns and Policy Solutions in the Financial Crisis*, Report of Expert Group, Paris: OECD.

OECD (Organisation for Economic Co-operation and Development) (2011) *Together for Better Public Services: Partnering with Citizens and Civil Society*, Paris: OECD.

OECD (Organisation for Economic Co-operation and Development) (2012) *Recommendation of the Council on Principles for Public Governance of Public-Private Partnerships*, Paris: OECD.

OECD (Organisation for Economic Co-operation and Development) (2013a) *Government at a Glance*, Paris: OECD.

OECD (Organisation for Economic Co-operation and Development) (2013b) *Water Security for Better Lives*, OECD Studies on Water, Paris: OECD.

OECD (Organisation for Economic Co-operation and Development) (2015a) *Effective Delivery of Large Infrastructure Projects: The Case of the New International Airport of Mexico City*, OECD Public Governance Reviews, Paris: OECD.

OECD (Organisation for Economic Co-operation and Development) (2015b) *Towards a Framework for the Governance of Infrastructure*, Paris: OECD.

OECD (Organisation for Economic Co-operation and Development) (2015c) *Education Indicators in Focus*, no 5., July, Available from: https://www.oecd-ilibrary.org/docserver/5k43k8r4k821-en.pdf?expires=1589713914&id=id&accname=guest&checksum=4F02667A15A7CF599075EF16E3801E87 (accessed 17 November 2020).

OECD (Organisation for Economic Co-operation and Development) (2017a) *Public Procurement for Innovation: Good Practices and Strategies*, OECD Public Governance Reviews, Paris: OECD.

OECD (Organisation for Economic Co-operation and Development) (2017b) *OECD Transfer Pricing Guidelines for Multinational Enterprises and Tax Administrations 2017*, Paris: OECD.

OECD (Organisation for Economic Co-operation and Development) (2017c) *Caring for Quality in Health*, Paris: OECD.

OECD (Organisation for Economic Co-operation and Development) (2018) *SMEs in Public Procurement: Practices and Strategies for Shared Benefits*, OECD Public Governance Reviews, Paris: OECD.

OECD (Organisation for Economic Co-operation and Development) (2019) *Reforming Public Procurement: Progress in Implementing the 2015 OECD Recommendation*, OECD Public Governance Reviews, Paris: OECD.

OECD (Organisation for Economic Co-operation and Development) (2020) *The Territorial Impact of COVID-19: Managing the Crisis Across Levels of Government*, Paris: OECD.

OECD (Organisation for Economic Co-operation and Development) (2020b) 'International Student mobility Education at a glance'. https://data.oecd.org/students/international-student-mobility.htm (accessed 12 November 2020).

OECD/WTO (Organisation for Economic Co-operation and Development/World Trade Organisation) (2019) *Facilitating Trade Through Regulatory Cooperation: The Case of the WTO's TBT/SPS Agreements and Committees*, Paris and Geneva: OECD.

OFT (Office of Fair Trading) (2006) 'Independent schools: exchange of information on future fees report on case'. Available from: https://www.gov.uk/cma-cases/independent-schools-exchange-of-information-on-future-fees (accessed 14 December 2020).

Ogden, S. G. (1995) 'Transforming frameworks of accountability: the case of water privatization', *Accounting, Organizations and Society*, 20(2–3): 193–218.

Oldfield, A. (1990) *Citizenship and Community: Civic Republicanism and the Modern World*, Abingdon: Routledge.

O'Neill, M. (2016) 'The road to socialism is the A59: the Preston model', *Renewal*, 24(2): 69–78.

Opoku, A. and Guthrie, P. (2018) 'The Social Value Act 2012: current state of practice in the social housing sector', *Journal of Facilities Management*, 16(3): 253–68.

Osborne, D. and Gaebler, T. (1993) *Reinventing Government: How the Entrepreneurial Spirit Is Transforming the Public Sector*, New York: Addison-Wesley,

Oshri, I., Kotlarsky, J. and Willcocks, L. P. (2015) *The Handbook of Global Outsourcing and Offshoring* (3rd edn), Basingstoke: Palgrave Macmillan.

Overbeek, H. (1993) 'Atlanticism and Europeanism in British foreign policy', in H. Overbeek (ed) *Restructuring Hegemony in the Global Political Economy*, London: Routledge, pp 124–47.

Packham, D. E. (2003) 'GATS and universities: implications for research', *Science and Engineering Ethics*, 9(1): 85–100.

Page, E. and Jenkins (2005) *Policy Bureaucracy: Government with a Cast of Thousands*, Oxford: Oxford University Press.

Page, E. and Wright, V. (eds) (2006) *From the Active to the Enabling State: The Changing Role of Top Officials in European Nations*, Basingstoke: Palgrave Macmillan.

Painter, J. (1991) 'Compulsory competitive tendering in local government: the first round', *Public Administration*, 69(2): 191–210.

Palley, T. I. (2005) 'From Keynesianism to neoliberalism: shifting paradigms in economics', in A. Saad-Filho and D. Johnston (eds) *Neoliberalism: A Critical Reader*, London: Pluto, pp 20–9.

Panchamia, N. and Gash, T. (2012) 'Competition in prisons', Institute for Government. https://www.instituteforgovernment.org.uk/sites/default/files/publications/Prisons%20briefing%20final.pdf (accessed 12 November 2020).

Paris, C. (2017) 'The super-rich and transnational housing markets: Asians buying Australian housing', in R. Forrest, S. Y. Koh and B. Wissink (eds) *Cities and the Super-Rich: Real Estate, Elite Practices and Urban Political Economies*, New York: Palgrave Macmillan, pp 63–83.

Parker, D. (1990) 'The 1988 Local Government Act and compulsory competitive tendering', *Urban Studies*, 27(5): 653–67.

Parker, D. (1991) *Privatisation Ten Years On: A Critical Analysis of Its Rationale and Results*, Cranfield: Cranfield University Press.

Parker, D. (2000) *Reforming Competition Law in the UK: The Competition Act 1998*, Bath: University of Bath, Centre for the Study of Regulated Industries.

Parker, D. (2009) *The Official History of Privatisation*, vol. 1: *The Formative Years 1970–1987*, London: Routledge.

Parker, D. (2012) *The Official History of Privatisation*, vol. 2: *Popular Capitalism 1987–1997*, London: Routledge.

Parry, R. (2004) 'The civil service and intergovernmental relations', *Public Policy and Administration*, 19(2): 50–63.

Patz, R. and Goetz, K. (2015) 'From politicised budgeting to political budgets in the EU?'. https://www.ippapublicpolicy.org/file/paper/1434615065.pdf (accessed 12 November 2020).

Pellegrin, J. (2016) *The Political Economy of Competitiveness in an Enlarged Europe*, Basingstoke: Palgrave Macmillan.

Pelling, H. (1979) 'The working class and the origins of the welfare state', in *Popular Politics and Society in Late Victorian Britain*, London: Palgrave Macmillan, pp 1–18.

Pendleton, A. (1997) 'The evolution of industrial relations in UK nationalized industries', *British Journal of Industrial Relations*, 35(2): 145–72.

Penny, J. (2017) 'Between coercion and consent: the politics of "Cooperative Governance" at a time of "Austerity Localism" in London', *Urban Geography*, 38(9): 1352–73.

Penny, J. (2018) 'The "cooperative" or "cop-out" council? Urban politics at a time of austerity localism in London', in T. Enright and U. Rossi (eds) *The Urban Political: Ambivalent Spaces of Late Neoliberalism*, Cham: Palgrave Macmillan, pp 147–69.

PHE (2015) 'Local action on health inequalities: using the Social Value Act to reduce health inequalities in England through action on the social determinants of health', Practice Resource Summary.

Pilkington, C. (1999) *The Civil Service in Britain Today*, Manchester: Manchester University Press.

Pirvu, D. and Clipici, E. (2016) 'Social enterprises and the EU's public procurement market', *Voluntas: International Journal of Voluntary and Nonprofit Organizations*, 27(4), 1611–37.

Plaitzky L. (1980) *Non-Departmental Public Bodies*, London: HMT.

Pliatzky, L. (1992) 'Quangos and agencies' *Public Administration*, 70(4): 555–63.

Pliatzky, L. (1988) 'Optimising the role of the public sector: constraints and remedial policies', *Public Policy and Administration*, 3(1–2): 35–45.

Polidano, C. (1999) 'The bureaucrat who fell under a bus: ministerial responsibility, executive agencies and the Derek Lewis affair in Britain', *Governance*, 12(2): 201–29.

Pollitt, C. (1994) 'The Citizen's Charter: a preliminary analysis', *Public Money & Management*, 14(2): 9–14.

Pollitt, C. and Bouckaert, G. (2000) *Public Management Reform: A Comparative Analysis*, Oxford: Oxford University Press.

Pollock, A. M. and Godden, S. (2008) 'Independent sector treatment centres: evidence so far', *BMJ*, 336(7641): 421–4.

Pollock, A. M., Clements, L. and Harding-Edgar, L. (2020) 'Covid-19: why we need a national health and social care service', *BMJ*, 369: m1465.

Porteous, C. (2018) 'Is commercial/private sector access to administrative data inevitable?', *International Journal of Population Data Science*, 3(2). doi: 10.23889/ijpds.v3i2.563.

Porter, T. and Webb, M. (2008) 'The role of the OECD in the orchestration of global knowledge networks', in R. Mahon and S. McBride (eds) *The OECD and Transnational Governance*, Vancouver: University of British Columbia Press, pp 43–59.

Preeg, E. H. (2012) 'The Uruguay Round negotiations and the creation of the WTO', in M. Daunton, A. Narlikar and R. M. Stern (eds) *The Oxford Handbook on The World Trade Organization*, Oxford: Oxford University Press, pp 122–40.

Price, C. W. (2005) 'The effect of liberalizing UK retail energy markets on consumers', *Oxford Review of Economic Policy*, 21(1): 128–44.

Prison Reform Trust (1991) 'The Woolf Report', London: Prison Reform Trust. Available from: http://www.prisonreformtrust.org.uk/portals/0/documents/woolf%20report.pdf (accessed 14 December 2020).

Propper, C., Croxson, B. and Shearer, A. (2002) 'Waiting times for hospital admissions: the impact of GP fundholding', *Journal of Health Economics*, 21(2): 227–52.

Quinn, J. B. and Hilmer, F. G. (1994) 'Strategic outsourcing', *MIT Sloan Management Review*, 35(4): 43–55.

Radnor, Z. and Johnston, R. (2013) 'Lean in UK government: internal efficiency or customer service?', *Production Planning & Control*, 24(10–11): 903–15.

Rashman, L. and Radnor, Z. (2005) 'Learning to improve: approaches to improving local government services', *Public Money and Management*, 25(1): 19–26.

Raynsford, N. (2006) 'The future of local government', Speech given at NLGN Annual Conference.

Regan, P. and Ball, E. (2010) 'Liberating the NHS; commissioning, outsourcing and a new politics debate', *British Journal of Community Nursing*, 15(10): 503–5.

Rhodes, R. A. W. (2018) *Control and Power in Central-Local Government Relations*, Abingdon: Routledge.

Rhodes, R. A. W. (2001) 'United Kingdom: "everybody but us"', in R. A. W. Rhodes and P. Weller (eds) *The Changing World of Top Officials. Mandarins or Valets?*, Buckingham: Open University Press, pp 111–51.

Ridley, N. (1992) *My Style of Government: The Thatcher Years*, London: Hutchinson.

Rippon, G. (1973) 'Opening address', in *Creating the New Local Government*, RIPA Conference Report, London: RIPA, pp 1–3.

Rittenberg, L. E. and Covaleski, M. (1999) 'Outsourcing the internal audit function: the British government experience with market testing', *International Journal of Auditing*, 3(3): 225–35.

Ritzer, G. (1983) 'The "McDonaldization" of society', *Journal of American Culture*, 6(1): 100–7.

Roberts, J. (2004) *The Modern Firm*, Oxford: Oxford University Press.

Robinson, C. and Adams, N. (2008) 'Unlocking the potential: the role of universities in pursuing regeneration and promoting sustainable communities', *Local Economy*, 23(4): 277–89.

Robinson, G. and Burnett, R. (2007) 'Experiencing modernization: frontline probation perspectives on the transition to a National Offender Management Service', *Probation Journal*, 54(4): 318–37.

Robinson, G., Burke, L. and Millings, M. (2016) 'Criminal justice identities in transition: the case of devolved probation services in England and Wales', *British Journal of Criminology*, 56(1): 161–78.

Robinson, H. S. and Scott, J. (2009) 'Service delivery and performance monitoring in PFI/PPP projects', *Construction Management and Economics*, 27(2): 181–97.

Rodwin, V. G. and Le Pen, C. (2004) 'Health care reform in France: the birth of state-led managed care', *New England Journal of Medicine*, 351(22): 2259–62.

Roelich, K. and Bale, C. S. E. (2015) 'Municipal energy companies in the UK: motivations and barriers', in T. E. Dolan and B. Collins (eds) *International Symposium for Next Generation Infrastructure Conference Proceedings: 30 September–1 October 2014*, Schloss Laxenburg, Vienna: International Institute of Applied Systems Analysis (IIASA), UCL.

Rowe, J. K., Peredo, A. M., Sullivan, M. and Restakis, J. (2017) 'Cooperative development, policy, and power in a period of contested neoliberalism: the case of Evergreen Cooperative Corporation in Cleveland, Ohio', *Socialist Studies*, 12(1): 54–77.

RTPI (2019) The UK Planning Profession in 2019. https://www.google.com/search?q=rtpi+uk+planning+profession+in+2019&rlz=1C1GGRV_enGB751GB751&sxsrf=ALeKk03zexZV1R9mIV-Rl NJcZ1YQlVu4hg:1605616567445&tbm=isch&source=iu&ictx=1& fir=-i4o4vZ0OvAfSM%252CMr2PBJMyBS8qpM%252C_&vet=1 &usg=AI4_-kRUYnkKwXGIpfumSIGu9Fsu2-ntxw&sa=X&ved=2a hUKEwiSopfpy4ntAhUNYsAKHfVrDM4Q9QF6BAgCEAM#img rc=-i4o4vZ0OvAfSM (accessed 17 November 2020).

Rudd, T. and O'Brien, S. (2019) 'The system crisis 2020: the end of neoliberal higher education in the UK?', *Journal for Critical Education Policy Studies*, 17(3), 24–49.

Ruddock, L. (1994) 'Performance and efficiency measurement in local authority building organisations', Doctoral dissertation, University of Salford. http://usir.salford.ac.uk/id/eprint/14709/1/DX192999.pdf (accessed 17 November 2020).

Rydin, Y. (1998) *Urban and Environmental Planning in the UK*, London: Macmillan International Higher Education.

Sage, J., Smith, D. and Hubbard, P. (2012) 'The diverse geographies of studentification: living alongside people not like us', *Housing Studies*, 27(8): 1057–78.

Saintier, S. (2017) 'Community energy companies in the UK: a potential model for sustainable development in "local" energy?', *Sustainability*, 9(8): 1–18.

Saint-Martin, D. (2012) 'Governments and management consultants: supply, demand, and effectiveness', in T. Clark and M. Kipping (eds) *The Oxford Handbook of Management Consulting*, Oxford: Oxford University Press, pp 447–64.

Samii, R., Van Wassenhove, L. N. and Bhattacharya, S. (2002) 'An innovative public–private partnership: new approach to development', *World Development*, 30(6): 991–1008.

Sandel, M. J. (2012) *What Money Can't Buy: The Moral Limits of Markets*, Basingstoke: Palgrave Macmillan.

Sanderson, I. (2001) 'Performance management, evaluation and learning in "modern" local government', *Public Administration*, 79(2): 297–313.

Sanderson, I. (2002) 'Evaluation, policy learning and evidence-based policy making', *Public Administration*, 80(1): 1–22.

Sandford, M. (2017) 'Combined authorities'. House of Commons Library Briefing Paper 06649, London: House of Commons Library.

Sands, V., O'Neill, D. and Hodge, G. (2019) 'Cheaper, better, and more accountable? Twenty-five years of prisons privatisation in Victoria', *Australian Journal of Public Administration*, 78(4): 577–95.

Sauter, W. (2008) *Services of General Economic Interest and Universal Service in EU Law*, Tilburg: Tilburg University.

Sauvé, P. (2002) 'Trade, education and the GATS', *Higher Education Management and Policy*, 14(3): 47–76.

Saxby, S. (2006) 'Public policy and the development of a UK national geographic information strategy', *International Journal of Law and Information Technology*, 14(2): 147–94.

Schildhaus, A. (1989) '1992 and the Single European Act', *The International Lawyer*, 23(2): 549–55.

Schulten, T., Brandt, T. and Hermann, C. (2008) 'Liberalisation and privatisation of public services and strategic options for European trade unions', *Transfer: European Review of Labour and Research*, 14(2): 295–311.

Schütze, R. (2009) 'Subsidiarity after Lisbon: reinforcing the safeguards of federalism?', *The Cambridge Law Journal*, 68(3): 525–36.

Scott, A., Peterson, J. and Millar, D. (1994) 'Subsidiarity: a Europe of the regions v. the British constitution', *JCMS: Journal of Common Market Studies*, 32(1): 47–67.

Seal, W. (1999) 'Accounting and competitive tendering in UK local government: an institutionalist interpretation of the new public management', *Financial Accountability & Management*, 15(3–4): 309–27.

Seddon, J. and Brand, C. (2008) 'Debate: systems thinking and public sector performance', *Public Money and Management*, 28(1): 7–10.

Seldon, A. and Collings, D. (2014) *Britain Under Thatcher*, London: Routledge.

Selsdon Group (1973) 'The Selsdon Group manifesto – 19th September 1973', 25th Anniversary Reprint. https://www.selsdongroup.co.uk/manifesto.pdf (accessed 12 November 2020).

Shanahan, E. A., Jones, M. D. and McBeth, M. K. (2011) 'Policy narratives and policy processes', *Policy Studies Journal*, 39(3): 535–61.

Shanks, M. (1961) *The Stagnant Society: a Warning*, London: Penguin Books.

Shapps, G. (2020) 'Rail franchising reaches the terminus as a new railway takes shape', 21 September. Available from: https://www.gov.uk/government/news/rail-franchising-reaches-the-terminus-as-a-new-railway-takes-shape (accessed 14 December 2020).

Shaw, K., Fenwick, J. and Foreman, A. (1994) 'Compulsory competitive tendering for local government services: the experiences of local authorities in the North of England 1988-1992', *Public Administration*, 72(2): 201–17.

Shearmur, J. (1997) 'Hayek, Keynes and the state', *History of Economics Review*, 26(1): 68–82.

Sheffield, H. (2017) 'The Preston Model: UK takes lessons in recovery from rust-belt Cleveland', *The Guardian*, 11 April. https://www.theguardian.com/cities/2017/apr/11/preston-cleveland-model-lessons-recovery-rust-belt (accessed 17 November 2020).

Shleifer, A. (2009) 'The age of Milton Friedman', *Journal of Economic Literature*, 47(1): 123–35.

Siciliani, L., Chalkley, M. and Gravelle, H. (2017) *Competition Policy in Five European Countries: What Can Be Learned for Health Policy in England?*, London: The Health Foundation.

Silverman, S. and Griffiths, M. (2019) *Immigration Detention in the UK*, Oxford: UK Migration Observatory.

Siverbo, S. (2004) 'The purchaser-provider split in principle and practice: experiences from Sweden', *Financial Accountability & Management*, 20(4): 401–20.

Smith, M. J. (2011) 'The paradoxes of Britain's strong centre: delegating decisions and retaining control' in Dahlström et al pp 166–90.

Smith, M. and Jones, R. (2015) 'From big society to small state: conservatism and the privatisation of government', *British Politics*, 10(2): 226–48.

Smith, M. J. (2010) 'From big government to big society: changing the state–society balance', *Parliamentary Affairs*, 63(4): 818–33.

Smith, M. P. (1998) 'Autonomy by the rules: the European Commission and the development of state aid policy', *JCMS: Journal of Common Market Studies*, 36(1): 55–78.

Smith, P. (1988) 'Assessing competition among local authorities in England and Wales', *Financial Accountability & Management*, 4(3): 235–51.

Smulian M. (2020) 'Good Law Project and Runnymede Trust send pre-action letter over appointment of head of National Institute for Health Protection', *Local Government Lawyer*. 4 November.

Smyth, A. and Kelleher, L. (2012) 'School choice, education reform, and fiscal austerity: UK perspective on their implications for school transport', The National Academies of Sciences, Engineering, and Medicine (No. 12-4143).

Sorrentino, M., Sicilia, M. and Howlett, M. (2018) 'Understanding co-production as a new public governance tool', Policy and Society, 37(3): 277–93.

Stern, J. (2004) 'Regulatory forbearance: why did Oftel find it so hard?', Telecommunications Policy, 28(3–4): 273–94.

Stern, J. and Cubbin, J. (2005) Regulatory Effectiveness: The Impact of Regulation and Regulatory Governance Arrangements on Electricity Industry Outcomes, Washington, DC: The World Bank Policy Research Working Paper.

Stewart, J. and Walsh, K. (1992) 'Change in the management of public services', Public Administration, 70(4): 499–518.

Stivers, C. (2008) Governance in Dark Times: Practical Philosophy for Public Service, Washington, DC: Georgetown University Press.

Stojanovic, A. (2020) State Aid Rules After Brexit, London: Institute for Government.

Stoker, G. (1989) 'Creating a local government for a post-Fordist society: the Thatcherite project?', in J. Stewart and G. Stoker (eds) The Future of Local Government. Government Beyond the Centre, London: Palgrave Macmillan, pp 141–70.

Stoker, G. (2006) 'Public value management: a new narrative for networked governance?', The American Review of Public Administration, 36(1): 41–57.

Stone, D. (1998) 'Principles and pragmatism in the "privatisation" of British higher education', Policy & Politics, 26(3): 255–71.

Stone, D. (2000) 'Non-governmental policy transfer: the strategies of independent policy institutes', Governance, 13(1): 45–70.

Stratton, A. (2010) 'Labour to rebrand Lambeth as "John Lewis" council', The Guardian, 17 February.

Stringfellow, A., Teagarden, M. B. and Nie, W. (2008) 'Invisible costs in offshoring services work', Journal of Operations Management, 26(2): 164–79.

Swyngedouw, E. (2005) 'Dispossessing H2O: the contested terrain of water privatization', Capitalism Nature Socialism, 16(1): 81–98.

Szymanski, S. (1996) 'The impact of compulsory competitive tendering on refuse collection services', Fiscal Studies, 17(3): 1–19.

Szymanski, S. and Wilkins, S. (1993) 'Cheap rubbish? Competitive tendering and contracting out in refuse collection–1981–88', Fiscal Studies, 14(3): 109–30.

Talbot, C. (2009) 'Public value—the next "big thing" in public management?', *International Journal of Public Administration*, 32(3–4): 167–70.

Talbot, C. and Talbot, C. (2019) 'One step forward, two steps back? The rise and fall of government's Next Steps agencies', Civil Service World. https://www.civilserviceworld.com/articles/opinion/one-step-forward-two-steps-back-rise-and-fall-government%E2%80%99s-next-steps-agencies (accessed 27 September 2019).

Taylor, D. (2018) 'Worse than prison: life inside Britain's 10 deportation centres', *The Guardian*, 11 October.

Taylor, R. (1996) 'The Heath government, industrial policy and the "new capitalism"', in S. Ball and A. Seldon (eds) *The Heath Government, 1970-1974: A Reappraisal*, Harlow: Longman, pp 139–60.

Theakston, K. (1995) *The Civil Service Since 1945*, Oxford: Blackwell.

Theakston, K. (2000) 'Permanent secretaries: comparative biography and leadership in Whitehall', in R. A. W. Rhodes (ed) *Transforming British Government*, vol. 2: *Changing Roles and Relationships*, London: Palgrave Macmillan, pp 125–45.

Thomas, C. (2019) The 'Make Do and Mend' health service Soving the NHS' capita crisis. London: IPPR.

Thompson, J. R. (2000) 'Quasi markets and strategic change in public organizations', In J. L. Brudney, L. J. O'Toole Jr and H. G. Rainey (eds) *Advancing Public Management: New Developments in Theory, Methods, and Practice*, Washington, DC: Georgetown University Press, pp 197–214.

Thompson, M., Nowak, V., Southern, A., Davies, J. and Furmedge, P. (2020) 'Re-grounding the city with Polanyi: from urban entrepreneurialism to entrepreneurial municipalism', *Environment and Planning A: Economy and Space*, 52(6): 1171–94.

Thorburn, M. (2020) 'Privatisation reforms and health work in schools: the end of the beginning', *Discourse: Studies in the Cultural Politics of Education*, 41(2): 299–309.

Thornton, M. (2011) *Privatising the Public University*, Abingdon: Routledge.

Tiefer, C. (1996) 'The GATT agreement on government procurement in theory and practice', *University of Baltimore Law Review*, 26(3): 31.

Timmins, N. (2001) *The Five Giants: A Biography of the Welfare State*, London: HarperCollins.

Timmins, N. (2005) 'Challenges of private provision in the NHS', *BMJ*, 331(7526): 1193–5.

Tomkinson, R. (2007) *Shared Services in Local Government: Improving Service Delivery*, Aldershot: Gower.

Topham, G. (2017) 'British rail is nationalised all over again – by foreign states', *The Guardian*, 1 April.

Torres, L. and Pina, V. (2002) 'Delivering public services—mechanisms and consequences: changes in public service delivery in the EU countries', *Public Money and Management*, 22(4): 41–8.

Trybus, M. (2010) 'From the indivisible Crown to Teckal: the In-House provision of works and services in the United Kingdom', in M. Comba and S. Treumer (eds) *The In-house Providing in European Law*, Copenhagen: Djøf, pp 187–212.

Tyler, I. E. (2018) 'Deportation nation: Theresa May's hostile environment', *Journal for the Study of British Cultures*, 25(1). https://eprints.lancs.ac.uk/id/eprint/125439/ (accessed 12 November 2020).

Tyrrall, D. (2004) 'The UK railway privatisation: failing to succeed?', *Economic Affairs*, 24(3): 32–8.

Utton, M. (2000) 'Fifty years of UK competition policy', *Review of Industrial Organization*, 16(3): 267–85.

Uyarra, E., Edler, J., Gee, S., Georghiou, L. and Yeow, J. (2014) 'UK public procurement of innovation: the UK case', in V. Lember, R. Kattel and T. Kalvet (eds) *Public Procurement, Innovation and Policy: International Perspectives*, Berlin and Heidelberg: Springer, pp 233–57.

Van der Heijden, J. (2010) 'Privatisation of building code enforcement: a comparative study of regimes in Australia and Canada', *International Journal of Law in the Built Environment*, 2(1): 60–75.

Van Middelaar, L. (2013) *The Passage to Europe: How a Continent Became a Union*, London: Yale University Press.

Vaughan, A. (2018) 'The heat is on for fans of publicly owned energy companies', *The Guardian*, 22 August.

Vize, R. (2019) 'The road to Wigan cheer. The council transforming lives despite £140m cuts', *The Guardian*, 5 July. https://www.theguardian.com/society/2019/jul/05/wigan-council-transforming-lives-despite-cuts-austerityize (accessed 12 November 2020).

Waelde, T. W. and Kolo, A. (1998) 'Renegotiating previous governments' privatization deals: the 1997 UK windfall tax on utilities and international law', *Northwestern Journal of International Law & Business*, 19(3): 405–24.

Waite, D., McGregor, A. and McNulty, D. (2018) 'Issues paper on city deals and inclusive growth', Glasgow: Policy Scotland.

Walford, G. (1988) 'The privatisation of British higher education', *European Journal of Education*, 23(1–2): 47–64.

Wall, S. (2008) *A Stranger in Europe: Britain and the EU from Thatcher to Blair*, Oxford: Oxford University Press.

Wallace, H. (1973) *National Governments and the European Communities*, London: Chatham House/PEP.

Wallace, H. (1988) 'The European Community and EFTA: one family or two?', *The World Today*, 44(10): 177–9.

Wallace, H. and Young, A. R. (1996) 'The single market: a new approach to policy', in H. Wallace and W. Wallace (eds) *Policy Making in the European Union*, Oxford: Oxford University Press, pp 125–55.

Walsh, K. (1989) 'Competition and service in local government', in J. Stewart and G. Stoker (eds) *The Future of Local Government. Government Beyond the Centre*, London: Palgrave Macmillan, pp 30–54.

Walsh, K. (1995) *Public Services and Market Mechanisms: Competition, Contracting and the New Public Management*, London: Macmillan International Higher Education.

Ward, J. (2020) 'The British state and the recentralisation of power: from Brexit to COVID-19', *British Politics and Policy at LSE*. http://eprints. lse.ac.uk/106410/1/politicsandpolicy_centralisation_of_power_brexit. pdf (accessed 18 November 2020).

Ward, R. C. (2007) 'The outsourcing of public library management: an analysis of the application of new public management theories from the principal-agent perspective', *Administration & Society*, 38(6): 627–48.

Warner, M. E. and Hefetz, A. (2008) 'Managing markets for public service: the role of mixed public–private delivery of city services', *Public Administration Review*, 68(1): 155–66.

Warner, N. (1984) 'Raynerism in practice: anatomy of a Rayner scrutiny', *Public Administration*, 62(1): 7–22.

Wass, D. (2008) *Decline to Fall: The Making of British Macro-Economic Policy and the 1976 IMF Crisis*, Oxford: Oxford University Press.

Waterman, J. (2008) 'Procurement capability: in search of solutions', Proceedings of the 3rd International Public Procurement Conference. http://www.ippa.org/IPPC3/Proceedings/Chaper%203.pdf (accessed 12 November 2020).

Watt, P. A. (2005) 'Information, cooperation and trust in strategic service delivery partnerships', *Public Policy and Administration*, 20(3): 106–23.

Weerakkody, V. and Dhillon, G. (2008) 'Moving from e-government to t-government: a study of process reengineering challenges in a UK local authority context', *International Journal of Electronic Government Research (IJEGR)*, 4(4): 1–16.

Weiss, L. (1999) 'Globalization and national governance: antinomy or interdependence?', *Review of International Studies*, 25(5): 59–88.

Wensley, R. and Moore, M. (2011) 'Choice and marketing in public management: the creation of public value', in J. Benington and M. Moore (eds) *Public Value: Theory and Practice*, Basingstoke: Palgrave Macmillan, pp 127–43.

Wettenhall, R. (2003) 'The rhetoric and reality of public-private partnerships', *Public Organization Review*, 3(1): 77–107.

Whalley, J. and Curwen, P. (2017) 'From phones to football: the changing strategic focus of BT', *Telematics and Informatics*, 34(5): 798–809.

White, A. and Dunleavy, P. (2010) 'Making and breaking Whitehall departments: a guide to machinery of government changes', London: Institute for Government and LSE Public Policy Group.

Whitfield, D. (2012) 'UK Social Services: the mutation of privatisation', *Studies in Social Services*. https://www.european-services-strategy.org. uk/wp-content/uploads/2012/09/uk-social-services-mutation-of-privatisation.pdf (accessed 17 November 2020).

Whitfield, D. (2014) UK outsourcing expands despite high failure rates PPP strategic Partnerships PPP database 2012-2013. European Services Strategy Unit https://european-services-strategy.org.uk.archived. website/ppp-database/ppp-partnership-database/ppp-strategic-partnerships-database-2012-2013.pdf (accessed 17 November 2020).

WHO (World Health Organization) (2012) *European Action Plan for Strengthening Public Health Capacities and Services*. https://www.euro. who.int/en/health-topics/Health-systems/public-health-services/ publications/2012/european-action-plan-for-strengthening-public-health-capacities-and-services (accessed 17th November 2020).

WHO (World Health Organization) (2020) *COVID-19 Strategy Update 14 April*. Available from: https://www.who.int/publications/i/item/ covid-19-strategy-update---14-april-2020 (accessed 14 December 2020).

Wilkins, A. (2017) 'Rescaling the local: multi-academy trusts, private monopoly and statecraft in England', *Journal of Educational Administration and History*, 49(2): 171–85.

Wilkins, S., Shams, F. and Huisman, J. (2013) 'The decision-making and changing behavioural dynamics of potential higher education students: the impacts of increasing tuition fees in England', *Educational Studies*, 39(2): 125–41.

Wilks, S. (1996) 'Britain and Europe: an awkward partner or an awkward state?', *Politics*, 16(3): 159–65.

Williams, B., Whatmough, P. and Pearson, J. (2001) 'Emergency transfer from independent hospitals to NHS hospitals: risk, reasons and cost', *Journal of Public Health Medicine*, 23(4): 301–5.

Wilson, D. and Game, C. (2011) *Local Government in the United Kingdom*, London: Macmillan International Higher Education.

Wilson, G. K. (1983) 'Planning: lessons from the ports', *Public Administration*, 61(3): 265–81.

Wilson, J. (1999) 'From CCT to best value: some evidence and observations', *Local Government Studies*, 25(2): 38–52.

Wilson, T., Roland, M. and Ham, C. (2006) 'The contribution of general practice and the general practitioner to NHS patients', *Journal of the Royal Society of Medicine*, 99(1): 24–8.

Wingfield, P. (1995) 'Externalisation: the Berkshire experience of compulsory competitive tendering', in *Incorporated Engineers and Technicians 1995 National Conference Tomorrow's Engineers Today – papers*, London : Thomas Telford Publishing. https://www.icevirtuallibrary.com/doi/abs/10.1680/ieat1995nctetp.43459.0001?mobileUi=0& (accessed 17 November 2020).

Winham, G. R. (2014) *International Trade and the Tokyo Round Negotiation*, Princeton, NJ: Princeton University Press.

Wishlade, F. G. and Michie, R. (2009) 'Pandora's box and the Delphic oracle: EU cohesion policy and state aid compliance', University of Strathclyde EPRC Paper 24(2). Available from: https://pureportal.strath.ac.uk/en/publications/pandoras-box-and-the-delphic-oracle-eu-cohesion-policy-and-state- (accessed 14 December 2020).

Woolcock, S. and Hodges, M. (1996) 'EU policy in the Uruguay Round', in H. Wallace and W. Wallace (eds) *Policy Making in the European Union*, Oxford: Oxford University Press, pp 301–24.

WTO (2020) 'GATS sectors detailed policy education services: EU commitments'. https://www.wto.org/english/tratop_e/serv_e/serv_commitments_e.htm (accessed 17 November 2020).

Young, R. and Leese, B. (1999) 'Recruitment and retention of general practitioners in the UK: what are the problems and solutions?', *British Journal of General Practice*, 49(447): 829–33.

Young, S. (1986) 'The nature of privatisation in Britain, 1979–85', *West European Politics*, 9(2): 235–52.

Zifcak, S. (1994) *New Managerialism: Administrative Reform in Whitehall and Canberra*, Buckingham: Open University Press.

Index

A

academies 136, 143–7, 180
academy chains 134, 144, 147
Accenture 62
accessibility 54
accountability 3, 12, 53–6, 58, 61–2, 67, 91, 93, 108–9, 151, 181, 190
accounting systems 54, 61, 87
Adam Smith Institute 5, 23, 35, 106
Adur Council 100, 172
agencification 8, 14, 44, 53, 55–6, 78, 103–4, 108, 112–13, 123, 181, 187
agriculture 17, 36
Airbnb 42
aligned budgets 171
Amazon 32, 94
anchor institutions 162, 168–70
apprenticeships 159, 176
Armed Forces Covenant 158
arm's length organisations 12, 60, 76, 78, 108, 117, 119, 183
asset lock 167
assets 5, 18, 21–2, 39–40, 44, 50, 67, 97, 166–7, 170, 180, 183
asylum 114, 116
Atkinson Review 70, 95
Audit Commission 53, 76, 80, 97, 126
austerity vii, 2, 8, 10, 100–1, 117, 150–2, 155–6, 164, 166–7, 174–5, 179, 188, 193
Australia 19, 27, 82, 84, 86, 88, 103, 106, 109, 117–18, 129, 137, 139

B

Babtie 77
back office services 11, 13–14, 86, 92, 94–9, 172
Barnet, LB 173
BBC 22, 151, 189
benchmarking 28, 65, 72, 78–9, 83, 100
best value 10, 95, 97, 126, 149
Big Society 144, 149, 151, 154
Birmingham 160, 173
Blair, Tony 81, 153, 180
blue-collar workers 71–2
Bournemouth 100
Boyne, G. 2–3, 73, 75–6, 78, 80–3, 87, 97
Brexit vii, 10, 30, 131, 147, 156, 170, 175, 182, 184, 190–1, 193
British European Airways (BEA) 37
British Petroleum (BP) 37, 39
British Rail 22, 37
  see also railways
British Sugar Company 39
British Telecom (BT) 42, 47–9, 97
Browne Report 2010 135, 137
building control 85–6, 100
building schools for the future 90, 143, 149
buses 37, 49
business cases 7, 91–4, 98, 145

C

Cabinet Office 40, 46, 55, 63–4, 153–4, 159, 184

Cable and Wireless 37, 47
Callaghan, James 21
Canada 84, 86, 118, 137, 145
Capita 62, 87, 92, 97, 131, 173
care homes 155–6, 163, 169, 192
Carillion 62, 87, 92, 97, 131, 173
Cave Review 2011 46
central–local relations 77, 182
Centre for Policy Studies 5
charities 62, 119, 123, 134, 136, 153,
    160, 192
charter schools 144–5
children 66, 115, 133–4, 138, 143, 180
China 88, 138, 138
choice 11, 54, 63, 75, 78, 87, 121,
    124, 127, 137, 146, 156, 160–1,
    165, 189
citizen-centred 46, 52–3, 55, 75, 83,
    93–4, 96, 120, 160, 188
Citizen's Charter 10, 53, 63, 73, 82,
    124, 182
city technology colleges 136, 144
civil service 7, 9–10, 14, 22–3, 25, 37,
    41, 43, 45, 51, 53–63, 73, 83–4,
    86, 103–4, 106–8, 112, 129,
    183–4, 187
    Fulton Report 25, 53, 112
    permanent secretaries 24, 61–2, 65,
        104–5, 107–8, 114
    revolving doors 62
    senior civil service 41, 45, 105,
        112–13
civil society 153
Clarke, Kenneth 108
Cleveland, Ohio 167
client 3, 13, 60, 75, 77–8, 82, 88–90,
    92–4, 96, 113, 123, 156, 185,
    188–90
climate 6, 28, 42, 59
coal 16, 22, 37, 124
    see also National Coal Board
Coalition Government 100, 124, 144,
    149–50, 154–5, 170, 174
Cockfield, Lord 26–7, 51, 183
commissioning 5, 55, 121–6, 128, 130,
    159–60, 165, 171, 179, 190

Community Interest Companies (CIC)
    167, 176–7
Community Rehabilitation Companies
    (CRC) 110–11
Competition Act 1980 16–17
Competition Act 1998 17, 49
competitive tendering 12, 53, 76,
    121
compliance 9, 26, 28, 41, 44–6, 49,
    56, 83, 88, 97, 99, 122, 127,
    166, 188, 191
compliant environment 114–15, 187,
    189
comprehensive schools 134, 143
Compulsory Competitive Tendering
    (CCT) 69, 71–2, 74–7, 79–83,
    86, 97, 101
concession contracts 8, 70, 164–6,
    172
Conservative Party 2, 4–5, 12, 20, 25,
    31, 35–8, 43, 65, 71, 75, 80–1,
    106, 116, 150, 154, 173, 181–2,
    186, 192
contract workers 123
contractors 3, 11, 14, 21–2, 72–80, 85,
    91, 93, 99, 108, 111, 114, 128,
    150, 156, 158, 161, 184, 169,
    185, 190
construction 5, 16, 18, 88–90, 96, 107,
    128–9, 159, 165, 173
consumers 41, 45–6, 50, 177
cooperatives 152, 154, 168, 162, 170
Cooperative Society 154
co-production 160, 171
core executive 64, 79, 180
corruption 81, 184–5
COVID-19 3, 10, 30, 32, 112, 138, 150,
    156, 163, 179–80, 185–6, 188–91
Crosland, Anthony 5, 19
cross-border 27, 93, 153
Crown Agents 16
Crown Commercial Service (CCS)
    159, 164–6
customer focus 63
customers 2, 13, 41, 47, 75, 87, 94, 98,
    100, 169, 188

D

DEFRA 44–5
Deloitte 62
Denmark 32, 189
depoliticisation 58
deportation centres 11, 114–16
devolution 10, 84, 151, 184, 190
DHSC 119
DHSS 57
digital technology 158
disadvantaged groups 152, 159, 164
dispute resolution 17, 33, 100, 191
diversification 48, 144
Dorset 100, 172
Dr Foster 130–1
drought 46

E

East Kent Services 172
easyCouncil 173
e-government 65, 87, 93–5
education 14, 52, 56, 62, 107, 149–50,
        180
effectiveness vii, 2, 6, 8, 10, 45, 52,
        62, 65, 86–8, 91, 96, 104, 122,
        142–3, 163, 188
efficiency vii, 2, 6, 8, 10, 20, 24, 27,
        36, 45, 52, 56–7, 60–1, 65, 67,
        71–2, 86–7
efficiency unit 63
electricity 22, 37
electronic patient record 130
eligibility 3, 150, 164, 187, 189
emergency support 126, 157
employees 3, 13, 25, 42, 76–7, 107,
        113, 119, 156, 163, 165
employment practices 77, 187
energy 29, 39–42, 49, 52, 150, 154,
        166–8, 170, 176–8
England 3, 100–11, 43–4, 71, 76, 82,
        84, 93, 105, 110, 119, 137, 144,
        146, 150–1, 158, 164, 166, 174,
        190, 193
environment 27, 29, 43–4, 53, 56, 59,
        114–16
Environment Agency 44

EU
    ECJ 26, 64, 152, 154, 191
    enlargement 27, 31
    ERDF 44, 84
    Open Method of Coordination
        135, 153
    Single European Act (SEA) 26, 37
    Single European Market (SEM) 17,
        19, 25–7, 30–1, 44, 48, 51, 74,
        79, 88, 91, 93, 120, 122, 127,
        135, 147, 149, 151, 158, 182–4
    Treaty of Rome 25–6, 29, 31
Evergreen 167–9

F

facilities management 66, 91, 122
failures vii, 11, 30, 33, 46, 56, 60,
        63–4, 66–7, 88–9, 91, 95–6, 99,
        105–6, 108, 110–11, 114, 121,
        127, 145, 147, 161, 163, 165,
        176, 180, 186, 188
Financial Management Initiative 24,
        54, 58–9
financial services 13, 25
Flinders, M. 55–8, 88–9, 127
flooding 45, 163
France 8, 23, 30, 46, 70, 120, 151,
        160, 166, 182
franchise 163, 166, 184, 188
free schools 144–7, 180, 188
Friedman, M. 4–5, 20
fuel poverty 177
fundholding 122–9, 133,

G

G4S 106–7, 109, 116–17
Gamble, A. 1–2, 22, 52, 58, 86,
        149–50, 164
gas 37, 41, 159
gateway reviews 66
GATS 8–12, 16–17, 24–33, 45, 48–58,
        60, 62–6, 69, 74, 78–86, 88, 91,
        95, 105–6, 109, 111, 114, 120–4,
        127–9, 133–5, 142, 146–52, 158,
        164, 166, 171, 180, 187, 192

GATT 2–6, 8, 10, 12, 15, 17–19,
  22–3, 25, 27, 35–6, 38–9, 51, 69
  Kennedy Round 4
  Tokyo Round 2, 4–5, 8, 12, 15, 17,
    23–5, 29, 33, 35–6, 38–9, 71
  Uruguay Round 18, 22, 24–5, 29,
    51, 69
Germany 8, 30, 152, 164, 166, 169,
  182
Gershon, Peter 65–6, 86, 95, 97
Glass–Steagall Act 20
globalisation 13, 18–19, 28, 168
Google 131–2
GPA 8–12, 15–27, 29–31, 33, 36, 38,
  40, 42–58, 63–6, 69, 71, 73–4,
  77–83, 91, 103, 120, 122, 127–9,
  149, 151, 157, 164, 166–7, 171,
  174, 180, 182, 184, 187, 191
GPC 17, 36
GP fundholding 125–6
grammar schools 134
Greater London Authority (GLA)
  177
greenhouse gas emissions 159
Grenfell Tower fire 11, 86, 188

H
Haddon, C. 3, 24, 51–2, 54, 60–1, 63,
  104, 122
Harvey, D. 4–5, 11, 15, 20, 31
Hayek, von, F. 4
HBOS 32
Heath, Edward 35–6, 39, 43
Help to Buy 42, 174
Heritage Foundation 5
Heseltine, Michael 59
highways 71, 73
HM Prison Service 106–9
HMPPS 106, 110
Home Office 47, 94, 103, 105–9,
  114–17
Hong Kong 53
Hood, Christopher 3, 56, 69, 72,
  155
Hoover Institute 5

housing 5, 21, 29, 56, 67, 71, 73, 80,
  86–7, 90, 92, 139–40, 150, 159,
  164, 167–80, 187, 193
  homelessness 174–6
  right to buy 2, 10, 80, 174, 176,
    183
Howard, Michael 108

I
ideology vii, 1–2, 4, 7–10, 12, 15,
  20–3, 35, 37, 45, 52, 69–70,
  78–9, 90, 109, 122, 142, 149,
  154, 157, 181–2
Immigration Removal Centres 115–16
India 138
in-house 13, 64, 72, 74–6, 89, 92, 112,
  162, 166, 187, 193
infrastructure 4–5, 21, 29–31, 40,
  45–7, 51, 61, 90, 127, 129, 165,
  176, 179
innovation 10, 28, 46–7, 139, 153,
  157, 167
Institute of Economic Affairs (IEA) 5,
  23, 35
institutional reform 7, 8, 35, 79, 83,
  100–1, 183
International Monetary Fund 1, 21,
  24, 27, 37, 174
international students 137–9
Ireland 32, 160
IT platforms 27

J
John Lewis 154, 173
joint ventures 96, 101, 130, 187
Joseph, Keith 5, 36
judicial review 41
just in time 27

K
Kemp, Peter 24, 41, 53, 60–1
Kent County Council 97, 134, 172
Keynesian 4, 20

Knowsley Council 169
Korea 138
KPMG 144

L

Labour Government 1–2, 5, 8, 15, 21, 25, 36, 49–50, 62, 65, 69, 76, 79–81, 90, 92, 123, 126–7, 136, 149–50, 154–5, 162, 170, 173, 181
Labour Party 37, 62, 81
Lambeth LB 173
Lancashire County Council 170, 175
lean 95–6
leisure centres 175–6
level playing field 159
Liberal Democrats 144, 154
libraries 94, 97, 152, 155–6
Lloyds Bank 32
Local Enterprise Partnerships (LEPs) 170
Local Government Association (LGA) 3, 11, 13, 67, 74, 99–100, 160, 163–4, 171–2, 176, 178
Localism Act 2011 150, 152, 154, 167, 175
local strategic partnership 82, 162, 170
lowest price 18, 66, 74, 80–2, 151, 185, 188
Luxembourg 32

M

Machinery of Government 23
Macmillan, Harold 25
Major, John 27, 52, 72, 87, 110, 122, 182
Malaysia 137
management consultants 16, 62
managerialism 55
Manchester 107, 135
market distortion 50
market making 31, 44, 53, 85, 189
marketisation 63, 75, 135
market testing 54, 63–4, 72, 80, 106–7

May, Theresa 116
McDonaldization 20
mental health 117, 158, 160
Mercury communication 48
mergers 49, 100, 135
migration services 11
military covenant 4, 2, 158
ministerial directions 10
Ministry of Justice 105–6, 109, 110, 112–13
Mitie 114
mixed economy 11, 119, 133, 156, 163, 165, 179–80, 186
monetarist 4, 35
monopolies 16–17, 31, 39–40, 42, 44–9
mortgage finance 13, 25, 139, 174
most favoured nation 17
Mount, F. 2, 20, 35, 181, 183, 190
municipal entrepreneurialism 150, 166–7
mutual enterprise 158, 173

N

NAFTA 25, 27
National Coal Board (NCB) 37
National Enterprise Board 37, 39
National Offender Management System (NOMS) 106, 108–10
National Water Council 43
nationalised industries 16, 23, 36–40, 49, 104
national security 40
neighbourhoods 152
neoliberalism 3–4, 20, 81, 83, 181
Netherlands 8, 32, 88, 138, 152, 164
New Public Management 8, 69, 72, 78–9, 81, 180
New Towns Corporation 14, 39
New Zealand 19, 53, 78, 103, 137, 145
Next Steps Agencies 24, 54, 60, 103
non-departmental public bodies 58, 183
non-tariff barriers to trade 4–5, 18–19, 93

Northern Ireland 10, 43–4, 84, 120,
147, 150–1, 166, 190
nurseries 133, 153

O
Ofcom 47–8
Office of the Third Sector 149, 154
offshoring 11, 13, 98
OFT 135–6
Oftel 48
Ofwat 41, 44–6
OGC 66–7
older people 66, 95, 107
one stop shop 93
Operational Efficiency Programme
67
Osborne, George 150, 155

P
Parker, David 1–2, 4–5, 12–13, 16, 19,
21–2, 31, 35, 37–48, 71–3, 75,
77, 86, 104, 177
Parkinson, Cecil 38
part-time workers 77
partnership 37, 81–2, 88–9, 92,
95–100, 127, 162, 165, 170,
173–4, 187
patient choice 121, 124, 127
Patients' Charter 123
performance management vii, 8, 11,
70, 72, 78, 83–5, 87, 93, 103–4,
122–3, 189
PFI 89–92, 107, 120, 122, 127–9, 143,
149, 163, 184, 188
Philippines 156
Pickles, Eric 155
Pliazsky, Leo 5, 12, 40, 44, 52, 55–6,
59, 63, 104
policy
design 7–8
failure 11
making 23, 51, 61, 66, 146
metanarrative 8–10, 180, 188,
190

narrative 2–3, 8–9, 55, 88, 121,
146–7, 149, 154, 163, 180, 184,
188, 190
punctuation 1
Poole 100
Portsmouth City Council 178
Post Office 22, 57
post-political 173
poverty 26–7, 150, 177
PPP 88–9, 127
Preston Council 169–71
price manipulation 40
pricing 19, 28, 32, 45, 47, 66, 120,
171, 189
Primary Care Trust 124, 126
prison service 106–9, 115, 183
probation service 50, 89, 106, 109–13,
163, 184
professionals 17, 63, 65, 72–3, 77, 85,
94, 106, 110–13, 169, 182
provincialism 168–9
public administration 156, 160, 162
public choice theory 75, 78, 87
public engagement 160
Public Health England 119, 158
public sector 1–12, 15–25, 36–7, 42,
44, 53, 60, 69–70, 75, 78–82,
85, 87–93, 95, 107, 111, 113,
121, 127–9, 134, 142–4,
149–64, 169, 179, 180–3, 186,
188–93
Public Services (Social Value) Act 2012
74, 144, 157–9, 169
public value 153–4, 156–7, 160, 162,
180, 189
Public Works Loans Board 91
PUMA 79
purchaser provider split 61, 162
PWC 62

Q
quality 1, 3, 18, 29, 53, 63, 73, 97, 99,
115, 129, 131, 134, 139, 144–5,
157, 160, 164, 169, 176–7, 191,
193

quangos 55, 57–8, 78, 183

R

railways 11, 50, 16, 21–2, 37, 40, 163, 166, 184, 188
Rayner, D. 24, 54, 57, 59
    the Rayner scrutinies 8, 58, 103
redress 54, 63
Redwood, John 37
regional water authorities (RWA) 43
regulators 40–8, 50, 86, 129, 177
regulatory framework 42, 47, 191
restrictive practices 16
Rhodes, R. A. W. 3, 14, 24, 51, 56, 64–5, 104–5, 113, 182
Ridley, Nicholas 12, 17, 20, 35–7, 49
RIEP 95, 97, 100
risk 14, 46, 50, 87–92, 96, 98–9, 110, 127–8, 160, 185

S

salami slicing cuts 155
Scandinavian 20, 43, 72
    see also Sweden
schools 21, 62, 74, 90, 94, 126, 133–8, 141–9, 169, 175, 180, 188
    see academy chains; charter schools; city technology colleges; free schools; grammar schools
Scotland 10, 14, 43–4, 75, 84, 120, 136, 138, 147, 150–1, 189–90
scrutiny 24, 41, 57–8, 60, 82, 103, 116, 187
Selsdon Group 20, 35, 37
Serco 62, 109, 115, 117, 144
service delivery 3, 19, 52–3, 55, 70–3, 75, 78, 81, 83, 97, 92, 95–6, 99, 101, 106, 151, 153–4, 160–3, 165–6, 171–1, 179, 189
service design 11, 156, 189
services of general economic interest (SGEI) 29, 40, 152–3
sewerage 43–4
shared services 171

Singapore 27, 88
single national accounts (SNA) 69–70
skills 66–7, 73, 85, 89, 145, 158, 176
small and medium sized enterprises (SMEs) 28, 31, 149, 152, 158–9
small state 149–50, 155, 164–5
social care 117, 119, 120–1, 124, 126, 129, 143, 153, 156, 163, 167, 169, 187
social enterprises 152–3, 158–9, 161, 171
social exclusion 153
social media 27, 187
social value 3, 8, 10, 70, 74, 80, 144, 149, 151–2, 157–9, 161, 169, 176, 186, 191
SOCITM 94
soft power 27, 167, 182
South Africa 103
Southend on Sea Council 71
Spain 129
specification 11–13, 55, 72–4, 80, 89, 92, 99, 115, 123, 156, 158, 161, 165, 159, 180–1, 186, 192
Spending Review 65, 67, 86, 155
SSPs 96–9
standards 18–19, 21, 26–7, 41, 45, 53–4, 65, 67, 75–6, 81, 83, 95, 109, 129, 142–3, 146, 158, 169, 172, 182, 186
steel 16, 37, 159
Stoker, G. 71, 84, 87, 92–3, 162
strikes 37, 47, 59
student accommodation 139–40
students 133–41, 147, 169
studentification 140
sub-contracting 159
subsidiarity 70, 81, 84, 121, 150–1, 164
subsidies 29, 33, 42, 189
supply chain 158–9, 192
Sweden 8, 20, 31, 53, 70, 78, 84, 120, 145–7, 152, 169, 189
sweetheart deals 22
Switzerland 32

T

target culture 114
taxation 14, 19, 30, 32, 36, 39, 44, 50, 54, 71, 104, 134, 137, 155, 167, 172, 176
Teckal exemption 172–3, 176
telecommunications 27, 42, 47
telephones 37, 93–4
temporary workers 77, 141
tenders 12, 22, 50, 54, 66, 70, 74, 81, 156, 158, 180
Thatcher, Margaret vii, 1–2, 5, 8, 19–22, 24, 38, 53, 55, 57–8, 60, 69–71, 75, 77, 87, 122, 167, 174, 180, 181, 194
Thatcherism 53
Theakston, K. 23, 51, 54–5, 57, 60–4, 104–5
think tanks 5, 20, 23, 35, 92, 106, 144
Third Sector 149, 151–5, 157, 160–4
third way 153
trades unions 76–7, 108, 113
trading accounts 73
training 140, 159, 164, 168–9, 176
transfer pricing 19, 28, 32, 189
Treasury, HM 39, 44, 47–8, 55, 59–60, 63–5, 70, 86–7, 95, 143, 151, 184
tuition fees 137–8, 141
TUPE 8, 76, 107, 110

U

Uber 42
unemployment 21, 153
United Nations (UN) 6, 69, 82, 150
United States (US) 4–5, 20, 22–3, 27, 33, 37, 39, 52, 57, 78, 82, 84, 94, 104, 106, 109, 118, 132, 138, 140–1, 144–5, 168, 170, 184, 191
Upper Clyde Shipbuilders 37
UK Border Agency 114, 117

V

value for money (VFM) 45, 56–7, 67, 72, 84, 91, 114, 128
Virgin Healthcare 32
voluntary sector 62, 72, 82, 134, 144, 158–9, 186, 192–3

W

Wales 43–4, 71, 82, 84, 105, 110, 120, 147, 150–1, 166, 189–90
Wandsworth 71, 172
Water Act 2014 43, 46
welfare state 2, 4–5, 10, 26, 54, 78, 155, 157, 165, 173–4, 181–3, 190
Welland partnership 99
wellbeing 40, 158, 190
West Midlands Combined Authority (WMCA) 117
white-collar workers 72, 77
Whitehall 2–3, 22–3, 43, 47, 57, 63, 65, 73, 142, 155, 181, 183, 190–1
WHO 121
Wigan Metropolitan Borough Council 95, 160, 170–1, 173
windfall taxes 50
Windrush 115–16, 188
World Bank 44
Work Foundation 154
Worthing Council 100, 172
WTO
    Doha Round 120, 135

Y

Yes Minister 105
youth services 155

Z

zero hours contracts 13, 156, 163, 192